"No first-book jitters for Sharma. . . . His smooth, almost chummy style suits him ideally for guiding civilians through the sometimes-arcane thicket of the dismal science, looking for those emerging markets likely to disappoint or exceed expectations in the coming years. . . . Sharma refreshingly comes across as that rare thing Harry Truman once sought: a 'one-handed economist' willing to stake his reputation without resort to 'on the other hand' equivocation." —*Kirkus Reviews*

"Ruchir Sharma's *Breakout Nations* is unarguably an epoch-defining book—unusual for a comparative study of nations based on ground-level data collected from personal experience." —Srivatsa Krishna, *Outlook* magazine (India)

"Excellent." —Rana Foroohar, *Time* magazine

"An insightful analysis of why some countries excel while others languish." —GlobalPost.com

"Every year for two decades, experts have told me that China's economy was set to crash, felled by huge imbalances and policy errors. . . . Ruchir Sharma . . . makes a different and more persuasive case in his new book, *Breakout Nations*, pointing not to China's failures but to its successes." —Fareed Zakaria, *Washington Post*

"As [Sharma's] book jumps from one country to the next, it throws up some intriguing juxtapositions." —*The Economist*

"This is a great road-map to the new and better-balanced world in which we will all live, and an encouraging one." —Hamish McRae, *Independent* (UK)

"There is no better book for country-by-country accounts of emerging markets (and riskier ones called frontier markets)." —S. A. Aiyar, *Times of India*

"Sharma . . . provides valuable perspective for investors and all others who seek to understand today's global world."   —Mary Whaley, *Booklist*

"The breadth of *Breakout Nations* is impressive . . . the analysis is nuanced, the arguments persuasive, the anecdotes revealing and the writing breezy."
—*Straits Times* (Singapore)

"It's as handy an emerging-markets travel guide as one can hope to find. . . . Sharma deftly takes readers on a quick tour of many of the world's evolving economies while managing to avoid most of the usual, clichéd landmarks."   —*The Deal* magazine

"In *Breakout Nations*, [Sharma] takes us on a fascinating gallop through the countries at the edges of the developed world. Not only does he challenge the accepted wisdom—that China and India will motor on, ad infinitum—but he comes up with some surprising candidates for the next decade's economic stars."   —Danny Fortson,
Sunday Times (UK)

"Accessible to newbies and revelatory for veterans, Sharma's observations upend conventional wisdom regarding what it takes to succeed in the relentlessly competitive global marketplace."   —*Publishers Weekly*

"An investor's lonely planet guide to the world for the new century."
—Bloomberg Radio

"Information-packed and fun, too. . . . For all smart readers."
—*Library Journal*

"These are the perfect few pages you want to read before you set out to visit the country, a Fodor's guide to recent economic history. The book's greatest strength is its refreshing antidote against herd behaviour and hype."   —Pratap Bahnu Mehta, *Indian Express*

"It is really the focus of economic attention around the world. It is a whole new look at which economies are going to be winners and which are going to be losers."   —NDTV

"This is among the best books to understand the emerging world. . . . Sharma matches the brilliance of Thomas L. Friedman, author of the widely cited *The World Is Flat*."   —CNN-IBN

BREAKOUT
NATIONS

BREAKOUT NATIONS

In Pursuit of the
Next Economic Miracles

RUCHIR SHARMA

W. W. NORTON & COMPANY

New York   London

Copyright © 2013, 2012 by Ruchir Sharma

Photograph credits: p. xii: Michael Nichols / National Geographic / Getty Images; p. 16:
Panos Pictures; p. 36: Mary Evans Picture Library; p. 60: Martin Adolfsson /
Gallery Stock; p. 74: Jon Lowenstein / Noor Images BV; p. 84: Donald Weber /
VII Photo Agency LLC; p. 98: Mark Power / Magnum Photos; p. 112: Redux Pictures LLC;
p. 130: Panos Pictures; p. 154: Liu Jin / AFP / Getty Images; p. 172: Benedicte Kurzen /
VII Network; p. 186: Panos Pictures; p. 222: Jan Cobb Photography Ltd / Photographer's Choice /
Getty Images; p. 240: Comstock Images / Getty Images.

For information about permission to reproduce selections from this book,
write to Permissions, W. W. Norton & Company, Inc.,
500 Fifth Avenue, New York, NY 10110

For information about special discounts for bulk purchases, please contact
W. W. Norton Special Sales at specialsales@wwnorton.com or 800-233-4830

Manufacturing by Courier Westford
Book design by Helene Berinsky
Production manager: Julia Druskin

Sharma, Ruchir.
Breakout nations : in pursuit of the next economic miracles / Ruchir Sharma. — 1st ed.
p. cm.
Includes bibliographical references and index.
ISBN 978-0-393-08026-1 (hardcover)
1. Developing countries—Economic conditions. 2. Economic forecasting.
3. Economic history—21st century. I. Title.
HC59.7.S4465 2012
330.9172'4—dc23

2012005810

ISBN 978-0-393-34540-7 pbk.

W. W. Norton & Company, Inc.
500 Fifth Avenue, New York, N.Y. 10110
www.wwnorton.com

W. W. Norton & Company Ltd.
Castle House, 75/76 Wells Street, London W1T 3QT

3 4 5 6 7 8 9 0

CONTENTS

PROLOGUE

It's been a long time since the farmers left the "farmhouses" of Delhi, and though the name lives on, it now describes the weekend retreats of the upper class, playgrounds on the fringes of the city where unmapped dirt lanes wind through poor villages and suddenly open onto lavish mansions with sprawling gardens and water features; in one case I even came upon a garden with a mini-railroad running through it. This is the "Hamptons" of Delhi, the city's party central, where event planners will re-create Oscar night, Broadway, Las Vegas, even a Punjabi village for the homesick, complete with waiters in ethnic garb.

On a foggy night in late 2010 I made my way to one of these famously decadent bashes, where the valets were juggling black Bentleys and red Porsches, and the hosts invited me to try the Kobe beef they had flown in from Japan, the white truffles from Italy, the beluga caviar from Azerbaijan. It was hard to talk over the pulsating techno-beat, but I managed to engage in a chat with a twenty-something son of the farmhouse demimonde—he was a classic of the type, working for his dad's export business (it always seems to be "exports"), wearing a tight black shirt, hair spiky with grooming gel. After determining that I was a New York–based investor back in town to search for investment opportunities, he shrugged and remarked, "Well, of course. Where else will the money go?"

"Where else will the money go?" I left the party around midnight, well before the main course was served, but the comment stayed with me. It should have stroked my sense of self-importance as an emerging-market investor. After all, the size of my team's fund had surged more than three-fold over the past decade, and if the trend continued—something the par-tying youth seemed to take for granted—then emerging-market investors would be the masters of the universe.

Instead an Urdu couplet came back to haunt me: "I am so stunned by my prosperity that my happiness has begun to make me anxious." I began my investing career in the mid-1990s, when one developing country after another was hit by economic crisis and emerging markets were seen as the problem children of the financial world. By the end of that decade some of my colleagues were rechristening these orphaned assets the "e-merging markets" in an attempt to pick up some of the stardust from the tech boom in the United States.

Emerging markets were spoofed in investment circles as an inversion of the 80/20 rule, which states that 80 percent of your profit comes from the top 20 percent of your clients. For much of post–World War II history, emerging markets accounted for 80 percent of the world's population but only 20 percent of its economic output. When Latin America was on the rise in the 1960s and 1970s, Africa and large parts of Asia were on the decline, and when broad swaths of Asia were growing at a rapid clip, in the 1980s and 1990s, Latin American nations could not seem to get their growth act together, while Africa was dismissed as the "Hopeless Con-tinent." Even as late as 2002 the big-money investors—pension funds, college endowments—saw emerging markets as too small to move the needle on multibillion dollar funds, or just too dangerous, because vast countries like India were seen as the "Wild East" of investing.

So here I was only a few years later, standing with some spoiled kid in the fog and the pounding din, and he is feeling on top of the world because his dad is one of some thirty thousand dollar-millionaires in Delhi, most of them newly minted. He has seen little of the world beyond the isolated farmhouses, and yet he knows enough to parrot the sentiment of emerg-ing markets everywhere: "Where else will the money go?"

Well, he had recent trends on his side. Private capital flows into devel-oping countries had surged from an annual pace of $200 billion in 2000 to nearly a trillion dollars a year in 2010. Even on Wall Street, all the experts were saying the West was in terminal decline, so the money was bound to flow east and south.

It also occurred to me how the dramatic change in sentiment was affecting the attitudes of politicians and businesspeople in the emerging world. When I visited Egypt nearly a decade ago, I was made to feel like an honored state guest of Prime Minister Ahmed Nazif, who invited dozens of media photographers for a ten-minute photo-op, and used my face on the financial pages to demonstrate that foreign investors were beginning to pay attention to his country. Flash forward to October 2010, when I made a televised presentation to Russian prime minister Vladimir Putin in Moscow, in which I was not exactly exuberant about his country's future. Some local media responded with taunts, saying that Russia could do without my fund's money.

By the middle of the last decade it seemed that every man and his dog could raise money for emerging markets. By the end, it appeared that just the dog would do. Yet history suggests economic development is like a game of snakes and ladders. There is no straight path to the top, and there are fewer ladders than snakes, which means that it's much easier to fall than to climb. A nation can climb the ladders for a decade, two decades, three decades, only to hit a snake and fall back to the bottom, where it must start over again, and maybe again and again, while rivals pass it by. That kind of failure happens a lot more often than making it to the top. There is a huge pool of competitors, and only a few nations defy the long odds against success. Those are the rare breakout nations, and they beat the game by growing faster than rivals in their own income class, so that a nation whose per capita income is under $5,000 competes with rivals in that class. The growth game is all about beating expectations, and your peers.

The perception that the growth game had suddenly become easy—that everyone could be a winner—is built on the unique results of the last decade, when virtually all emerging markets did grow together. But that was both the first and, in all probability, the last time we will ever see such a golden age: the next decade will almost certainly not bring more of the same.

For the last fifteen years I have typically spent one week every month in a particular emerging market, obsessing about it, meeting all sorts of local characters, and traveling the breadth of the country, mostly by road. As the writer Aldous Huxley put it, "To travel is to discover that everyone is wrong about other countries." Reading Excel spreadsheets in the office can't tell you, for example, whether a political regime gets the connection between good economics and good politics.

No one can pinpoint the precise mix of reasons why nations grow, or fail to grow. There is no magic formula, only a long list of known ingredients: allow the free-market flow of goods, money, and people; encourage savings, and make sure banks are funneling the money into productive investments; impose the rule of law and protect property rights; stabilize the economy with low budget and trade deficits; keep inflation in check; open doors to foreign capital, particularly when the capital comes with technology as part of the bargain; build better roads and schools; feed the children; and so on. This is armchair academics, clichés that are true but that offer only a long list of dos with no real insight into how these factors will or will not combine to produce growth in any given country at any given time.

To identify breakout nations it is key to travel with an eye toward understanding which economic and political forces are in play at the moment, and whether they point to growth, and at what speed. In a world reshaped by slower global growth, we need to start looking at the emerging markets as individual cases. This book tours the world to examine which nations are likely to flourish—or disappoint—in the new era of diverging economic prospects. Along the way I will offer a few plain-English rules of the road for identifying emerging markets with star potential. My point is to take you with me on my travels in search of the next breakout nations, and to answer that simple but difficult question, "Where else will the money go?"

BREAKOUT NATIONS

Not all trees grow to the sky.

1

The Myth of the Long Run

THE OLD RULE OF FORECASTING was to make as many forecasts as possible and publicize the ones you got right. The new rule is to forecast so far into the future that no one will know you got it wrong.

The super-long view inspires some of the most influential forecasts of our time, which look back to the overwhelming economic might of China and India in the seventeenth century as evidence that they will reemerge as dominant global powers in 2030 or 2050. In 1600 China accounted for more than one-fourth of global GDP, and India accounted for just under a fourth. Though their shares have fallen dramatically since then, the super-long view skips past the messy recent centuries. The reasoning seems to be that seventeenth-century performance offers some guarantee of future results. Sweeping extrapolation has become a staple argument for the many companies, politicians, and high-profile public intellectuals who believe we are entering a Pacific Century or even an African Century. I recently received a report from a major consulting firm forecasting that Nigeria could be one of the top-ten economies in the world by 2050. Well, yes, but almost anything could happen by 2050.

The irony is that the extra-long views have a growing impact even on Wall Street, where in general the way people think about time has become increasingly narrow, even breathless. For example, the average length of time that American investors, both large and small, hold stocks has been falling for decades, from a peak of sixteen years in the mid-1960s to under four months today.* At the same time, Americans and Europeans have been pouring money into emerging nations at a wildly accelerating pace, inspired in no small part by forecasts for the year 2050. The total amount of funds flowing into emerging-market stocks grew by 92 percent between 2000 and 2005, and by a staggering 478 percent between 2005 and 2010. Apparently, for many investors, it is inspiring to imagine that their investments are well grounded in the remote past and the distant future, but in the real world it is not practical for investors or companies to tell clients to come back and check their returns in forty years. Forecasts are valuable, indeed unavoidable for planning purposes, but it doesn't make much sense to talk about the future beyond five years, maybe ten at the most.

The longest period that reveals clear patterns in the global economic cycle is also around a decade. The typical business cycle lasts about five years, from the bottom of one downturn to the bottom of the next, and the perspective of most practical people is limited to one or two business cycles. Beyond that, forecasts are often rendered obsolete by the appearance of new competitors (China in the early 1980s) or new technologies (the Internet in the early 1990s) or new leaders (the typical election cycle is also about five years). The super-long view is being popularized largely by economic historians and commentators and has become faddishly influential in business circles as well. But the reality is that most CEOs still limit their strategic visions to three, five, or at most seven years, and big institutional investors judge results based on one-, three-, and five-year returns. As much as we all love the speculative titillation of futurology, no one can forecast the next century with any credibility and, more important, be held accountable for it.

Today we are at a very revealing moment. For the last half century, the early years of each decade saw a major turning point in the world economy and markets. Each began with a global mania for some big idea, some new change agent that reshaped the world economy and generated huge

---

*Throughout the book, "now" and "today" refer to the best-available information as of late 2011. The "last decade" means the 2000s; the "last year" or "last five years" means the period through mid- to late 2011.

profits. In 1970 the mania was for the top U.S. companies like Disney, which had been the "go-go stocks" of the 1960s. In 1980 the hot play was natural resources, from gold to oil. In 1990 it was Japan, and in 2000 it was Silicon Valley. There were always a few doubters shouting from the wings, warning that other changes were overtaking the change agent—that spiking oil prices will self-destruct by strangling the world economy, that a patch of Tokyo real estate can't be worth more than the entire state of California, that tech start-ups with zero earnings can't possibly justify stock prices in the four figures. But by this point in the mania, there were so many billions of dollars invested in the hot new thing that few people wanted to listen to the Cassandras.

Most gurus and forecasters are willing to give people what they want: exotic reasons to believe that they are in with the smart crowd. The mania appears to make sense, for a time, until the exotic reasoning crumbles. In all the postwar booms just cited, the bubble went bust in the first few years of the new decade.

The Miracle Year of 2003

The mania at the start of the 2010s was the big emerging markets, in particular the belief that the economies of China, India, Brazil, and Russia would continue growing at the astonishingly rapid pace of the previous decade. This was a unique golden age, unlikely to be repeated yet widely accepted as the new standard by which poorer nations should measure growth. The emerging-market mania began with China, which for two decades starting in 1978 grew rapidly, but erratically, anywhere from 4 to 12 percent a year. Then in 1998 China began an unbroken run of growth at 8 percent or more each year, almost as if the lucky Chinese number 8 had also become an iron rule of Chinese economics.

Starting in the year 2003, an underappreciated turning point in the course of the world, this good fortune suddenly spread to virtually all emerging nations, a class that can be defined a number of different ways but here broadly means countries with a per capita income of less than $25,000.* Between 2003 and 2007, the average GDP growth rate in these

* See appendix A for a full list of the emerging markets.

countries almost doubled, from 3.6 percent in the prior two decades to 7.2 percent, and almost no developing nation was left behind. In the peak year of 2007, the economies of all but 3 of the world's 183 countries grew, and they expanded at better than 5 percent in 114 countries, up from an average of about 50 countries in the prior two decades. The three outliers were Fiji and the chronic basket cases of Zimbabwe and the Republic of Congo, all exceptions that proved the rule. The rising tide lifted nation after nation through a series of normally difficult development stages: Russia, to cite the most dramatic example, saw its average annual income soar effortlessly from $1,500 to $13,000 in the course of the decade.

This was the fastest, most all-encompassing growth spurt the world has ever seen. Even more unusual, these economies were taking wing at the same time that inflation, a constant threat in periods of rapid growth, was falling back everywhere. The number of nations that beat inflation—containing the annual rate of price increases to less than 5 percent—rose from 16 in 1980 to 103 in 2006. This was the same high-growth and low-inflation "Goldilocks economy" that America enjoyed in the 1990s, only with much faster growth and expanded to a planetary scale, including much of the West. It was a chorus of all nations, singing a story of stable high-speed success, and many observers watched with undiscriminating optimism. The emerging nations were all Chinas now, or so it seemed.

This illusion, which in large part persists to this day, is fed by the fashionable explanation for the boom—that emerging markets succeeded because they had learned the lessons of the Mexican peso crisis, the Russian crisis, and the Asian crisis in the 1990s, all of which began when piles of foreign debt became too big to pay. But starting in the late 1990s, these formerly irresponsible debtor nations cleaned up the red ink and became creditors, even as former creditor nations, led by the United States, began sinking into debt. Thus the emerging nations were poised, as never before, to take advantage of the global flows of people, money, and goods that had been unleashed by the fall of Communism in 1990.

Former president George W. Bush tells a story about Vladimir Putin that illustrates how completely the global economy had been turned on its head. In mid-2011 at a conference in the Bahamas, I moderated a discussion featuring President Bush, who told us that when he first met the Russian leader in 2000, Russia was struggling to recover from a massive currency crisis and Putin was obsessed with its national debt. By early 2008, Russia's economy was booming, its budget was deep in the black, and the first thing Putin wanted to talk about was the value of U.S. mortgage-backed securities, which would soon collapse in the debt crisis. Putin's focus had shifted 180 degrees, from cutting Russian debt to enquiring about the risk of holding American debt, and he was growing cocky about Russia's economic expansion. The Russian leader, who had met Bush's little terrier, Barney, on an earlier visit to Washington, introduced his black Lab to Bush later in the decade with the remark, "See, bigger, stronger, faster than Barney."

Swelling pride was the norm across all emerging nations, and the declining national debts, at least, were a sign of real progress. Some countries (including, for a time, Putin's Russia) were learning to spend wisely, investing in the education, communication, and transportation systems necessary to raise productivity—the key to high growth with low inflation. But the most important factor behind the boom went overlooked: a worldwide flood of easy money.

The easy money that set the stage for the Great Recession of 2008, by fueling the American housing bubble, still flows freely, now dispensed by central banks attempting to engineer a recovery to the growth rates of the last decade, which were not sustainable anyway. What is apparent now is that while central banks can print all the money they want, they can't dictate where it goes. This time around, much of that money has flown into speculative oil futures, luxury real estate in major financial capitals, and other nonproductive investments, leading to an inflation problem in the emerging world and undermining the purchasing power of consumers across the globe. As speculation drives up oil prices, consumers now spend a record amount of their income on energy needs.

The easy money flows from a sea change in the way the United States sees hard times. The old view was that recessions were a natural phase in the business cycle, unpleasant but unavoidable. A new view started to emerge in the Goldilocks economy of the 1990s, when after many straight years of solid growth, people started to say that the Federal Reserve had beaten back the business cycle. Under Alan Greenspan and his successor, Ben Bernanke, the Fed shifted focus from fighting inflation and smoothing the business cycle to engineering growth. Low U.S. interest rates and rising debt increasingly became the bedrock of American growth, and the increases in total U.S. debt started to dwarf the increases in total U.S. GDP: in the 1970s it took $1.00 of debt to generate $1.00 of U.S. GDP growth, in the 1980s and 1990s it took $3.00, and by the last decade it took $5.00. American borrowing was getting less and less productive, focused more on financial engineering and conspicuous consumption.

U.S. debt became the increasingly shaky pillar of the global boom. Low interest rates were driving growth in the United States, pressuring central banks around the world to lower their rates as well, while fueling an explosion in U.S. consumer spending that drove up emerging-market exports. It was no coincidence that the emerging markets began to levitate in mid-2003, after aggressive U.S. interest-rate cuts—aimed at sustaining a recovery after the tech bubble burst two years earlier—started the worldwide flood of easy money, much of which poured into emerging markets. The flow of private money into emerging markets accounted for 2 percent of emerging-market GDP in the 1990s—and jumped to 9 percent of a far higher GDP in 2007.

Now the credit house of cards has collapsed—a casualty of the Great Recession. There is much talk in the West of a "new normal," defined by slower growth as the big economies struggle to pay down huge debts. Real GDP growth in the rich nations is expected to fall this decade by nearly a full percentage point, to about 2 to 2.5 percent in the United States and 1 to 1.5 percent in Europe and Japan. What observers have not realized, however, is that emerging markets also face a "new normal," even if they are not ready to accept that reality. As growth slows in rich nations they will buy less from countries with export-driven economies, such as Mexico, Taiwan, and Malaysia. During the boom the average trade balance in emerging markets nearly tripled as a share of GDP, inspiring a new round of hype about the benefits of globalization, but since 2008 trade has fallen back to the old share of under 2 percent. Export-driven emerging markets, which is to say most of them, will have to find a new way to grow at a strong pace.

The $4,000 Barrier

This is not just a seasonal shift. It is a fundamental change in the dynamic that has driven the rise of emerging markets for several decades now. The basic laws of economic gravity are already pulling China, Russia, Brazil, and other big emerging markets back to earth. The first is the law of large numbers, which says that the richer a country is, the harder it is to grow national wealth at a rapid pace.

China and many other big emerging markets are following an export-driven growth model similar to those adopted by Japan, South Korea, and Taiwan after World War II. All these boom economies began to slow from 9 or 10 percent growth to around 5 or 6 percent when their per capita incomes reached upper middle-income levels, which the World Bank defines as a country with a per capita income of $4,000 or more in current dollar terms. Japan hit that wall in the mid-1970s; Taiwan and South Korea hit it over the subsequent two decades. Note that these are the greatest success stories in the history of economic development, so they represent the best-case scenario.

In all three cases the major warning sign of a slowdown was what economists call "structural inflation": the sudden rise in worker demands for higher pay, indicating that there was no longer a bottomless pool of labor available to staff the export factories at rock-bottom wages. China exceeded the $4,000 mark in 2010, just as the latest outbreak of labor strikes for higher wages was accelerating. Yet many observers still choose to believe that China can blow beyond the $4,000 barrier at near-double-digit speed.

At the same time, investors in the West have lost faith in the dynamism of the United States and Europe and are turning east and south, partly in desperation. In 2009 and 2010 hundreds of billions of dollars went into emerging-market funds that made little or no distinction between Poland and Peru, India and Indonesia. Such "macro mania"—an obsession with global macro trends—operates on the assumption (at least temporarily correct during the boom years) that knowledge of the broad movements in the world economy is all you need to evaluate any particular asset class. The result is that the prices of stocks in all the mainstream emerging markets have been moving together in increasingly synchronized formations.

In the first half of 2011 the difference between the best-performing and the worst-performing major stock markets in the emerging world was just 10 percent, an all-time low and a dangerous indicator of herd behavior.

This is exactly the same mistake the world made in the run-up to the Asian crisis of 1997–1998, when all the emerging "tiger" economies were seen, one way or another, as the next Japan. Encouraged by Wall Street marketers and best-selling books, today many analysts and investors are thinking big about the shift of wealth from the West to the East, and the coming "convergence" of rich and poor nations—the idea that the average incomes of emerging nations are rapidly catching up to those of rich nations. This is a great sales gimmick, but it distorts the reality, which is that emerging markets could not be more different from one another.

For a start, these nations are all over the development map. Russia, Brazil, Mexico, and Turkey, with average annual incomes above $10,000, have much slower growth potential than India, Indonesia, or the Philippines, whose average incomes are well under $5,000. But high incomes do not necessarily translate into technological strength: Hungary is in the same income class as Brazil and Mexico, but 90 percent of Hungarians have access to mobile communications, compared with only 40 percent of Brazilians and Mexicans.

The debt loads of emerging markets vary widely—even recent success stories like China and South Korea carry as heavy a burden of personal and business loans, relative to GDP, as many troubled developed countries. The typical South Korean has more than three credit cards and carries debts larger than the average annual income, while fewer than one in three Brazilians has even one card. The nature of emerging-market vulnerability to troubles in the West also takes many forms. Many Asian countries still depend on exports to the West, while several eastern European countries rely more on lending from the West to fund growth.

Not All Trees Grow to the Sky

There has also been a halt to the reforms that set many developing countries on the "emerging" path in the first place. After Deng Xiaoping began experimenting with free-market reform in the early 1980s, China went on to launch a "big bang" reform every four to five years, and each new opening—first to private farming, then to private businesses, then to for-eign businesses—set off a new spurt of growth. But that cycle has run its course.

The unthinking faith in the hot growth stories of the last decade also ignores the high odds against success. Very few nations achieve long-term rapid growth. My own research shows that over the course of any given decade since 1950, on average only one-third of emerging markets have been able to grow at an annual rate of 5 percent or more. Less than one-fourth have kept that pace up for two decades, and one-tenth for three decades. Just six countries (Malaysia, Singapore, South Korea, Taiwan, Thailand, and Hong Kong) have maintained this rate of growth for four decades, and two (South Korea and Taiwan) have done so for five decades. Indeed, in the last decade, except for China and India, all the other countries that managed to keep up a 5 percent growth rate, from Angola to Tanzania and Armenia to Tajikistan, are new to this class. In many ways the "mortality rate" of countries is as high as that of stocks. Only four companies—Proctor & Gamble, General Electric, AT&T, and DuPont—have survived on the Dow Jones index of the top-thirty U.S. industrial stocks since the 1960s. Few front-runners stay in the lead for a decade, much less many decades, and identifying those few is an art rather than a science.

Over the next few years the new normal in emerging markets will be much like the old normal, dating back to the 1950s and 1960s, when growth was averaging around 5 percent, and the race was in its usual state of churn. The subsequent decades saw growth that was either unusually weak or unusually strong: In the 1980s and 1990s, growth in emerging markets averaged only 3.5 percent, weighed down by the collapse of the Soviet Union and serial financial crises in countries ranging from Mexico to Thailand to Russia. That was followed by the liquidity-fueled, turbocharged boom of the last decade, which is now unraveling as the cost of funding growth rises. Once a financial soufflé collapses, it can only rise again once memories of the collapse fade. Given the depths of the Great Recession of 2008, however, another debt binge is extremely unlikely in the next decade.

The return of emerging-market growth rates similar to those in the

1960s does not imply a revival of the image of the "Third World," consisting of uniformly dark and backward nations at the bottom of the heap and destined to stay that way. During the 1950s and 1960s the biggest emerging markets—China and India—were struggling to grow at all. Nations like Iran, Iraq, and Yemen put together long strings of strong growth, but those runs came to a violent halt with the outbreak of war, and these countries are now more closely associated with conflict than finance. The chaos overshadowed the takeoff in places like South Korea and Taiwan, both of which were largely unrecognized in their early years. While there are no reliable growth data on emerging markets from before 1950, the available evidence suggests that never have so many nations grown so fast for so long as they did in the last decade. Yet today analysts are still looking for this miracle of mass convergence to happen all over the globe.

Meanwhile, scores of "emerging" nations have been emerging for many decades now. They have failed to gain any momentum for sustained growth or their progress has begun to stall since they became middle-income countries. Malaysia and Thailand appeared to be on course to emerge as rich nations until the crony capitalism at the heart of those systems caused a financial meltdown in the crisis of 1998. Their growth has disappointed ever since. In the 1960s, the Philippines, Sri Lanka, and Burma were billed as the next East Asian tigers, only to see their growth falter badly, well before they could reach the "middle-class" average income of about $4,000. Failure to sustain growth is the general rule, and that rule is likely to reassert itself in the coming decade.

While India is widely touted as the next China, the odds are even that India could regress to be the next Brazil. While in recent years Brazil has been widely touted as a rising regional superpower, on the relevant fundamentals Brazil is the anti-China, a nation that invested in the premature construction of a welfare state rather than the roads and wireless networks of a modern industrial economy. Nations that have grown dependent on booming prices for raw materials such as oil and precious metals—namely, Russia and Brazil—face a hard decade ahead. These countries had two of the world's top stock markets in the last decade.

The next decade is full of bright spots, but you can't find them by looking back at the nations that got the most hype in the last decade, and

hope they will hit new highs going forward. These stars are the breakout
nations, by which I mean the nations that can sustain rapid growth, beating or at least matching high expectations and the average growth rates
of their income class; for a nation like the Czech Republic, in the income
class of $20,000 and more, breaking out will mean 3 to 4 percent growth
in GDP, while for China, in the class of $5,000 and less, anything less
than 6 to 7 percent will feel like a recession.

One of the great economic stories of the century is largely overlooked,
because the European Union is widely spoofed as an "open-air museum"
and in late 2011 is in the throes of a severe debt crisis. But the EU is also
a stabilizing model and still an inspiration for some new members, particularly Poland and the Czech Republic, which are in that rare class of
nations poised to break through and join the ranks of the rich elite. Not
every little EU member is a Greece.

The Rules of the Road

The main rule for identifying breakout nations is to understand that economic regimes—the factors driving growth in any given country at any
given time—are in constant flux. Different operating rules apply in different nations, depending on rapidly changing circumstances. Economic
regimes are like markets. When they are on a good run they tend to over-
shoot and create the conditions for their own demise. Popular understanding tends to lag well behind the reality: by the time a regime's rules have
been codified by experts and hashed over in the media, it is likely already
in decline. That dynamic underpins Goodhart's law (a cousin of Murphy's
law), coined by former Bank of England adviser Charles Goodhart: once
an economic indicator gets too popular, it loses its predictive value.

In a period of impending change, like this one, with the painful ending of a golden age of easy money and easy growth, it is typical for people
to cling to dated ideas and rules for too long, particularly notions that
minimize or explain away potential risks. The most dramatic recent example is the idea that the basic tools of economic stimulus—lowering interest rates and raising public spending—can end a business cycle, not only
in the United States but also in the developing world. In the emerging
markets, there has long been a disturbing tendency among leaders to take

credit for boom times and blame bad times on the West: that phenomenon was widespread in late 2011, as many leaders attributed any slowdown in emerging markets to contagion from Europe, forgetting that lending from European banks was a key driver of the boom in the first place.

Another dated idea is the rise of demographic analysis as a financial-consulting industry. Because China's boom was driven in part by a particularly large generation of young people entering the workforce, there is now a small army of consultants who scour census data looking for similar population boomlets as an indicator of the next big economic miracle. These forecasts often assume that these workers have the necessary education and skills to be employable, and that governments will find gainful employment for them. In a world where a rising tide was lifting all economies, this made brief sense, but economic conditions will change. They always do.

One way or another all the rules flow from understanding the current economic regime—recognizing the pace of change; determining whether it is moving in productive or destructive directions, and whether it is creating balanced growth across income classes, ethnic groups, and regions, or precarious imbalances. It's not just a cultural oddity that new wealth in Warsaw is boring and understated while the style of the Moscow elite is garish and overstated: it's a sign that Poland has a more serious future than Russia does, because Poland is spending money more wisely. On the other hand, it is not always a good sign when celebratory headlines announce that such-and-such company is "going global": in countries like Mexico or South Africa, which still have underdeveloped consumer markets, companies going global may be a bad sign if they are voting with their feet against the way politicians are governing the national economy.

It's also not just a nasty shock for European tourists that everything from a Bellini (a peachy champagne brunch cocktail) to a taxi ride feels like it costs a fortune in Rio: it's a symptom of the overpriced Brazilian currency, the real, and of the general rule that a cheap currency is a sign of competitive strength. Brazil's economy has gotten a bit fat and slow, even as hot money-flows rendered the real overpriced and uncompetitive. So that expensive Bellini is not only a sign of weakness for Brazil, it's a sign of strength for competitors, even of potential revival in Detroit, as the

United States regains competitiveness against major emerging markets. After falling in value by a third since 2001 versus the currencies of its major trading partners, by mid-2011 the U.S. dollar was at its cheapest inflation-adjusted rate since the early 1970s.

The consensus is typically a step behind the next big change in the economic scene, and one increasingly inescapable conclusion is that the prevailing pessimism about the United States is probably overwrought. Over the last decade several major emerging-market currencies have risen against the dollar—none more than the Brazilian real—which is the main reason why the long-term decline in the U.S. share of global exports bottomed out in 2008 at 8 percent and has since been inching higher. U.S. dependence on foreign energy has steadily fallen from 30 percent a decade ago to 22 percent today, owing to new discoveries of oil and gas trapped in shale rock and the development of new technologies to extract it. The United States has now overtaken Russia as the number one producer of natural gas, and could reemerge as a major energy exporter in the next five years. Basic American strengths—including rapid innovation in a highly competitive market—are producing the revival of its energy industry and extending its lead in technology; all the hot new things from social networking to cloud computing seem to be emerging once again from Silicon Valley or from rising tech hotspots like Austin, Texas. As some of the big emerging markets lose their luster over the next decade, the United States could appear quite resilient in comparison.

For a truly rounded view of emerging markets, my approach is to monitor everything from per capita income levels to the top-ten billionaire lists, the speeches of radical politicians, the prices of black-market money changers, the travel habits of local businessmen (for example, whether they are moving money home or offshore), the profit margins of big monopolies, and the size of second cities (oversized capital cities often indicate excessive power in the hands of the political elite). This is an approach based on experience on the ground, not on theory or numbers alone. In one form or another, every major investor works essentially the same way: learn the macroeconomic numbers, then go to the country and kick its tires, get a feel for "the story." Locals are the first to know. In 2003, my team saw that the global rush of easy money was about to sweep up

Brazil when the black-market money changers, who had been demanding a premium for dollars, suddenly started quoting prices for the real that were higher than the official exchange rate.

A nuanced perspective on individual nations may not have mattered so much even a decade ago, when developing economies represented less than 20 percent of the global economy and merely 5 percent of the world's stock market capitalization. As of 2011 emerging markets represent nearly 40 percent of the global economy and just under 15 percent of the total value of the world's stock markets. These economies are now too big to be lumped into one marginal class, and are better understood as individual nations.

2

China's After-Party

Nothing captures the over-the-top quality of the long boom in China better than the maglev train that zips from Longyan Road in Shanghai to Pudong International Airport in eight minutes. I had often seen the maglev as a white blur, flying by as I drove to the airport, but I had never taken it. There is no practical reason to ride the maglev—Longyan Road is in the middle of nowhere, twenty minutes from the city center, and the walk from the train station at the airport to the terminal is longer than the maglev ride itself. But on a 2009 visit I finally found the spare time to take the world's fastest operational train. And boy was it fun.

A big digital screen ticks off the speed until it hits a maximum of about 270 miles per hour, but if you don't look out the window you can't tell you're moving. No rocking, no rattling, indeed no sound at all, particularly in my car, where my colleague and I were the only riders apart from the conductor, who was dressed like a flight attendant. Locals say the train typically runs half full, attributable to the inconvenience and the relatively steep ticket price of $8.00 ($13.00 in first class, compared to $1.50 for the metro trains). "Maglev" means "magnetic levitation," and promotional videos that describe it as "flying at zero altitude" capture the sensation pretty well, because the magnets float the train a fraction of an inch off the ground. It was like a cool amusement-park ride, but I have taken it only that one time.

*The myth of the missing consumers: they are easy to
find everywhere in China.*

It is easy to spoof this cross between public transport and slingshot coaster as another Chinese extravagance—alongside the "ghost cities" of unsold apartment blocks, and the vacant sports venues left over from the 2008 Olympics. However, my point here is to highlight how entirely unique it is that China, a nation in the same income class (around $5,000 annual per capita income) as Thailand and Peru, was able to build and maintain an experimental technology that none of the richest nations have yet managed to put into commercial operation. Britain ran a maglev in Birmingham from 1984 to 1995, and Germany pondered one for Berlin in the 2000s, but both gave up for cost reasons. With 1.2 billion people in an economy that has been growing at a double-digit pace for more than a decade, China has been generating a national income stream that allowed it to experiment in exciting ways unthinkable even for richer nations.

But as the economy has matured, the high-speed fun and games are coming to a close. Plans to extend the Shanghai line have been put off, apparently because of local protests over electromagnetic radiation from the trains, and concern about the expensive nature of such projects. China is moving to a new stage, one in which costs and public reaction matter, and the scope for multibillion-dollar experiments is narrowing.

A rethink is already under way in China. It was back in 2008 that Premier Wen Jiabao described Chinese growth as "unbalanced, uncoordinated and unsustainable," and the situation has grown more precarious since. To a degree most observers have underestimated, many critical factors now point to a slowdown in China. Total debt as a share of GDP is rising fast, and the advantage of cheap labor, a key to the Chinese boom, is rapidly disappearing, as the labor shortage gives workers the upper hand in contract negotiations. In late 2011 the head of a small construction glass company in Shentou, a factory town outside Shanghai, complained to a member of my team, "Three years ago you could shout at your workers, now they can shout at you."

These costs are starting to spill over into higher inflation, and Beijing has openly acknowledged that all this points to a slowdown in the economy. Yet such is the overblown faith in China's economic stewards that the China bulls seem to think Beijing can achieve growth targets the country itself no longer aims to achieve. The amazing story of China's relentless reform—which had persisted in good times and bad since the landmark reign of paramount leader Deng Xiaoping and his immediate successors appears to have exhausted itself in the last few years.

China boomed the old-fashioned way, by building roads to connect factories to ports, by developing telecommunication networks to connect business to business, and by putting underemployed peasants to work in better jobs at urban factories. Now all these drivers are reaching a mature stage, as the pool of surplus rural labor dries up, factory employment reaches maximum capacity, and the highway network reaches a total length of 46,000 miles, the second largest in the world behind the 62,000 miles in the United States. The demographic trend that in recent decades tipped the population balance toward young, income-earning workers is nearly past, and a growing class of pensioners will soon start to work its decaying effect on growth.

The exports that have powered Chinese growth will also slow as the West struggles with its debts. Over the past decade China's exports have grown at an average yearly pace of 20 percent, and that is bound to come down. The bulls say China can continue to grow by changing its focus from export markets to domestic consumers, but this hope rests on a myth: that the Chinese consumer has been suppressed. In fact, Chinese consumption has been growing at the near-double-digit rate expected of a boom economy. These are natural barriers that cannot be overcome.

The current debate on China's future has two basic camps: the extremely bullish camp and the bearish camp. The extremely bullish camp likes to extrapolate past trends endlessly into the future, forecasting continued growth of 8 percent or better. The economists who are most bullish on China predict the economy will grow by 15 percent in dollar terms every year, or 8 percent growth in GDP plus 5 percent appreciation of the yuan and 3 to 4 percent inflation, which would be enough for China to "eclipse" the United States in a decade. The bulls leave no room for recession or reversal, and they forecast a kind of endless boom in the urban real estate market, assuming that tens of millions of rural Chinese will migrate to the cities over the next two decades as they have done in the last two. The bearish camp was a shrill minority until recently, but it's growing. One common line of the bearish argument is that China's over-investment, surging debts, and rising home prices are very similar to what occurred in Thailand and Malaysia before the 1997–1998 Asian crisis, which brought those economies to a grinding halt. I think the truth probably lies in the middle.

Too Big to Boom

The most likely path for China is the trajectory Japan followed in the early 1970s, when its hot postwar economy began to slow sharply but still grew at a rapid clip, an entirely expected course for any maturing "miracle" economy. China is on the verge of a natural slowdown that will change the global balance of power, from finance to politics, and take the wind out of many economies that are riding in its draft. The signs of the coming slowdown are already clear, and it is likely to begin in earnest within the next two or three years, cutting China's growth from 10 percent to 6 or 7 percent. As a result the millions of investors and companies betting on near-double-digit growth in China could be wiped out.

It is said that it takes money to make money, but for nations to grow rapidly it is much easier to be poor—the poorer, the better. Per capita income is the critical measure because a growing pie doesn't change a nation's circumstances if the number of mouths it needs to feed is growing just as fast. To grow 10 percent from an average annual personal income of $1,000, a nation needs to earn an extra $100 per person, assuming zero population growth; at $10,000 the nation needs to make an extra $1,000.

It makes no sense to think of India ($1,400 per capita income, with a high-growth population) in the same way as Russia ($13,000, with a shrinking population). The richer the country, the tougher the growth challenge, and it is possible to be too big to grow fast. It becomes a question not only of scale but also of balance, of devouring an outsized share. In 1998, for China to grow its $1 trillion economy by 10 percent, it had to expand its economic activities by $100 billion and consume only 10 percent of the world's industrial commodities—the raw materials that include everything from oil to copper and steel. In 2011, to grow its $6 trillion economy that fast, it needed to expand by $600 billion a year and suck in more than 30 percent of global commodity production.

Academic literature warns that in the early stages of development, emerging nations can narrow the income gap with rich nations with relative ease, by borrowing or copying the technology and management tools of cutting edge nations. At a certain point, however, emerging nations have borrowed all they can and need to start innovating and inventing on their own, and many fail at this challenge. Their economies suddenly stop growing faster than those in the rich nations, and thus they stop catching up. They have hit the "middle-income trap," where they can idle for years, like unhappy residents of a lower-middle-class suburb.

Typically the middle-income trap is said to spring at an income level equal to between 10 and 30 percent of the income level in the world's "leading nation," the one that sets the gold standard in technology and management. Today that nation is the United States, and 10 to 30 percent of the average U.S. income is $5,000 to $15,000, which clues you in to the problem with this academic concept. The range of incomes is so large that the middle-income trap is not terribly useful as a guide to which nations really have the potential to continue growing at a rapid pace.

The middle-income trap also ignores the separate phenomenon of the middle-income deceleration. The economies of many nations have slowed down to a lower cruising speed, even if they did not stop catching up entirely. This has been the experience of even the most successful growth stories in modern history, including those of Japan, Korea, and Taiwan, which witnessed an early deceleration at an income level equivalent to where China is today. After adjustments are made for changes in the exchange rate, China is at roughly the same income level—of around $5,000—as Japan in the early 1970s, Taiwan in the late 1980s, and Korea in the early 1990s. Though they all continued to catch up to the United States, they did so much more slowly, with growth rates falling from around 9 percent to 5 percent for many years. Given the similarities between China and these export-driven East Asian predecessors, one could argue that these are the cases most directly relevant to China, where a four-percentage-point slowdown would take the growth rate to 6 percent. China can continue to push for double-digit growth by paying workers to build trains to nowhere (as Japan built bridges to nowhere in the 1980s, with disastrous results), or it can change its growth targets— and that appears to be the plan.

In the last decade the main driver of China's boom was a surge in the investment share of GDP from 35 percent to almost 50 percent, a level that is unprecedented in any major nation. Investment spending includes everything from transportation and telecommunication networks to office buildings and equipment, factories and factory machinery—all the stuff that lays the foundation for future growth, which is why this is a critical indicator. China was spending more on new investment—basically pouring more concrete—than the far-larger economies of the United States and Europe, where the investment shares of GDP were about 15 and 20 percent, respectively. The investment effort focused on building the roads, bridges, and ports needed to turn China into the world's largest exporter, doubling its global export-market share to 10 percent in the last decade.

This spending spree can't continue. By 2010 the government had already laid out plans to cut back, lowering the pace of new road construction from about 5,000 miles in 2007 to 2,500 miles in 2010, and announcing a 10 percent cut in spending on new railways for 2011. By late 2011, the *Wall Street Journal* was reporting that as a result of funding cuts and safety concerns in the wake of a deadly collision of high-speed trains in July, builders had been forced to suspend work on 6,200 miles of track, half of it on new high-speed lines.

The Fountain of Youth Runs Dry

China's changing demographics also point to a slowdown. The surge of rural workers to better-paid jobs in the cities is slowing dramatically. China is closing in on what is known as "the Lewis turning point," named for the Saint Lucian economist Arthur Lewis, which is the point when most underemployed farmers have already left the farm. According to estimates by an independent research and consulting firm, Capital Economics, of the rural Chinese who are no longer needed as farm workers, 150 million have already moved to cities, 84 million have found nonfarm jobs in the countryside, and only 15 million are left in the "surplus" pool. The rate of urban migration has slowed dramatically to about 5 million a year, a pace that is still fast enough to exhaust the surplus labor pool soon. When it runs out, urban wages, which are already rising sharply, are likely to jump even higher.

As the countryside is emptying out, China's two postwar baby-boom generations are getting ready to retire. The first boom in the 1950s was brought to a halt by the famine that broke out in 1958, and the second was encouraged by Mao Zedong, who strongly believed that a large population was a key to economic and military might. By the late 1960s and early 1970s, the average Chinese woman was having six children, and it was that generation that would boost the size of China's young labor force starting in the 1980s. Even before Mao died in 1976, however, the Communist Party mandarins were turning against his ideas on population, which led to the establishment of the one-child policy in 1979 and the end of significant baby booms. The result is that only five million people between the ages of thirty-five and fifty-four will join China's core labor force this decade, versus ninety million in the previous decade.

So China is losing its edge in youth. For decades the population of the very old and very young had been decreasing relative to the most productive age groups (fifteen to sixty-four), who pay for pensions and preschools. But that trend—toward an increasingly young and productive population—is expected to reverse over the next three years. The aging of the population will put pressure on the working class to increase its productivity, in order to support all those new retirees, and the shrinking labor pool will put pressure on businesses to raise wages.

Why Inflation Points to a Long-Term Slowdown

The declining size of its workforce is the key reason why, for the first time in decades, China is seeing wage-driven inflation: as of late 2011 the average wage was rising at an average annual rate of about 15 percent, and prices were rising at a recent-record pace of more than 5 percent. A sudden rise in factory wages was the most important warning sign that at the peak of their boom decades, economic growth in Japan, Korea, and Taiwan was about to slow sharply. China is hitting that same point.

In addition, wages have been growing faster for unskilled than for skilled workers. The gap between the wages of migrants working off-the-books jobs and those of college graduates has been closing, while the wages of farmhands have been rising faster than what migrants earn. That means that the return on moving to the city, and on getting a college education (the additional income one can expect with a degree), has dropped. For Chinese employers this means paying more and more for less and less.

Lately employers have started paying just to get workers to return to work. Every year tens of millions of migrant workers go home to see their families for the New Year holidays. In the award-winning 2009 documentary *The Last Train Home*, director Lixin Fan captures the utter chaos of the holiday season in China. For most, the cheapest and fastest route home is by train, but the impossible crowds strain the system past the breaking point. Police use bullhorns, batons, verbal abuse—whatever means necessary—to keep the vast mob under control. Many migrants camp at the railway station for weeks, waiting to buy tickets. Others give up in despair, crippled by exhaustion. Those who get a ticket often have to climb through a window to get on the train, for a ride that can last up to three days but seems much longer. Many have to stand day and night, for lack of space on the floor to sit. Some wear diapers to avoid using the lavatory, and struggle to keep their sanity during the ride.

When the documentary was filmed, an estimated 130 million people made the holiday journey—but each year the numbers were growing by double digits, like so much else in China. Now, as rural incomes rise and living conditions improve in the countryside, factory owners are increasingly worried that workers will go home and stay. To prevent that from happening, they are offering all kinds of perks, from films to food, to make factory life more appealing. Shenzhou Limited, a large manufacturer of apparel, runs a fleet of comfortable buses, stocked with food, beverages, and movies, to take workers home for New Year's and pick them up at the end of the holidays.

This growing need to cater to workers is a reflection of the increasing bargaining power of labor, as strikes and walkouts erupt in the manufacturing belt of the southeastern coast. Although discussion of Chinese wage hikes typically centers on manufacturing, wage inflation is at least as high (about 20 percent per year) in low-skilled service industries such as basic retail, catering, and hospitality. In fact hourly wages are now rising twice as fast as productivity, or hourly output per worker, which is forcing companies to raise prices just to cover the cost of higher wages.

Sharply increasing wages call into serious question the future of a Chinese economy built on cheap labor and exports. Improved productivity made it possible for China to grow fast with low inflation, but that era is coming to a close. Rising wages are compelling manufacturers to move plants to cheaper labor markets in nations like Indonesia and Bangladesh, so the export-manufacturing boom in China has probably hit its limit and may start to reverse. Typically it is difficult for any nation to expand the manufacturing share of its labor force much beyond 20 percent, and China's is already at around 23 percent.

One Price Beijing Won't Pay Is Social Revolt

The worst case of consumer price inflation is in the property market, which has given rise to a house-flipping culture that makes America's recent mania seem rational by comparison. To maintain growth as the global financial crisis struck in 2008, Beijing ordered banks to open the tap on loans so wide that in the subsequent three years the nation issued new credit to the tune of nearly $4 trillion—almost the size of its entire economy in 2009—making the credit binge bigger than the U.S. credit expansion during the 2003–2007 boom. There is now more money in circulation in China ($10 trillion) than in the United States ($8 trillion).

Much of that money found its way into real estate. In 2010 approximately 800 million square feet of real estate was sold in China, more than in the rest of the world combined. Urban real estate prices in major Chinese cities such as Beijing and Shanghai rose past the level (relative to their underlying economy) that Japan hit in the late 1980s, when the land under the Imperial Palace in Tokyo would have sold for more than all of California.

Property prices in premier Chinese cities doubled between 2003 and 2008, then jumped by another 40 percent in 2009 and 2010, making houses increasingly unaffordable for the vast majority of the locals. Some cities have been imposing caps on property price increases to calm the market. The most popular television show in China in the late 2000s was *Woju*, or "Snail's Home," which depicted the despair of average Chinese people over spiraling apartment prices (apparently a bit too vividly—it was taken off national TV channels in late 2009). The despair is perhaps particularly acute for the growing legions of young Chinese men who can't find a mate because they can't afford a house: 70 percent of single Chinese women say that the first thing they look for in a man is the deed to an apartment. Meanwhile cash-rich Chinese are buying multiple homes.

The mismatch between the cost of new homes and the content of the typical Chinese wallet is complete. Developers are building "ghost cities"—vast tracts of apartment high-rises and malls that remain largely vacant because the average Chinese worker can't afford them. One reason prices are so high is that when the government privatized the housing market between 1998 and 2003, it sold off state-owned urban apartments to their occupants at well below market rates. When the occupants turned around and resold the units at higher prices, they could afford new apartments well beyond their income range, pushing prices skyward. Having triggered this upward spiral, Beijing stepped in to mitigate the problem in 2010, launching an ambitious plan to build 15.4 million low-cost "social housing" apartments by 2012.

But local governments and developers are making such fat margins on the booming market that few want to free their land or time to build social housing. Since many of the developers are now private companies, as a result of the 1998 reforms, they don't take orders directly from Beijing. In response the government is employing land-use laws to force developers to build social housing. This leads to a final mismatch. Few young Chinese aspire to live in public tract homes, so some of these cheaper developments may become new ghost cities. To control the runaway housing market, Beijing has been hiking interest rates through the central bank, which will slow investment and overall economic growth.

Outsiders who think Chinese leaders care only about fast growth overlook their mounting concern about the anger over inflation, and the threats to social stability. Beijing recently banned billboards advertising luxury goods, not to restrain spending but to avoid stirring up resentment. Whereas Deng Xiaoping proclaimed that "it's glorious to be rich," his successors are making sure no one gets too rich. Not a single billionaire in China has a net worth of more than $10 billion; compare that to eleven billionaires with a net worth of more than $10 billion in Russia and six in India, which have far smaller economies. Only one tycoon who made China's list of top-ten billionaires five years ago was still on the roster in 2011. The government appears to be both creating competitive churn among the very wealthy and restricting their maximum wealth. To be sure, there is crony capitalism in China, or wealth built on friendly ties to the government. Some reports even suggest that a majority of the Chinese worth more than $10 million are children of high-level Communist Party officials. Still, it's clear that Chinese leaders are acutely aware of the growing wealth gap. The ruling party won't countenance growth at any cost, if one of the costs is stoking popular revolt.

The Illusion of China's $2.5 Trillion Surplus

The extent of China's indebtedness is also poorly understood. Because China now sits on $2.5 trillion in foreign-currency reserves, and is a major creditor to the United States, no one thinks of it as having a debt problem. But it does. Though official government debt is low (about 30 percent of GDP), that is a small part of the story. The debt of companies (many of them owned by the government) and households combined amounts to 130 percent of China's GDP, among the highest levels in emerging markets, and that is just the official number.

The real number may be much higher because the government data do not count China's unique and exploding "shadow banking sector." Described as "social financing" by China's central bank, this sector is not necessarily shady but it is off the official books, and it includes a great variety of sometimes new credit channels that can involve loans from one corporation to another, or one depositor to another, with the bank playing the middle man rather than putting up any money. This gray sector has exploded since 2008, when the state began trying to slow regular bank lending. If the shadow banks are included, the ratio of China's debt to GDP rises to 200 percent, off the charts for a developing economy.

Many outside observers remain convinced that Chinese leaders can continue to engineer near-double-digit growth rates, even when those leaders have made it clear that they need to dial back the spending and lending that produced that growth. Talk to Chinese CEOs and big domestic investors, and they don't share the outsider's see-no-downside, hear-no-downside optimism. Most outsiders bet on China by buying stocks sold in other countries (say, commodity companies listed in Australia and Canada) because the Shanghai market is still largely closed to outsiders, but that makes Shanghai a very good barometer of domestic investor confidence in the future. The Chinese stock market has flat-lined since late 2006, up zero percent through late 2011.

The End of the Deng Dynasty

China, more than most countries, has been willing to confront the downside of its economic performance ever since Deng Xiaoping made pragmatism the reigning national ideology. But the sense of mission

Deng inspired is dissipating. Only a handful of nations have summoned the will to push reform over many decades, and China is perhaps the only country in which reform has followed a predictable cycle, pegged roughly to the gatherings of the National Congress of the Chinese Communist Party, which sets the five-year plan for the economy. Since the National Congress meeting in 1977, the first one following the chaos and disastrous social experiments of the Mao years, every new congress has set an aggressive reform mission, and almost without fail the government has delivered.

It's not clear why China has been able to sustain this momentum. One explanation is that since communism has lost its power to inspire, the ruling party's legitimacy depends on delivering economic reform and growth. But plenty of ideologically bankrupt regimes have failed to reform, most recently in Tunisia and Egypt. Another explanation cites a burning national desire to recover the glory of past empires, but there are plenty of nations with proud pasts, such as Greece and Argentina, that never summoned the same desire.

For whatever reason, China's leaders have pushed through reform with metronomic determination despite the high risks. Indeed reform has consistently granted more power and freedom to the people and places— the peasants and the provinces—that have proved most threatening to Chinese regimes in the past.

Loosening the reins took tremendous courage and will, which China first found in the personality of Deng. The 1977 congress chose Deng as Mao's replacement, and within two years he had freed rural households to farm their own plots and keep the profits, leading to an explosion in farm income and productivity. He also allowed farmers to sell their own produce at markets in the city, opening a crack in the system of internal residency permits known as *hukou*, which had kept peasants confined to their own land. The lack of hukou still relegates most urban migrants to second-class status, because the permits are required for access to public services in most cities. But the rules have relaxed sufficiently to allow the vast internal migration that has reshaped China. In a country with a long history of peasant rebellion, it was bold indeed for the top leaders to allow this much freedom of movement.

At the next meeting of the National Congress, in 1982, Deng began to promote a generation of younger, like-minded leaders who in the coming years would extend reform to the cities while expanding it in the country-side: easing central control over state enterprises, opening the door to the rise of township and village enterprises, and lifting regulations on prices for food and other goods.

The Tiananmen Square protests of 1989, which ended in a harsh military crackdown, forced reformers to lie low for a while. But Deng jump-started the economic reform process with his landmark 1992 trip to the southern coast, during which he powerfully endorsed the market experiments under way there. Deng had earlier opened the door to the creation of export-manufacturing zones on the coast, which made perfect economic sense, given the need to move exports efficiently through ports to the rest of the world, and the fact that every major industrial power has most of its population clustered on the coastline.

The coast was the logical place to start building a modern economy, yet it defied a common pattern. Many countries, particularly socialist countries, have tried to achieve "spatial balance" for political reasons, prematurely seeking to spread the wealth to downtrodden regions, including remote inland areas that would never be logical targets for development funds. The China scholar Yukon Huang argues that spatial balance "was an obsession of planners in the former Soviet Union" and a prime objective of leaders in Egypt, Brazil, India, Indonesia, Mexico, Nigeria, South Africa, and other developing nations. Huang says Deng was virtually alone in his understanding that rising regional inequality was a necessary political risk, at least in the short term. He also clearly knew that the boom in these coastal zones would serve as a magnet to rural migrants.

The congress in 1997 coincided with the onset of the Asian financial crisis and the collapse of currencies across the region. As falling global demand idled plants around the country, Beijing began to downsize bloated state factories, laying off tens of millions, and sold many small state firms to private owners. It also privatized the real estate sector, allowing individual property ownership for the first time. The sight of the Communist Party slashing state jobs and bankrolling the rise of a home-owning bourgeoisie showed that communism as Mao knew it was truly finished. Yet perhaps the most radical move in this period was China's push to enter the World Trade Organization in 2001, which required Beijing to gradually roll back barriers to trade, sector by sector. The Middle Kingdom was officially open to unfettered foreign trade.

If there is a single thread that runs through the twenty-five years of reform—from 1978 through 2002—it is the Deng dynasty. As Matthew Gertken and Jennifer Richmond of the STRATFOR consulting firm have pointed out, any leader who had Deng's stamp of approval had broad public legitimacy, and though Deng died in 1997, he not only handpicked his successor as paramount leader, Jiang Zemin, but also was a mentor and guide to Jiang's successor, the current president Hu Jintao. Deng created tremendous momentum for reform, but it is largely gone. The bold moves—opening to the world, relaxing the internal passport system, allowing increased inequality—have been replaced by efforts to increase social welfare, lower the environmental impact of rapid growth, and redistribute portions of the economic pie. For example, with the exception of the crisis year of 2008, China has raised the minimum wage by 18 percent or more every year since 2003. Early evidence from the provinces suggested it would rise 21 percent in 2011. This move—toward reforms that make life easier rather than making the economy more competitive—are quite common as nations grow more wealthy. And after Hu's presidency, the Deng dynasty and its generations of hard reformers will be history.

There Is No Magic in the System

The success of command-and-control capitalism in China has set off a vigorous debate over which political system is most likely to produce growth—but it's not the type of system that matters, it is the stability of the system and, even more important, whether the leaders running it understand the basics of economic reform. The chance that any particular system—democratic, authoritarian, or any other—will have a positive impact on a country's breakout potential is about 50/50.

I've been working by this rule for a long time, but for the purposes of this book I decided to look at high-growth nations—emerging markets growing at a rate better than 5 percent—for the last three decades. Based on Central Intelligence Agency classifications, my team labeled each country democratic or authoritarian (including monarchies and military governments). We found that in the 1980s, thirty-two nations were growing at a rate faster than 5 percent, and 59 percent of them were democracies; in the 1990s, 59 percent of the thirty-nine high-growth nations were democracies; and in the 2000s, 43 percent of fifty-three were democracies. The total for the three decades: 64 (52 percent) of 124 high-growth countries were democracies, pretty much what I expected.

Still, there is a widespread belief that political systems matter for economic success. It's a deep-seated faith of American politics that democracy and capitalism not only are superior systems, but also go hand in hand. Many economists, however, favor the opposite view—that well-managed authoritarian systems are more likely to produce rapid economic growth, particularly at early stages of development, a view born of the fact that many of the most successful development stories—South Korea, Taiwan, Singapore—were authoritarian states, at least in their early years, and that China is one now.

However, a closer look at the countries that have posted high growth since 2000 shows nations in every stage of transition from authoritarian to democratic rule (or from democratic to authoritarian rule). There are democracies in India and Indonesia, autocracies in China and Russia. Even the economies of inept autocracies like Myanmar and Kazakhstan grew at better than 10 percent for the decade, a sign of how little it took to expand an economy from a small base during this go-go decade. Adam Przeworski of the University of Chicago and New York University has pointed out very similar evidence for the postwar era: of the eight countries that quadrupled their incomes between 1950 and 1990, two (Taiwan and Singapore) were ruled by dictators during the entire period, one (South Korea) was ruled by a dictator during most of it, two (Japan and Malta) were democracies throughout the period, and three (Thailand, Portugal, and Greece) waffled back and forth between autocracy and democracy. Authoritarian control is not necessarily an advantage, and for every China there is a Vietnam, which as we will see later in the book is a command economy that is not working.

The Case of the Missing Consumer

The market's faith in the China boom is currently sustained by the belief that Beijing can shift from banging out exports to building a consumer society. This would rebalance the economy not only of China but also of the world, giving slow-growing Western economies more opportunity to sell to Chinese consumers. But this hope rests on a misconception, namely, that up to now China has deliberately prevented the emergence of a consumer economy by compelling people to save, creating a huge pool of funds ready to be invested in new export factories.

The suppressed Chinese consumer does not exist. For the last thirty years Chinese consumer spending has increased at an average annual rate of almost 9 percent, which is about as fast as it can grow without triggering runaway inflation. It is also a full percentage point faster than the average rate in Japan, and about the same as the rate in Taiwan, during their boom decades. The idea that Beijing has somehow starved its consumer class also defies the widely available and well-known evidence of a consumption boom. China continues to replace the United States or Europe as the leading market for one major multinational company after another: the latest example is Rolls-Royce, which in 2010 sold more cars in China than in Britain for the first time. By some estimates China already has a 25 percent share of the global luxury market. The scale of this expansion is hardly unusual or limited to luxury goods, and it is transforming Chinese society in many ways. Despite widespread concern that China already has too many hotels, developers plan to build another 7,500 at an estimated cost of $60 billion, opening new swaths of the nation to foreign tourists and catering to the growing thirst of the Chinese to see their own country.

In the last decade China began to widen development from the southeast coast to the interior, and retailers are following. Louis Vuitton now boasts seventeen stores in cities beyond the major urban centers of Beijing and Shanghai, including Nanjing, Shenyang, and Tianjin. Chinese men are rethinking themselves in a new, more fashionable light too; sales of skin-care products for men grew at 40 percent in early 2011—five times faster than sales for women, according to L'Oréal. In short, the evidence of an ongoing consumer revolution is so well known, it's a wonder anyone can imagine that Beijing has the option of sustaining growth by unshackling the Chinese consumer: any shackles fell away some time ago.

China bulls respond to that argument by pointing out that domestic consumption in China is falling as a share of GDP, and now stands at just 40 percent, well below the 55 to 60 percent share in Korea and Japan during their boom years. The statistic is correct, but it misleads: Chinese consumption is growing fast, as we saw above; it is falling as a share of GDP only because investment has been growing even faster. Over the past decade investment grew at an annual rate of 15 percent, up from 12 percent over the preceding two decades. So if investment growth is bound to slow—as Chinese leaders have already announced it will—and consumption can't grow any faster, the conclusion is inescapable: the overall growth rate in China is set to move to a lower plane.

No one gains if the slowdown comes hard and fast, and some China bears think it will, given the scale of the boom and the related credit excesses, especially in housing. One commentator compares China's possible fall below the recent growth rate of over 8 percent to the Hollywood thriller *Speed*, in which a bomb on a bus is set to detonate if the vehicle slows to below fifty miles an hour. In China the bomb would be triggered by the slump in job creation and explode in the form of labor unrest, which is already bubbling in the form of strikes and protests.

The China Slowdown Won't Devastate China

The bears are probably as wrong as the bulls, because China still has plenty of room to grow, albeit at a slower rate. Again the comparison to Japan is telling. Back in the early 1970s Japan was forced by the United States and its other leading trading partners to revalue the exchange rate as it was running large trade surpluses. At the time, Japan was buying billions of dollars to hold the value of the yen at 360 to the dollar, the level at which the yen had been pegged since 1949 to help the economy recover from the war.

Many economists viewed revaluation as a natural step, given the fact that larger economies require greater currency flexibility to tailor domestic money and credit conditions to local needs. By the end of the 1970s the value of the yen had risen by 80 percent against the dollar, making

Japanese exports much more expensive and less competitive. Other factors, including the fact that Japan has no oil and was particularly vulnerable to the oil-price shocks of the late 1970s, also conspired to slow the economy. Over the next fifteen years GDP growth downshifted—first to 5 percent, then to 4—before Japan fell into the stagnation that continues to this day. (Japan has averaged just 1.2 percent annual growth since 1990, and less than 1 percent since 2000.)

China's economy is not likely to slow to 4 percent growth for some time. While China has also moved toward greater exchange-rate flexibility—the yuan has risen in value steadily since 2005—it has done so more gradually than Japan. And it still has a long way to go before it achieves anywhere near the level of modernization that Japan had reached in the mid-1970s. China started its modernization drive in 1978 from a much lower base than Japan, which was already a relatively advanced industrial economy at the beginning of its high-growth period in 1955, with modern textile, steel, and shipbuilding sectors.

Compared with Japan in the 1970s, China is also less heavily urbanized and is aging less rapidly. China's leaders also see what is happening: they are trying to manage a slowdown to a healthy middle-income growth rate rather than continuing to aim for a target befitting a less developed economy, and that makes the collapse scenario far less likely.

The slowdown of China will lower the trajectory of a star that has altered the arc of human progress, for better and worse, rapidly reducing global poverty while rapidly accelerating the threats of environmental destruction and global warming. China is the equivalent of a company with revolutionary technology: it has been highly disruptive, destroying competitors while lifting up nations that supply and feed off its growth momentum. China's rise as an export-manufacturing power has not slowed the long-term decline of global manufacturing (which has slipped in inflation-adjusted terms from 17.5 percent to 16.9 percent of world GDP since 1970); it has simply eaten more and more quickly into the share of steel, TVs, cars, and other goods manufactured in the West. A slower China means a less disruptive China, producing less geopolitical friction, fewer trade battles, and less fear of a rising "Red Dragon." So perhaps this is not a bad thing.

If China moves to a 6 to 7 percent growth path in the coming years, it will first feel like a mild recession for that economy, and there will be some transition pains. But it will hardly be a cataclysmic event for the global economy. After all, as the Chinese proverb goes, "A dead camel is still larger than a horse." The bigger picture is that the Chinese economy is now so large—worth around $6 trillion a year—that even at a 6 percent growth rate, it will remain the largest single contributor to global growth in the coming years. So the shock will be partly psychological: nations, politicians, and investors who feared China's rise (or its possible collapse) will experience tremendous relief. Those who bet everything on riding the coattails of China growing at 8 percent or better will face a much nastier surprise.

3

The Great Indian Hope Trick

IN THE LATE NINETEENTH CENTURY, the story of a startling new magic trick emerged from India and spread, as one Western visitor after another returned home and swore they had seen it. There were many versions of the tale, but in its full-blown incarnation a street performer coils a thick rope into a basket and begins to play his flute. The rope starts to dance like a cobra and climbs to a great height. The mischievous boy assistant scrambles to the top of the rope and disappears. The magician bows to applause and calls for the boy, and calls some more. He grows impatient, then furious, grabs a large knife, scrambles up the rope, and vanishes too. Then limbs, a torso, and a head fall out of the sky. The magician reappears, reassembles the body parts, covers them in a sheet, and from under the bloody sheet the boy reappears, grinning. It would be one hundred years before "the great Indian rope trick" was fully exposed as a hoax: a composite pasted together in the imagination of Western visitors from the full menu of tricks executed by Indian street magicians. Magic societies have offered hefty rewards, but no one has ever been able to perform "the world's greatest illusion."

In recent years visitors have been returning from India in a similar state of awe, overwhelmingly impressed by the nation that perhaps has been most deeply transformed by the emerging-market levitation act of the last decade. India has, for good reason, come to be seen as the every-

The tale of the "world's greatest illusion" was eventually exposed as a hoax, a composite pasted together in the imagination of Western visitors from the full menu of tricks performed by Indian street magicians.

man of emerging nations, an archetype that captures the best and worst tricks of all the most dynamic young economies. Indian stocks move up and down more closely in sync with the global emerging-market average than the stocks of most other countries do, because its market is deep and diverse. It has more than 5,000 listed companies, including more than a thousand in which foreigners have invested, and nearly 150 with total stock market values of over $1 billion. (China's local market is the only other one this big, but since it is largely closed to foreigners, no one sees it as a reflection of global trends.) Moreover, while many emerging-nation stock markets list companies predominantly from a single industry—oil in Russia, tech in Taiwan—India's market has everything, from cars to drug companies.

Sheer size and diversity make it possible to assemble almost any picture of India, a melting pot for all the pitfalls and promise of emerging markets, from the medieval backwardness of Bihar to the Infosys campus in Bangalore. The state of Uttar Pradesh, with a population of two hundred million, would on its own represent the world's sixth most populous country, and West Bengal's population of ninety million is a good deal larger than Germany's. This is an incredibly diverse country in which youths still have a choice between world-class engineering schools and Maoist rebellion, yet the broad command of English among the elites can make it appear highly uniform and easily accessible to the outside world. Foreign analysts vie to predict how fast India will rise as an economic power, and how soon it will regain the might it wielded three centuries ago, when it accounted for nearly one-quarter of world economic output. Every society is complex, but one as big and sprawling as India defies straight-line, long-term forecasting more than most.

When historians dug into the origins of the Indian rope trick, they found previous versions of the tale that dated back to as early as the fourteenth century in China. India now risks falling for its own hype, based largely on the assumption that it is again performing a trick pioneered by China—a seemingly endless stretch of 8 to 9 percent growth—and is therefore destined to be the fastest-growing economy over the next decade. At least until the last months of 2011, when growth forecasts dipped below 7 percent and rattled investor confidence, the Indian elite seemed more focused on how to spend the windfall than on working to make sure the rapid growth actually happens.

The best example of this rosy thinking was the way the ongoing baby boom in India has been transformed from a "time bomb" into a "demographic dividend" in the minds of the elite. Until the 1990s the Indian government was still working hard to rally the nation against the dangers of overpopulation, but that fear has melted away, based on the argument that a baby-boom generation of new workers helped fuel China's rise and will do the same for India. Indeed China's baby boom is about to end— the "dependency ratio" of old pensioners to the young workers who support them is expected to start growing sharply in 2015—while India's baby boom still has legs. By 2020 the average Chinese will be thirty-seven years old; the average Indian will be twenty-nine (and the average European forty-nine). Many Indians now see demographics as a critical advantage in competition with the nation it regards as its chief rival: the hope is that China will get old before it gets rich, and India will reach middle-income status while it is still young.

India's confidence ignored the postwar experience of many countries in Africa and the Middle East, where a flood of young people into the labor market produced unemployment, unrest, and more mouths to feed. The conventional view is that India will be able to put all those people to work because of its relatively strong educational system, entrepreneurial zeal, and strong links to the global economy. All of that is real, but India is already showing some of the warning signs of failed growth stories, including early-onset overconfidence. Many outsiders were just as confident before the recent signs of trouble. I put the probability of India's continuing its journey as a breakout nation this decade at closer to 50 percent, owing to a whole series of risks that the Indian and foreign elites leave out of the picture, including bloated government, crony capitalism, falling turnover among the rich and powerful, and a disturbing tendency of farmers to stay on the farm.

The early signs of an unraveling have begun to emerge under the administration of Prime Minister Manmohan Singh, but not really because of it. Singh helped open India to global trade in the early 1990s, when he was finance minister. India was in crisis, and Singh oversaw sweeping changes that broke down the regime known as the "License Raj," a red tape–laden bureaucracy in which licenses spelled out not only who could manufacture which goods but also how much and at what price. In addition Singh lowered import tariffs from an average of 85 percent to 25 percent, and opened Indian stock markets to foreign investors. In the 1990s India's economy grew at about 5.5 percent per year, not much faster than in the 1980s, but the reforms prepared India to take off in the global boom that dawned in 2003 with the sudden surge of easy money flowing out of the West. India's growth rate rose to nearly 9 percent per year between 2003 and 2007, the second fastest rate of expansion in the world, after China.

When Singh was tapped to become prime minister in 2004, many hoped that he could continue to push reform, but in reality he became more of a figurehead, presiding over an economic boom unleashed by global rather than local forces. Critics said that his low-key, low-charisma style made him incapable of becoming a forceful prime minister, but in practice his power is quite limited. With no independent political base of his own, Singh owes his position entirely to Congress Party president Sonia Gandhi, an aggressive proponent of welfare-state policies that do little for growth. Singh could not force reform on a political class and culture that had grown deeply complacent, and he now reminds me of U.S. President Calvin Coolidge, the nondescript leader who was in office during the boom of the 1920s but did not use his power to correct widening fault lines that would eventually bring down the U.S. economy in the 1930s. A man of few words, Coolidge earned the moniker "Silent Cal," and Singh too is known for keeping his mouth shut. A cartoon that went viral in India shows Singh in a dentist's chair as the dentist pleads with him to open up at least when he is being examined.

The Inauspicious Indo-Brazilian Connection

India does have its reasons for self-confidence. By many indicators, from the number of TV sets in consumer hands to the number of cars on the road, to the large and increasingly young population, India does indeed look much like China of the 1990s, when China was poised to supplant Thailand as the world's fastest-growing economy. But to assemble a composite picture of India that looks just like 1990s China, one has to leave out many of the least-flattering images.

China is not the only possible model for India. Culturally and politically India has far more in common with the chaos and confusion of modern Brazil than with the command-and-control environment that defines China. While for decades China summoned the will to produce a new round of landmark economic reforms every four to five years, the reform cycle stopped in Brazil back in the 1970s, when it fell off the list of up-and-coming economies and into one of the worst bouts of hyperinflation the world has ever seen.

Both India and Brazil are "high-context" societies, a term popularized by the anthropologist Edward Hall to describe cultures in which people are colorful, noisy, quick to make promises that cannot always be relied on, and a bit casual about meeting times and deadlines. These societies tend to be family oriented, with tight relationships even beyond the immediate family, based on close ties built over long periods of time. In an environment this familiar, there is a lot that goes unsaid—or is said very briefly—because values are deeply shared and much is implicitly understood from context. The spoken word is often flowery and vague; apologies are long and formal. "Low context," in contrast, describes societies like the United States and Germany in which people are individual oriented, care about privacy, and are more likely to stick to timelines and their word. People tend to be on the move, to have many brief relationships, and thus rely on simple, open communications and codified rules to guide behavior. Drive from the German part of Switzerland north of Zurich to the Italian part close to Lugano, where suddenly the decibel levels get higher and everyone seems to be talking at the same time, and you see both high- and low-context societies on vivid display in one country. Indians and Brazilians are a lot more like the Italians than like the Germans.

High-context societies believe deeply in tradition, history, and favoring the in-group, whether it is one's family or business circle, and thus they are vulnerable to corruption. If this description sounds questionable to businessmen or tourists who know Brazil and India as open, familiar, and straightforward, that is because they've experienced only the low-context facade adopted by the outward-facing elites who need to deal in a clear way with foreigners. Everyone is welcome at Brazil's Carnival or an Indian wedding, and they may even be made to feel like an insider, but the reality is that it takes decades to become a real part of these cultures. Prime Minister Singh is fond of remarking that whatever can be said about his country, the exact opposite is also true. There is something to this—India is rife with contradictions, no doubt—but it is also classic high-context analysis, a way of avoiding overt confrontation with hard facts—or with the side of India that could drag it down.

Of course Brazil and India are far from the only high-context cultures—this style of social interaction is typical in much of Asia and Latin

America. Yet I'm convinced there is a particular bond between Brazil and India. I feel it all the time when I visit these countries, from the late dining habits and colorful personalities to the casual informality and cultural choices as well.

The most popular soap opera in Brazil in recent times has been *A Passage to India*, a Brazilian-Indian love story filmed in the Indian cities of Agra and Jodhpur in which Brazilian actors play the Indian roles and pass easily for North Indians. To Indians who have seen it, the show is a dead ringer, in terms of look, mood, and even lighting, for the style of the Indian producer Ekta Kapoor, who has turned out some of the most popular serial dramas in Indian TV history—and gave all the early ones titles starting with the letter "K" for superstitious reasons (it doesn't get more high context than superstition).

Indians and Brazilians are only loosely aware of their connection, if at all. In 2002 Google rolled out a California-based social networking site called Orkut, to compete with Myspace and Facebook in forty-eight languages; the site fizzled out in just about every country except India and Brazil, which together produce more than 80 percent of the traffic. Something about the site's look, feel, and features hits that Indo-Brazilian chord.

In politics there is also a distinct Indo-Brazilian connection: a desire for state protection from life's risks—social welfare for the nation as one big in-group—to a degree that I've rarely found in other high-context societies, such as China and Chile. The political elites of India and Brazil share a deep fondness for welfare-state liberalism, and both populations demand high levels of income support even though the economies do not yet generate the necessary revenue to support a welfare state. Per capita income is about $12,000 in Brazil and $1,400 in India. Lately India's governing Congress Party has turned to generous spending in an effort to recover the political backing it had lost to an array of regional parties in recent decades. Brazil offered what was probably the emerging world's most generous welfare program—the Bolsa Familia income supports—that is, until 2005, when the Congress Party in India pushed through the Mahatma Gandhi National Rural Employment Guarantee Act (MGN-REGA), which guarantees the rural poor one hundred days of public-sector employment each year, at an annual cost to the treasury of nearly $10 billion.

It was easy enough for India to increase spending in the midst of a global boom, but the spending has continued to rise in the post-crisis period. Inspired by the popularity of the employment guarantees, the government now plans to spend the same amount extending food subsidies to the poor. If the government continues down this path, India may meet the same fate as Brazil in the late 1970s, when excessive government spending set off hyperinflation and crowded out private investment, ending the country's economic boom. One of the key mistakes made in Brazil was indexing public wages to inflation, which can trigger a wage-price spiral. India's central bank voiced its fears of the same price spiral as the wages guaranteed by MGNREGA pushed rural wage inflation up to 15 percent in 2011.

Under the current regime of drift in India, crony capitalism has become a real worry. Widespread corruption is an old problem, but the situation has now reached a stage where the decisive factor in any business deal is the right government connection. When I made this observation in a September 2010 *Newsweek International* cover story titled "India's Fatal Flaw," I was greeted as a party spoiler. Top government officials told me that such cronyism is just a normal step in development, citing the example of the robber barons of nineteenth-century America. Prime Minister Singh, asked privately about the corruption problem, supposedly told people not to spoil India's image by going on and on about this.

Since 2010, the issue has exploded in a series of high-profile scandals, ranging from rigged sales of wireless spectrum to the shoddy construction of facilities for the Commonwealth Games that India hosted that year. India's place on Transparency International's annual survey of the most and least corrupt nations fell to number 88 out of 178 nations in 2010— down from number 74 in 2007. India is approaching the point that Latin America and parts of East Asia hit in the 1990s, when a backlash started to form against economic reforms because any opening up of the economy was seen to favor just a select few. The first stirrings of deep middle-class discontent appeared in 2011 as many urban Indians started to rally behind social activist Anna Hazare, who morphed quickly from being a hunger striker protesting corruption to the leader of a civil movement capable of paralyzing Parliament and damaging business confidence.

When Open Land Is More Attractive Than Movie Stars

As soon as companies from emerging nations start expanding their interests abroad, it is usually celebrated as a giant step for the whole country. But in India the moves suggest that many companies are going abroad in part to avoid the problems of doing business in the home market. Lately businessmen in Delhi and Mumbai have been complaining ever more bitterly that the cost of starting new businesses in India has gone up dramatically over time because of the sharp increase in the number of demands for government payoffs. Investment by Indian businesses has declined from 17 percent of GDP in 2008 to 13 percent now.

At a time when India needs its businessmen to reinvest more aggressively at home in order for the country to hit its growth target of 8 to 9 percent (foreign investment is well below the required totals), they are looking abroad. Overseas operations of all Indian companies now account for more than 10 percent of overall corporate profitability, compared with just 2 percent five years ago. Given the potential of the domestic marketplace, Indian companies should not need to chase growth abroad. (In 2010 more than a third of Indian households had, by local standards, a middle-class income equal to between $2,000 and $4,200, up from 22 percent in 2002.) But just over half the earnings of India's top-fifty companies are now "outward facing" or dependent on exports, global commodity prices, and international acquisitions.

When emerging nations start spending too little on investment at home, the big risk is a spike in inflation. As investment dries up, the nation is not putting enough money into the new factories and new roads that are required to make and deliver the goods desired by an increasingly prosperous middle class. Supply falls behind growing demand, and prices start to shoot up. The fall in investment won't reverse itself in an unstable business environment, and nothing is more destabilizing than government favoritism and graft. That's why graft is inflationary: it channels money away from productive investment. In 2010 and the first part of 2011, inflation in India was running at more than 9 percent, up from 5 percent during the 2003–2007 boom.

There are lots of stories that dramatize the spread of a graft-driven inflation threat in India. Lately Indian businessmen have been regaling one another with accounts of a leading politician from Mumbai who is known to have amassed huge wealth through property deals. At a private screening of a new Bollywood movie, this politician asked the producer to replay a particular song-and-dance number, over and over. When the producer asked if he was taken with the leading lady, the politician said no, he was eyeing the location and wondering where the producer had found such an attractive stretch of open space in Mumbai.

To avoid a crisis, India needs to create a society governed more by rules than by the personal connections that put potentially productive assets like land, factories, and mines in the wrong hands. One of the secrets of the successful East Asian growth stories was that Japan, Korea, and Taiwan all set up relatively fair systems for selling public land, and India's parliament to its credit is working on a law designed to prevent land grabs. India's large tribal and farmer population need to get some benefit from land acquisitions if they are going to support business development.

A Better Class of Billionaires?

In the global media India is closely associated with its dynamic technology entrepreneurs, the personalities who often grace the covers of international magazines. But this misses the retreat inward, the high-context side of India. Lately the enterprising moguls are getting replaced on the billionaire list by a new group: provincial tycoons who have built fortunes based on sweetheart deals with state governments to corner the market in location-based industries like mining and real estate. India has always been top-heavy with billionaires, which is partly a function of the way in-groups work to monopolize the economic pie for themselves. Also, the country has no wealth or inheritance taxes. But wealth at the top is exploding, perhaps faster than in any other country. In 2000 there were no Indian tycoons among the world's top-one-hundred billionaires, and now there are seven, more than in all but three countries: the United

States, Russia, and Germany. In this category India outranks China (with one) and Japan (with zero).

A rule of the road: watch the changes in the list of top billionaires, learn how they made their billions, and note how many billions they made. This information provides a quick bellwether for the balance of growth, across income classes and industries. If a country is generating too many billionaires relative to the size of its economy, it's off balance. (Russia has one hundred billionaires, about as many as China in an economy one-fourth the size.) If a country's average billionaire has amassed tens of billions, not merely billions, the lack of balance could lead to stagnation. (Russia, India, and Mexico are the only emerging markets where the average net worth of the top-ten billionaires is more than $10 billion.)

If a country's billionaires make their money largely from government patronage, rather than productive new industries, it could feed resentment (which is what sparked revolt in Indonesia in the late 1990s). Healthy emerging markets should produce billionaires, but their num-

THE BILLIONAIRES' INDEX

COUNTRY	NUMBER OF BILLIONAIRES	TOTAL NET WORTH (in US $ billions)	TOTAL NET WORTH (as % GDP)	AVERAGE NET WORTH (Of top 10, in US $ billions)
Russia	100	431.8	29.2	16.8
Malaysia	9	44.0	20.1	4.9
India	55	246.5	17.2	14.8
Taiwan	25	62.4	14.6	4.1
Mexico	11	125.1	12.5	12.4
Saudi Arabia	7	54.8	12.4	7.8
Turkey	38	63.7	8.7	2.8
Brazil	30	131.4	6.5	8.8
Philippines	4	11.4	6.0	2.9
Indonesia	14	32.3	4.6	2.8
Korea	16	39.6	4.0	3.2
China	115	230.4	4.0	6.0

Source: IMF World Economic Outlook, April 2011, available at www.forbes.com/wealth/billionaires/list.

ber must also be in proportion to the size of the nation's economy; the billionaires should face competition and turnover at the top; and ideally they should emerge predominantly from productive economic sectors, not cozy relationships with politicians. Creative destruction lies at the heart of a prospering capitalist society, and because well-connected incumbents have everything to gain from the established order, they are the enemies of capitalism.

Comparing the changes in the list of top-ten billionaires in India and China reveals how differently each economy is developing. China's top-ten list shows a lot of turnover, with names falling off or coming on all the time, and no one man or woman ever breaking through the ceiling of about $10 billion in net worth; indeed there is good reason to believe that China's leaders are enforcing an unwritten rule that caps total wealth. This is the only way to explain the fact that in the last fifteen years China has generated much more growth, much more overall wealth than any other country, but its richest man is now worth about $9 billion, far less rich than the billionaires in much smaller economies, ranging from Mexico to Russia to Nigeria. It is also telling that the man who held the title of richest man in China in the year 2007—discount-appliance king Huang Guangyu—is currently in jail on insider-trading and corruption charges, as is one of his predecessors, the flamboyant entrepreneur Mou Qizhong, who received a life sentence for bank fraud. That is not to say that the charges were baseless, only that in China's very freewheeling business culture, the authorities seem to pay particularly close attention to the wheeling and dealing when it generates fortunes approaching $10 billion. No doubt China's goal is to contain resentment against the rich and curtail their ability to influence the political scene. To an extent the strategy is succeeding; China faces widespread labor strikes and protests against corrupt local officials, but India faces a low-level rebellion by armed Maoists known as the Naxalites, who are strongest in some of the poor but resource-rich heartland states, such as Chhattisgarh and Jharkhand, where governance has in the past been weak and favored cronies have generated much of the new wealth.

India lags behind only Russia and Malaysia in terms of the wealth of its billionaires as a share of the economy. Turnover at the top has been slowing. Nine out of the top-ten Indian billionaires on the 2010 Forbes list are holdovers from the 2006 list, while the 2006 list had only five hold-overs. As of today many of India's super-rich still inspire national pride, not resentment, and they can travel the country with no fear for their safety, but this genial state of affairs can change quickly.

Crony capitalism is a cancer that undermines competition and slows economic growth. That is why the United States confronted the problem and moved to take down the robber barons by busting up their monopolies in the 1920s. Ever since the passage of the antitrust laws, the American economy has seen constant change in its ranks of the rich and powerful, including both people and companies. The Dow index of the top-thirty U.S. industrial companies is in constant flux and, on average, replaces half its members every fifteen years. India's market used to generate heavy turnover too, but in late 2011, twenty-seven—90 percent—of the top-thirty companies tracked by the benchmark Sensex index were holdovers from 2006. Back in 2006 the comparable figure was just 68 percent. Fur-ther, the top-ten stocks on the Sensex now account for two-thirds of the total value, while the top ten on the Dow account for just half the total value, showing a higher concentration of corporate wealth in India.

This is emblematic of a creeping stagnation at the upper echelons of the elite, which is a predictable tendency in a high-context society. Nepotism rules in Bollywood, where daughters and sons of film person-alities are widely favored, and in Parliament, where most young members are political princelings or "hereditary MPs" who took over seats formerly held by their fathers or other close relatives. *India: A Portrait*, a 2010 book by Patrick French, showed that while every member of the lower house of Parliament under thirty years old was a hereditary MP, the proportion declined steadily among older members, to just 10 percent among those seventy-one to eighty years old. In the ruling Congress Party the situation was more extreme: every member of Parliament in the Congress Party under the age of thirty-five was a hereditary MP.

It Looks Like Churchill Was Half Right about India

The Gandhis, the Congress Party's founding dynasty, were long treated as the nation's rightful ruling family, and they ran the country for almost three unbroken decades after independence in 1947. To this day the Congress Party remains highly centralized, its command-and-control structure revolving around the Gandhi family, now entering its fourth generation in power. The Gandhis are the only national brand in Indian politics, and they have demonstrated a great capacity for reinvention over the years, such that many see forty-one-year-old Rahul Gandhi, the party's general secretary, as the contemporary face of India.

This continuity at the top persists despite the growing hostility of Indians to incumbent politicians. The Congress Party suffered its first losses in a national election in the chaos of the late 1970s as a multiparty democracy took root, and over the next quarter century, Indians became the least loyal voters in the world, turning out the incumbent in 70 percent of elections, on both the national and the state level, due to their frustration with the poor standards of governance. Traditionally Parliament poses for a big photo-op before general elections, and in photographs from the 1990s many of the MPs looked like suspects before a firing squad, each member knowing that none of them were likely to survive for long. The rejection rate dropped to 50 percent amid the boom of the last decade, but it has since begun to rise again.

The reason family dynasties can survive in a country so aggressively inclined to vote against incumbents is that the politicians never quit politics. They just wait for the next election and stage a comeback. In many states political competition amounts to a merry-go-round, with two entrenched parties trading places in office. Often these are regional parties with a provincial focus, even in larger or richer states like Uttar Pradesh or Tamil Nadu. In Tamil Nadu, for example, a Tamil nationalist party called the DMK first beat the Congress Party in the late 1960s, and every election since then has pitted the DMK against a local splinter party, the AIADMK. In these places the Congress Party and its major national rival, the Hindu nationalist Bharatiya Janata Party (BJP), are at most junior parties.

Voters look less and less to the central government for answers to their problems, and increasingly the momentum for economic reform comes from the chief ministers of the country's twenty-eight states. In India state governments matter because they control more than half of all government spending, an unusually high share. As Indians come to see themselves first as citizens of Bihar or Tamil Nadu, they are turning to regional parties, or the few strong regional leaders of national parties such as the BJP and the Congress Party. The definition of the in-group is shifting from the national to the state level. Voter turnout runs 10 percent higher for regional elections than for national elections, and the gap is growing. As central power fades, India is again starting to look like a commonwealth of states with distinct identities and waning national consciousness.

It is important to remember that during centuries of Mogul and British rule, India was never a single nation-state. Even at the height of Mogul power in the seventeenth century, when India was a global economic force, it was an empire of many autonomous states, which to varying degrees wrote their own legal codes and collected their own taxes. Winston Churchill once observed that "India is just a geographical term with no more a political personality than Europe." That remark sounds increasingly relevant today. However, the growing strength of regional political forces is not tearing the country apart, as Churchill thought it might.

True, the waning of central power is making it more difficult for New Delhi to champion breakthrough reforms, but the secession movements in states like Kashmir, Punjab, and Tamil Nadu peaked decades ago. On the other hand, the rise of the regions is spreading the economic boom into every corner of the country, allowing new consumer subcultures to emerge (which is good for growth) alongside the rise of more unchecked cronyism (which isn't). The complexity of regionalization is a big reason why the future economic growth of this country is so tough to call, with some regions gaining and others losing momentum, and why its chances of remaining a breakout nation are 50/50.

The North-South Divide

The center of economic dynamism is shifting from the South and parts of the West to the major population centers of the central and northern heartland. If the corruption issue has discouraged many businesses from investing, there are many exceptions in provinces where competent new governors are actually cleaning up the local business scene, and where the consumer culture is exploding. In the 1980s, when India first began to reform, economic growth increased from 3 percent to 5.5 percent, propelled mainly by the emergence of technology and outsourcing industries in the southern states of Karnataka and Tamil Nadu. Back in 1981 incomes in the most-developed states were 26 percent higher than those in undeveloped states, and that gap had grown to 86 percent by 2008.

Predictably this produced a certain arrogance in the southern states, where it became commonplace to look with alarm and pity on the failure of the populous northern states to keep up. Southerners saw themselves as harder working, better educated, and more ready to compete in the world. Bihar, the biggest and most backward northern state, became the butt of southern jokes that India could end its running territorial dispute with Pakistan by giving up Kashmir, so long as Pakistan took Bihar too. Bihar was the only Indian state that not only sat out India's first growth spurt but also saw its economy shrink (by 9 percent) between 1980 and 2003. Soon thereafter things began to change, and in recent years the North has been growing faster than the South. Between 2007 and 2010 the average economic growth rate of the southern states decelerated from 7 percent to 6.5 percent, while that of the northern states accelerated from 4.5 percent to 6.8 percent.

The rise of the rest in India resulted from a number of factors, perhaps most important the election of better leaders. In a recent analysis Credit Suisse showed that over the last twenty years many Indian states have undergone rapid growth spurts, but only once under a Congress Party chief minister. This helps explain why Congress is now the governing party in only two of the ten major Indian states, down from eight in the 1980s and all ten in the 1960s. Meanwhile, there are dozens of examples of economic growth led by rival parties.

The most striking example comes from Bihar, a remote state that V. S. Naipaul once described as "the place where civilization ends." Chief minister Nitish Kumar stormed into office in 2005 on a wave of voter frustration with the general chaos, and launched an aggressive campaign to bring order and common sense to a lawless territory. He forced the police to start pursuing crooks, who in Bihar included both powerful members

of the state parliament and their business cronies. To punish these characters in a state with a nonfunctioning judiciary, Kumar created "fast
track" courts that worked so fast that critics called it unjust haste. He
has also implemented a law under which the property of a corrupt public
official can be seized, and indeed recently a palatial house of one such
bureaucrat was turned into a school for poor kids.

In a state government known for throwing up every possible bureau-
cratic obstacle to getting any project done, Kumar parted the sea of paper-
work through which state engineers had to swim just to build a bridge.
Lawless Biharis even started to pay their taxes, believing for the first time
that the money might find its way to the public purse, not private wallets.
Bridges and roads got built, Bihar started to function, then to fly. Now its
economy is growing at an 11 percent rate, the second fastest in India, and
Kumar is lauded as a model of what a straight leader can accomplish in a
crooked state.

Meanwhile India as a whole was going the opposite way, as the formerly dynamic southern states seemed to a hit a wall of complacency.
The economy in six Indian states grew faster than 10 percent in 2010,
but none of them were in the South. The southern states have also seen
a decline in the competence of their leaders, and growth has fallen
accordingly: over the past ten years, Karnataka, Andhra Pradesh, and
Tamil Nadu have seen growth rates slip, in some years to about half
their previous double-digit pace. Some southern Indians explain this
away by saying that they already had their big boom, but this is hardly
the way to follow China. In China the rich southern states experienced
a boom for three decades, not just one, and have reached annual per
capita income levels of $15,000 to $20,000—while India's southern
states still have a per capita income only slightly above the national
average of $1,400.

To an extent, isolation set up the remote states in the northern and
central parts of India for success: the global credit boom of the last decade
passed them by, which meant the crisis that followed didn't leave them
broke, and they have room to borrow to build new enterprises. The global
commodities boom has also worked to the advantage of these regions,
which are home to rich reserves of coal and iron, and most of India's new

steel and power-plant projects. Kumar and other new leaders are taking the simple steps required to start growing from a poor base—particularly building new roads and wireless telecom systems. Literacy rates are rising faster in the North than the South, evidence that the new leadership is taking advantage of their demographic potential: half of India's under-fifteen population resides in just five underdeveloped states—Uttar Pradesh, Bihar, Madhya Pradesh, Rajasthan, and Orissa.

The New Map of the Middle Class

There are three layers of life in India: the increasingly cosmopolitan cities, the faceless towns, and the often desperate villages in which, at first glance, not much seems to have changed in recent decades, except for the gradual construction of new roads between them. If you parachuted into the center of any town or village in India, your initial impression would be pretty much the same no matter where you landed. I've traveled the back roads all over the country, from the southeastern coastal boomtown of Nellore to the aptly named Bhagalpur ("abode of refugees") in Bihar, and everywhere I've seen the same wild variety of vehicles with and without motors, from motorbikes to the colorful Tempos, a three-wheeled car, all pouring through teeming streets into a central square graced by the bust of a major political figure, surrounded by shops built in the same utilitarian-concrete style.

It appears to be a nation without much sense of modern aesthetic, a stretch of sameness that runs two thousand miles north to south, yet look more closely, and diversity abounds. Beauty parlors mushroom at every corner, all offering regional spins on the latest hairdos and betraying a deep inner individuality and local personality. Walk in any door, scan any store shelf, and the stunning variety of regional tastes and styles jumps out: from local brands of cooking oil to hair oil, which is prized all over the country as a baldness cure, but the ingredients differ from state to state. Even within cities, the favored style of rice or pickles can vary from neighborhood to neighborhood. This is India at its tradition-minded extreme, still clinging to local codes, in baldness cures as in language.

The growing wealth of the Indian hinterlands finds expression in many ways. One is the rise of the Hindi-language press, for years an also-ran industry. In recent times the premium that advertisers pay to appear in English-language papers has fallen from 1,200 percent to 700 percent. Urban residents of poor states are now as likely to have mobile phones as are residents of rich states. While most multinationals have avoided entering the Hindi heartland, that's starting to change as well. Recently the English daily *Hindustan Times* carried a story about the first Domino's Pizza outlet in Patna, Bihar, accompanied by an editorial comparing the opening-day lines to the queues that used to form outside "Public Distribution Stores"—the ubiquitous state-run "ration shops" that sell goods like rice and kerosene to the poor at subsidized prices. It was a striking sign of modernity arriving in Bihar. Now "the place where civilization ends" has globally branded fast-food joints.

But a one-size-fits-all chain store won't always work in India. The CEO of a large Korean consumer company recently told me that while Chinese consumer tastes are growing more homogeneous, India's are not. In China, he says, he was surprised to find that magazines like *Vogue* and *Elle* are doing well in all major cities, while in India a different array of new publications is blossoming in every state. In China everyone is learning to speak Mandarin, which is even displacing Cantonese in its traditional heartland along the southern coast, including in Hong Kong. As Beijing relocates members of the Han Chinese majority—who constitute 90 percent of the population—to minority regions, even once-remote areas like Xinjiang and Tibet are entering the Han consumer mainstream, making the country ever more homogeneous. The growing sense of Chinese nationalism, based on pride in the revival of China as a major power, has helped to solidify the emergence of a unified national consumer culture, while the rise of provincial political powers in India is having the opposite effect. "When people say, let's go to India, I say, 'Okay, but where?'" says the CEO. In China, he points out, there are many popular national snacks, like the noodle packages put out by the Tingyi company. In India there are mainly regional snacks, as is the case across Europe.

Brand managers need to think of India as a United States of Europe and deal accordingly with the problem of selling goods in a nation where even the dates and names of the holiday seasons—as well as the peak seasons for brand advertising—shift state by state. The roster of festivals covers everything from the harvests in January and August to religious celebrations of gods and goddesses, the rites of spring, the bond between brother and sister, and the winter solstice. Many are celebrated in some states but not others, or go by different names in different places; the winter harvest festival called Pongal in Tamil Nadu goes by at least six other names in the rest of the country.

At the same time, rising incomes in the North have been accompanied by rising incomes in rural areas all over the country, partly a result of higher prices for rice and other crops, generous government support to farmers, and large salary increases for public and rural workers. This has allowed the new consumerism to penetrate the most rural and traditional corners of the country, where low incomes would have appeared to bar entry a few years ago. Demographers traditionally expected consumers to start asking for nonessential "aspirational" goods like deodorant and hair conditioner only after they entered the middle class, so they mapped demand for these goods by plotting the location of neighborhoods where incomes were rising to middle-class levels. In India that generally meant the cities and the South.

Instead, as access to modern media has spread, demand for aspirational goods has grown in regions that have not yet reached those levels of income. Car sales are increasing faster in the North than in the South. As of 2006, one of India's largest carmakers spent only 20 percent of its marketing budget outside the cities; today the share is split 50/50, with much of the new growth in the northern states. Even men with relatively low incomes are buying "fairness creams," increasingly popular items in color-conscious India. Where consumers want but can't afford these aspirational goods, companies are offering discount versions or smaller, less expensive packages of the same products. These sachets cost a few cents and are easier to distribute and store in India's highly fragmented retail market, which has more than 7.5 million outlets. Among increasingly brand-conscious young men in northern India it is popular to flaunt the red band of Jockey underwear over low-waisted denim jeans. In rural Bihar, where the Jockey brand is still out of reach, discount knockoffs with labels such as "Obama" enjoy brisk sales.

How the "Population Bomb" Became a Competitive Edge

The northern states such as Bihar are the epicenter of India's newfound excitement about population growth, just as they were once the focus of fear about the population bomb. During the 1970s and 1980s the growing population was seen as a threat to the economy, and this fear inspired extreme population-control measures during the dark period known as "the Emergency." In 1975, when Prime Minister Indira Gandhi was facing massive strikes and protests as the economy faltered under the pressure of the oil-price shocks, a state court convicted her of misuse of government authority in the 1971 election and disputed her victory. On the advice of family and close confidants, Gandhi struck back and imposed emergency rule that hot June, suspending Parliament and civil liberties, and in the ensuing months tens of thousands of activists, union leaders, and political opposition figures were tossed in jail.

The most controversial of the many Draconian measures imposed during "the Emergency" was the program of sterilization, led by Indira's son Sanjay. The program required every government employee to identify at least two candidates who had fathered two or more children. Candidates were then pressured to undergo the fifteen-minute surgery by roving sterilization teams, which had the power to withhold all manner of government privileges, from ration cards to business licenses.

Strikingly, many members of the middle class were in support of the program, on the grounds that India had to be saved from the "poverty trap" supposedly created by its exploding young population. It was often possible to hire a stand-in to undergo the sterilization for a measly sum, so this was not a sacrifice men of the middle class were forced to endure themselves. The government tried to break down the widespread resistance by offering volunteers a free radio. A common crack at the time, if a guy stumbled or walked strangely, was that "he must have a new radio."

The period of emergency rule ended in 1977, when Gandhi declared new elections, and the sterilization program ended with it, but not before 7.8 million men had been coerced or paid to undergo vasectomies. The Congress Party lost the 1977 election, ending its period of dominance and unleashing the centrifugal forces of regionalization that continue to erode central power today. Even into the 1980s the new government kept urging Indians to embrace population control as a civic duty. The catchiest advertising jingle of the decade was a public-service ditty that went like this: "After one, not now. After two, never again." People could not get that song, which rhymes neatly in Hindi, out of their heads.

In the last decade, however, the government dropped this theme, and the overwhelming consensus holds that population growth means more workers who can drive economic growth. The shelves of Indian libraries groan with research reports that argue for the inevitable wonders of this demographic dividend, citing the Chinese example as precedent, but ignoring the huge challenge of educating all the young people and expanding the job opportunities available to the ten million entering the labor force every year.

Yes, a growing pool of young workers can be a huge advantage, but only if a nation works hard to set them up for productive careers. A recent survey by the consulting firm Aon Hewitt shows that salaries of urban workers are rising faster in India than anywhere else in Asia, with average wages increasing by nearly 13 percent in 2011—a symptom of the fact that when so few workers are highly skilled, those who are can charge a premium.

The growth in demographic analysis as a global industry is striking. I can't count the number of demographers who have come to my offices in recent years, all offering some spin on the basic idea that population growth drives economic growth, and proffering tips on which nations will enjoy the biggest "demographic dividend." These fads come and go on Wall Street. In the 1970s and 1980s, every investment house had its own political economist, as a kind of coup and war forecaster, but they were gradually phased out in the 1990s as wars became more localized and political stability spread in the developing world. For now the demographers rule, and they love to talk about India. Consulting trends like these should be treated with the amused detachment they deserve, and the knowledge that this fad, too, shall pass. No doubt the phrase "population bomb" will be rediscovered before too long.

India Is a Political Chameleon, in a Good Way

India's boom has also sparked a rise in inequality, which to some extent is natural in the early stages of economic development; however, inequality can pose a threat to growth if it goes unchecked. Over the last decade, consumption levels have grown dramatically for all Indians, but 6 percentage points faster per year for the richest 10 percent than for the poorest 10 percent. The country's leaders have been working to contain the potential social tensions, mainly by increasing government handouts rather than by widening business and job opportunities. The Gandhi family has continued to show its trademark sensitivity to the poor, but in ways that may backfire against economic growth because it involves running up deficits. For the last five years government spending has been growing at a 20 percent annual pace, much faster than the economy. Over that time India's total fiscal deficit has ballooned from 6 percent to 9 percent of GDP, and the total public-debt-to-GDP ratio is now 70 percent—among the highest for any major developing country.

The development of this habit—deficit spending in good times as well as bad—was a major contributor to the current debt problems in the United States and Western Europe, and India can ill afford it. What's more, welfare schemes such as the rural employment guarantees create a perverse incentive for villagers to stay on the farm. As we've seen, China was able to convert its growing labor force into an economic miracle by encouraging a rapid mass migration of inland farmers to the more productive coastal cities. Over the past decade the share of the Chinese population living in urban areas rose from 35 to 46 percent. During the same period India's urban population grew much more slowly—from 26 percent to 30 percent of the whole.

India's hope for a big payoff from population growth ignores where people are living. Rising population helps drive growth when people are moving to higher-paying and more productive factory jobs in the cities, not languishing in farm regions. In China twenty-three cities have grown from a population of one hundred thousand to more than a million since 1950. These include some of the most dynamic urban areas, such as Shenzhen, which was a fishing village as recently as the 1970s. India has only six cities in this explosive growth category, and a more aggressive effort to encourage urbanization might have boosted India's long-term growth rate to double digits.

None of this seemed to matter too much to India's policy makers, who until recently were supremely confident that their country would become the fastest-growing major economy this decade. Even if they were ignoring the basic dynamics of how demographics, debt, and corruption can impact long-term growth, the optimistic view of India may still be right. China's economy is likely to slow down as the law of large numbers catches up with it, thereby more or less ceding the number one spot to India, which still has plenty of room to grow from a low base.

No other large economy has so many stars aligned in its favor, from its demographic profile to its entrepreneurial energy and, perhaps most important, an annual per capita income that is only one-fourth of China's. But destiny can never be taken for granted. Indian policy makers cannot assume that demographics will triumph and that problems such as rising crony capitalism and increased welfare spending are just sideshows instead of major challenges. These are exactly the factors that have prematurely choked growth in other emerging markets.

The wild card for India is its freewheeling democracy, an environment in which the zeitgeist can change very quickly. It was only in the last decade that India came to see itself as the next China, and came to see its growing population as a competitive advantage rather than as a threat. Only now is the southern sense of superiority over the North giving way to a newfound respect. The recent case of national overconfidence could give way just as fast to a healthier sense of urgency, with new leaders who see the complex picture of India for what it is. The great Indian rope trick may be impossible, in its mythical form, but Indian leaders don't need to come up with something that dazzling. Lesser versions of the rope trick—with no one disappearing into the sky and no falling body parts—are still impressive enough to keep audiences riveted to the show.

4

Is God Brazilian?

WHEN EVENTS ARE TURNING THEIR WAY, Brazilians like to joke that "God is Brazilian," and recent years have been blessed indeed. Brazil is a top exporter of every commodity that has seen dizzying price surges—iron ore, soybeans, sugar—producing a golden age for economic growth. Back in 2007 President Inácio Lula da Silva said this was Brazil's *momento magico*, but in the eyes of foreigners the magic would grow even stronger after Brazil weathered the 2008 crisis with relatively little damage. Foreign money-flows into Brazilian stocks and bonds climbed heavenward, up more than tenfold, from $5 billion a year in early 2007 to more than $50 billion in the twelve months through March 2011.

If there is a divine hand here, it is not necessarily working on Brazil's side. The flood of foreign money buying up Brazilian assets has made the currency one of the most expensive in the world, and Brazil one of the most costly, overhyped economies. Almost every major emerging-market currency has strengthened against the dollar over the last decade, but the real is on a path alone, way above the pack, having doubled in value against the dollar.

Economists have all kinds of fancy ways to measure the real value of a currency, but when a country is pricing itself this far out of the competition, you can feel it on the ground. Restaurants in São Paulo are pricier than those in Paris. Hotel rooms cost more in Rio than on the

In São Paulo, traffic has gotten so bad that CEOs have built an alternative transport system: a network of helipads atop their corporate headquarters.

French Riviera. Apartments in the chic Leblon area of Rio sell for more than Fifth Avenue co ops with views of Central Park. In early 2011 the major Rio paper, *O Globo*, ran a story on prices showing that croissants are more expensive than they are in Paris, haircuts cost more than they do in London, bike rentals are more expensive than in Amsterdam, and movie tickets sell for higher prices than in Madrid. On a recent visit I spent twenty-four dollars buying a Bellini for a girl from Ipanema, which seemed excessive. A rule of the road: if the local prices in an emerging-market country feel expensive even to a visitor from a rich nation, that country is probably not a breakout nation.

There is no better example of how absurd it is to lump all the big emerging markets together than the frequent pairing of Brazil and China. Those who make this comparison are referring only to the fact that they are the biggest players in their home regions, not to the way the economies actually run. Brazil is the world's leading exporter of many raw materials, and China is the leading importer; that makes them major trade partners—China surpassed the United States as Brazil's leading trade partner in 2009—but it also makes them opposites in almost every important economic respect: Brazil is the un-China, with interest rates that are too high, and a currency that is too expensive. It spends too little on roads and too much on welfare, and as a result has a very un-China-like growth record.

When Lula hailed his country's "magic moment" in 2007, Brazil had just put together a four-year run of 4 percent growth. But Russia, India, and China had averaged 8 percent growth over the same period. It may not be entirely fair to compare economic growth in Brazil with that of its Asian counterparts, because Brazil has a per capita income of $12,000, more than two times China's and nearly ten times India's. But even taking into account the fact that it is harder for rich nations to grow quickly, Brazil's growth has been disappointing. Since the early 1980s the Brazilian growth rate has oscillated around an average of 2.5 percent, spiking only in concert with increased prices for Brazil's key commodity exports. This is not the profile of a rising economic power.

While China has been criticized for pursuing "growth at any cost," Brazil has sought to secure "stability at any cost." Brazil's caution stems from its history of financial crises, in which overspending produced debt, humiliating defaults, and embarrassing devaluations, culminating in a disaster that is still recent enough to be fresh in every Brazilian adult's memory: the hyperinflation that started in the early 1980s and peaked in 1994, at the vertiginous annual rate of 2,100 percent. Prices rose so fast that checks would lose 30 percent of their value by the time businesses could deposit them, and so inconsistently that at one point a small bottle of sunscreen lotion cost as much as a luxury hotel room.

Wages were pegged to inflation but were increased at varying intervals in different industries, so workers never really knew whether they were making good money or not. As soon as they were paid, they literally ran to the store with cash to buy food, and they could afford little else, causing nonessential industries to start to die. Each new president came in with a plan—typically a different version of the same plan—which was basically to freeze prices and introduce a new currency, and this happened five times in ten years. The cruzeiro yielded to the cruzado, the cruzado to the new cruzado, the new cruzado to the cruzeiro, and then to the real cruzeiro, until finally the long process of trial and error ended in a plan that worked in 1994 and introduced the real, the currency that survives today. Hyperinflation finally came under control in 1995, but it left a problem of regular inflation behind. Brazil has battled inflation ever since by maintaining one of the highest interest rates in the emerging world. Those high rates have attracted a surge of foreign money, which is partly why the Brazilian real is so expensive relative to comparable currencies.

There is a growing recognition that China faces serious "imbalances" that could derail its long economic boom. Obsessed until recently with high growth, China has been pushing too hard to keep its currency too cheap (to help its export industries compete), encouraging excessively high savings and keeping interest rates rock bottom to fund heavy spending on roads and ports. China is only now beginning to consider a shift in spending priorities to create social programs that protect its people from the vicissitudes of old age and unemployment.

Brazil's economy is just as badly out of balance, though in opposite ways. While China has introduced reforms relentlessly for three decades, opening itself up to the world even at the risk of domestic instability, Brazil has pushed reforms only in the most dire circumstances, for example, privatizing state companies when the government budget is near collapse. Fearful of foreign shocks, Brazil is still one of the most closed economies in the emerging world—total imports and exports account for only 15 percent of GDP—despite its status as the world's leading exporter of sugar, orange juice, coffee, poultry, and beef.

While China is just starting to ponder the creation of a welfare state, Brazil has already built one that it can't really afford. Since the crises of the 1980s Brazil's government spending as a share of its economy has climbed steadily from nearly 20 percent—pretty typical for the emerging markets—to around 40 percent in 2010, among the highest in the developing world. This is not how Brazil used to be. In the 1950s and 1960s, the economy expanded at a double-digit growth rate, and professors of development economics from South Korea to Argentina held Brazil up as a paragon of economic virtue. But by the 1970s, as the oil shocks first started to drive up prices, Brazil lost its way and succumbed to the populist appeal of trying to lock in a comfortable lifestyle: the 1988 constitution guarantees free health care and university education, and today the minimum wage is so high that it applies to one in three workers. Economists don't agree on when big government equals bad government, but they do agree that government spending should track changes in per capita income, and for Brazil currently that would correspond to around 25 percent of GDP, not 40 percent. Hence, Brazil has long since entered a zone that should be considered excessive.

It's sometimes said that supporting a welfare state is a rich man's disease, but Brazil has a full-blown case without a rich man's income. To pay for its big government Brazil has jacked up taxes and now has a tax burden that equals 38 percent of GDP, the highest in the emerging world, and very similar to the tax burden in developed European welfare states, such as Norway and France. This heavy load of personal and corporate tax on a relatively poor country means that businesses don't have the money to invest in new technology or training, which in turn means that industry is not getting more efficient. Between 1980 and 2008 Brazil's productivity grew at an annual rate of about 0.2 percent, compared to 4 percent in China, a reflection of the fact that China was not only putting more people to work in factories and investing heavily in better equipment, as well as better roads to get the factory goods to market, but also figuring out how to make those workers and those machines work more efficiently. Over the same period, productivity grew in India at close to 3 percent and in South Korea and Thailand at close to 2 percent—one big reason why those three are real or potential breakout nations, while Brazil is not.

Why Brazil Overheats at Such Slow Speeds

On one level Brazil's failure to invest in roads and factories can give simple tasks, like moving about the country, a comic-opera quality. Truckers taking sugar to the seaport in São Paulo routinely wait two to three days at the gate because of a lack of warehouse space and mechanized cargo movers inside the port. Those who make it don't always arrive with a full load. A former executive of a major U.S. agribusiness says his company used to transport seeds from the Brazilian hinterlands by truck, but the roads were so bad that half of the seeds would fall out by the time the truck reached São Paulo. Scavengers would follow the truck, and he would later find his seeds on sale in Paraguay.

The low investment rate doesn't just lead to awful inefficiencies. It also means the economy can overheat at a very low rate of growth. If a nation's supply chain is built on aging factories and potholed roads, supply cannot keep up with demand, and prices will rise. If the nation invests too little in its schools and is producing too few highly skilled workers, then wages will rise. Brazil's economy seems to be hitting its limits on every front, as the aging airports of Rio and São Paulo—unimproved for decades now—struggle to keep up with increasing traffic, schools fail to graduate enough skilled workers, and businesses operate near capacity. In São Paulo traffic is so bad that the CEOs of major Brazilian businesses developed an alternative transport system: a network of landing pads on the rooftops of office skyscrapers, so that top executives can hopscotch from one corporate headquarters to another by helicopter. I've been forced to use this system myself on a number of visits, and while it works great for the business elite, it's a bad sign for Brazil, and a very inflationary way to get across town.

The arteries of the labor pool are just as clogged. With schools underfunded, the result is a massive skills shortage. Unemployment has fallen to a decade-low 6 percent, but businessmen now complain that they have no choice but to hire unprepared and unqualified applicants. The average student in Brazil stays in school for only seven years, the lowest of any middle-income country; in China, where average income levels are much lower, the average is eight years. There is a shortage of engineers and technical workers, and a visible decline in manufacturing and service standards. Wages are going up, helping persuade expat Brazilian pilots to return home from jobs in Asia and the Middle East, but standards in the domestic airline industry are falling anyway. The number of canceled and delayed flights rises at the end of each month because there aren't enough pilots, and there are legal limits on their monthly flying time. Even the service in high-end Rio hotels—which charge up to a thousand dollars a night for a room on Ipanema Beach—sometimes struggle to get rooms cleaned before the late afternoon.

It may seem counterintuitive, but the high cost of labor and transport in Brazil is a direct result of investing too little. While China's total investment (in everything from new factories to new schools) has gone too far, climbing to 50 percent of GDP in the last decade, Brazil's has stagnated for many years at just under 19 percent, one of the lowest rates in the emerging world. Specifically the share of that overall investment devoted to new infrastructure—roads, railways, ports—is just 2 percent of GDP in Brazil, compared with an emerging-market average of 5 percent, and 10 percent in China. The experience of driving on a smooth new highway, which is commonplace in the new China, is alien in Brazil. No wonder it takes two to three days for trucks to get into the port of São Paulo, and no wonder it seems like everything in Brazil is rushed, way behind schedule, out of stock. Given the country's track record, frequent visitors to Rio look at the empty fields where the stadiums for the 2016 Olympic Games are supposed to be built, and wonder if Brazil will really pull it off.

The broad measure of how fully an economy is employing its total stock of labor and equipment—a number called the capacity utilization rate—is running at a very high level of 84 percent in Brazil, or about 5 percentage points higher than the average in other emerging markets. And if businesses are short of everything, paying high prices for staff as well as goods, they are going to pass those costs on to customers. It's this basic lack of capacity that makes the economic engine overheat at a relatively slow speed in Brazil, pushing up prices when GDP growth approaches a rate of just 4 percent, compared with around 8 percent in China. This, in a nutshell, is why my Rio Bellini cost twenty-four dollars.

The Unambitious Brazilian Model

In China all the big reforms of the last thirty years provided big openings—freeing peasants to migrate to the cities, allowing foreigners to invest in China—while in Brazil all the signature reforms were about anchoring the economy to a stable foundation. The president most responsible for getting hyperinflation under control was President Itamar Franco, who ended the constant introduction of new currencies once and for all by creating the real and pegging it to the dollar in 1994. When a contagion swept through emerging-market currencies in the late 1990s and threatened Brazil, the new president, Fernando Henrique Cardoso, helped stabilize Brazil by pushing new measures to control spending, including a budget law that makes it difficult for the independent-minded Brazilian states to borrow heavily. The most dramatic example, though, is Lula, who won the 2002 election with a radical platform that included veiled threats of a debt default, which panicked foreign investors. Once in power, Lula reversed course and adopted a program of budget discipline indistinguishable from Cardoso's, for a very simple reason: he understood that inflation hits the poor and the working class—the core support of his Worker's Party—the hardest. Brazil seemed to achieve the impossible when its inflation rate fell to a low of 3 percent in April 2007—the same as in the United States.

Lula was delivering what the Brazilian people really wanted, which was stability. Since Brazil never recorded the gangbuster growth rates of other big commodity exporters like Russia, and did not borrow heavily during the Lula years, it found itself better able to cope with the credit crisis of 2008. Lula's background, as a child of the working class, gave him the street credibility to sell budgetary responsibility to his mass base. Lula left office in early 2011 widely viewed as a model for Latin America, and others would follow his path from radical to moderate. In Peru, Ollanta Humala campaigned for president in 2006 as a classic Latin firebrand, complete with red T-shirts; at the next election, in 2011, he came out in business suits, singing the praises of Brazilian-style macro-orthodoxy. But those who have come to admire the Brazilian model focus on its relatively strong recent economic growth of about 4 percent, not on the long-term record or its inherent weaknesses.

When Petrobras Is Worth More Than Turkey, Something's Wrong

Until recently the Brazilian elite seemed oblivious to the simple fact that all the money the government and consumers have been spending depends on high commodity prices, and it could disappear if commodity prices collapse. The dramatic change in the power of commodity exporters was captured well by Glenn Stevens, governor of the Reserve Bank of Australia, when he pointed out that five years ago the money received for one shipload of iron ore could buy 2,200 flat-screen TVs; in 2011 the payment for the same shipment could buy 22,000. Brazil, the world's largest exporter of iron ore, can afford a lot of TVs now. Over the last ten years the top-performing sectors in emerging markets were energy and materials, and Brazil rode that wave too. In 2008 the total stock market value of Brazil's state-owned oil giant, Petrobras, reached more than $300 billion. At the same moment, the total value of Turkey's stock market—all the publicly traded companies in the country—was less than $200 billion.

The commodity windfall is fun while it lasts, but it also carries the seeds of its own destruction. The strong demand for Brazilian coffee, steel, and iron ore drives up the value of the real, which makes all other Brazilian exports more expensive. That is hollowing out Brazilian factories, which can no longer find customers for their increasingly expensive exports. The manufacturing share of GDP peaked at 16.5 percent in 2004, and had fallen to 13.5 percent by the end of 2010. With all the money flowing into Brazil, chasing commodities and high interest rates, the strong real gives the Brazilian consumer greater purchasing power: the total value of imports is rising faster than exports, pushing the overall trade account into the red, from a surplus in 2007 to a $50 billion deficit in 2010. This, too, is the exact opposite of China, where the currency has increased in value only slightly, and the overall trade surplus is growing sharply.

Brazil's reliance on commodity exports is growing. Following major oil discoveries in recent years, Brazil is now estimated to have the world's tenth-largest reserves, and some experts have called it "the next Saudi Arabia." A decade ago Brazil was producing a million barrels per day. In 2011 it was expected to produce two million, and global forecasters are looking to Brazil to pump four million per day by 2015 and six million by 2020, at which point it would become a serious counterweight to unstable suppliers in the Middle East and Africa. That could be a good thing for the world—and for Brazil, but only if it learns to invest the windfall in ways that raise productivity: Saudi Arabia did not do so for many years, and it has about the same per capita income now that it had three decades ago.

The Unsolvable Trilemma

Right now Brazil offers a good example of one of the more popular projects in economics, which is attempting to solve the "trilemma." That's the problem leaders face in trying to manage and stabilize exchange rates, interest rates, and the flow of foreign money in and out of the country. The search for a solution looks a lot like a game of "whack a mole," in which hammering one mole on the head triggers another one to pop up out of another hole. If the authorities want to stabilize inflation, they raise interest rates, but that is going to attract foreign capital and drive up the exchange rate. If they want a more competitive currency, they hold down interest rates, at the risk of unleashing inflation. In a globalized world with huge international money flows, this game can go on indefinitely.

Brazil's puzzle is particularly difficult to solve because inflation kicks in at such a low rate of economic growth, so to fight inflation authorities raise interest rates quickly in an expansion cycle, pushing up the value of the currency and capping the potential speed at which the economy can grow. China faces the opposite problem: productive capacity is very high, and authorities want a cheap currency to keep those plants globally competitive and fully employed, but that makes it very difficult for the authorities to raise interest rates when inflation begins to threaten, as it did in 2011. China needs to cut back its investment binge and let its currency appreciate, even though many of its plants are already operating below capacity. Brazil needs more investment, lower interest rates, and a cheaper currency, but it will be tough to achieve all three. Foreign capital flows ensure that neither Brazil nor China can achieve their aims without harming themselves in some other way. They are both caught in the trilemma even though—as the world's biggest commodity importer and the world's biggest commodity exporter—they have the opposite problems.

It's not surprising, in these complex circumstances, that the Chinese and Brazilians can have a hard time understanding one another. One of the top executives at Brazil's largest bank recently told me a story to illustrate the problem: Chinese investors are bullish on Brazil, largely because the Chinese are spending so much money buying coffee and iron ore from Brazil, so they figure it has to be a good investment. But that's not necessarily the case, as one big Chinese investor learned when he came to the Brazilian bank, complaining about the lengthy delays at Brazilian ports. "Why can't you build better infrastructure?" the Chinese investor asked. The Brazilian banker explained, "We have to look at profitability, and high interest rates make the cost of capital here so prohibitive that it's very difficult to build anything quickly." The Chinese investor looked at him blankly: Profitability? Interest rates?

In China, with the state pouring capital into infrastructure projects, profitability is never an issue when the authorities want to build a port or a rail line. The government doesn't care about making a profit; it cares about getting the rail line up and running. And with the Chinese state holding real interest rates near zero, the cost of capital is never an issue either. The banker from the nation with one of the highest interest rates in the world and the investor from a nation where money is virtually free ended up talking straight past one another.

Where "CNBC Culture" Is a Complimentary Term

That conversation helps explain another 180-degree difference between these two countries: Brazil has been one of the hottest stock markets in the emerging world over the last decade, and China one of the coldest. For all the talk about how Chinese Communists have "embraced capitalism," they have not yet embraced bottom-line discipline. The Shanghai stock market lists mainly big state-owned enterprises that couldn't care less about profit margins; in Brazil the high cost of borrowing (and everything else) has forced publicly traded companies to be extremely disciplined, and as a result they are highly profitable. That's a big reason why the value of Brazil's stock market rose 300 percent in dollar terms from 2000 to 2010, more than triple the rise in China's market, despite Brazil's slower economic growth.

In this respect at least, Brazil represents a positive turn in emerging markets. Stock markets should rise in value when the economy is growing, but in recent decades in the emerging world, they often have not. A case in point was South Korea, where the benchmark KOSPI index peaked in 1989, while the economy continued to grow at a 6 percent pace until the outbreak of the Asian financial crisis in 1997. Companies saw the stock market as a place to raise quick money, not as a basic measure of the company's long-term value. Emerging-market companies focused on getting big—more employees, more sales, more market share—and didn't pay much attention to whether all that revenue was generating bottom-line profit, the metric stock market investors care about most. In recent years with a few glaring exceptions, such as China, that has begun to change: as companies from Brazil to South Korea have started to refocus on profit, stock markets have started to rise (and fall) with emerging economies.

The more accurately a stock market reflects the real economy, the more important it becomes as a signal of where the nation is headed. In places such as India, the stock market eventually became a kind of stand-in for public opinion polls: during the all-important annual budget season, the national media covers the stock market reaction as the ultimate verdict on whether the new budget makes sense. Perhaps for that reason Indian politicians are always asking themselves, "What will the market think?" Investors and market analysts are an increasingly important public voice and political constituency, because of the constant din that they generate on CNBC-style news channels, which are spreading fast in emerging markets, including India and Brazil.

The impact of this vocal investor class on critical national decisions is tough to quantify, but I think it's profound. The rise of leaders like Lula—who campaign as radicals and govern as moderates—reflects how the global market culture effectively narrows policy choices. As capital markets play an increasingly important role in funding growth, there is tremendous pressure to follow the orthodox international rules—open the economy, maintain budget discipline—in order to benefit from globalization. A growing class of stockholders is watching 24/7, and the market instantly punishes policy decisions that depart too far from the accepted norm.

"CNBC culture," the constant obsession with the zig and zag of the markets, is often used as a pejorative term. Critics see the reportage of every blip and blink in the markets as the ultimate expression of short-term thinking, and everything that is wrong with it. But in many developing nations, governments and companies have been so focused on growth at any cost that they have often ignored profit—an expression of efficient, sustainable growth. In these countries, the rise of the CNBC culture can also have positive fallout.

One of the more telling cases involves the richest businessman in Brazil, Eike Batista, who like most Rio tycoons travels with a posse of bodyguards because of widespread crime, mixed with resentment of the very well-off. (There is a reason why Brazil is the second-largest market in the world for armored cars.) He also goes everywhere with his guard dog, Eric, and his BlackBerry, constantly checking on the stock price of his vast holdings.

Batista is now one of the ten wealthiest men in the world. His ambition is to overtake the richest, Carlos Slim of Mexico, and he's clearly got the right focus to get there. For Eike, it's all about profit, productivity, and making the right strategic moves. It doesn't matter what drives him—the focus on profits and delivering value to shareholders offers a vast improvement over the approach of emerging-market tycoons before the crises of the 1990s, when all they cared about was building the biggest possible empire, no matter how inefficient, unfocused, or indebted. The CNBC driven obsession with efficiency could be a good thing for Brazil.

Time to Experiment

There is not much sign of a similar obsession taking hold in government circles. While Chinese leaders have recognized and vigorously debated the imbalances they face, Brazilians are only starting to recognize how overpriced their economy is. For the most part Brazilians seem content with this sluggish state of affairs, or they just find ways to get around the obstacles, like the rooftop helipad network in São Paulo.

Brazil needs to start experimenting, taking some risks to break out of its low-growth pattern. Despite Brazil's role as a major exporter, it is still one of the most protectionist "normal" economies in the world, short of the oddball cases, like North Korea. Brazil maintains a host of antiquated trade barriers, which is why trade as a share of GDP is just 20 percent, the lowest among all the emerging nations. The authorities are loath to lower barriers, for fear that a surge of imports will worsen the trade deficits, but a dose of foreign competition could help spark the innovation and experimentation Brazil lacks.

In a recent conversation Arminio Fraga, former governor of Brazil's central bank, pointed out to me that Brazil's per capita income had risen from 12 to 25 percent of U.S. per capita income during its first boom phase of the 1950s and 1960s, fell back to 16 percent in the lost decades, and then climbed back up to 20 percent in the last decade. Now he fears the cycle of big spending and complacency that stopped Brazil's first boom may start all over again. "In this regard we can't seem to shake off our Iberian roots," says Fraga, referring to the slow-moving welfare-state culture of Portugal, Brazil's original colonizer. If Brazil does not carry out the reforms, it will be hard-pressed to grow even at 4 percent per year—less than half as fast as China's recent growth. Unless God really *is* Brazilian.

5

Mexico's Tycoon Economy

EVERY NATION HAS ITS BIG TYCOONS, but to a rare degree Mexico is owned by them. The top-ten business families control almost every industry, from telephones to media, which allows them to extract high prices without much effort and to enjoy unusually high profit margins. That explains why Mexico has had one of the hottest stock markets and one of the most sluggish economies in the emerging world. Over the last ten years the Mexican stock market increased by more than 200 percent in dollar terms, while in the United States the S&P 500 was essentially flat, even though Mexico's economy did not grow much faster than that of its northern neighbor. This perverse disconnect between the stock market and the economy is unusual in the current global environment. In Mexico it reflects, to a large degree, the power of oligopolies.

While big Mexican companies use their fat profits at home to become major multinationals, Mexico itself has fallen behind. Cornered markets mean the oligopolists have little incentive to invest and innovate: domestic productivity growth has been virtually stagnant since the financial crisis of 1994, when excessive government borrowing led to an 80 percent drop in the value of the peso. The economy has been expanding at an average rate of barely 3 percent for the last decade, and it barely accelerated through the great boom from 2003 to 2007. With a population of 105 million, Mexico was once the richest country in Latin America, but in recent

A Petri dish for monopolies of all kinds:
The war on the cartels produces another drug bust.

years it has been surpassed by its largest regional rivals. Mexico now has a per capita income of $11,000, lower than both Brazil's ($12,000) and Chile's ($13,000).

The oligopolistic structure dates to the 1970s, when Mexico was still a largely socialist country and most industries were state monopolies, protected from foreign competition by high tariffs. As a result of the Mexican government's debt crises in the 1980s and 1990s, these businesses were sold off to the private sector, which in practice often meant a few wealthy families with access to capital, who wound up buying the businesses at prices well below their book value. The state monopolies became private monopolies, and today the top companies in telecommunications, beer, cement, and other industries control 50 to 80 percent of the Mexican market. They have used the cash generated from captive domestic consumers to push abroad, giving birth to the Mexican multinational. Today the Mexico City stock exchange lists the world's largest telecommunications company, America Movil; the third-largest cement company, CEMEX; the largest Coke bottler, Femsa; and the largest tortilla company, Gruma (which makes most of its money not in Mexico or Latin America but in the United States).

Another reason why the Mexican stock market is largely divorced from what's actually happening in Mexico is that many of the sectors that drive the local economy are not listed on the market. Manufacturing exporters, particularly the big American car companies that have plants along the border, are the largest part of the economy. But GM, Ford, and Chrysler are not listed on the Mexican stock market. The next-biggest sector is oil and utilities, led by the state oil company Pemex, which is not listed anywhere. The companies that dominate the stock market are focused on telecommunications and media within Mexico, but even they are becoming increasingly international. About 45 percent of the revenues of Mexican public companies are generated outside Mexico, mainly elsewhere in Latin America and in the United States.

This leaves Mexico with a growing concentration of global wealth in the hands of the few. Today the top-ten Mexican families account for more than a third of its total stock market value—one of the highest concentrations among emerging markets. Private cartels produce about

40 percent of the goods that Mexicans consume and charge prices that are 30 percent higher than international averages. Phones, services, soft drinks, and many foodstuffs cost more in Mexico than in the United States, where per capita income is five times higher. As U.S. corporations streamline operations and lay off workers in the wake of the Great Recession of 2008, American corporate profits are becoming politically controversial as they consume a growing share of the economic pie, and now represent about 12 percent of GDP. But Mexican corporations are taking an even larger share of the Mexican pie—about 25 percent of GDP.

Normally, rising inequality is a necessary but temporary downside of rapid development, but in Mexico the oligopoly culture is creating a self-perpetuating form of inequality. Mexico is a troubling outlier on the Kuznets curve, which shows that in the early stages of a country's development, a rising tide normally lifts all boats, but it lifts incomes of the upper class much faster than those of the working class. There are a few nations, including Taiwan and South Korea, that managed to beat the curve and produce fast growth with growing equality for many decades. Mexico has produced high inequality with little growth: indeed the entrenched power and wealth of its elite are major impediments to growth.

A rule of the road: strong companies and stock markets should—but do not necessarily—make for strong economies, so don't confuse the two. The clearest examples are countries dominated by oligopolies, like Mexico, South Africa, and to some extent the Philippines. In these economies, if competition increases and undermines the abnormally high profit margins of the large companies, that could lower consumer prices, raise overall productivity, and boost the country's growth potential.

The Revolutionary Party of Oligarchs

The roots of Mexico's oligopoly culture lie in politics. Until the elections of July 2000, the dominant Institutional Revolutionary Party (PRI) was itself a monopoly. It had ruled with little challenge for seventy years, and in that time Mexicans got very comfortable with the centralization of power. Leaders passed the mantle through a succession system in which the sitting president simply pointed *el dedazo*—"the big finger"—at his successor. The PRI maintained support by passing out privileges—

including parliamentary seats—to favored interests. It's hard to push for change when Parliament itself is a vast pool of patronage, with too many legislators (628), one-third of whom are picked from party lists rather than directly elected.

Many emerging markets have dominant families in big business, but in Mexico they are particularly powerful, and not only in business. Negotiating political deals was easy because all the various groups—the ruling party, big business, the public and private unions, the groups representing big farmers and peasants, the mighty teachers' union—had a very similar structure: top-down oligopolies. Cutting deals required only that the oligarchs meet in a back room and work things out. Such groups are entirely self-interested: The social security workers' union has won pensions that not only are much more generous than the average worker's but also are effectively subsidized by the average worker. The teachers' union won the right to national collective bargaining two decades ago, and one result is that Mexican students consistently rank at or near the bottom of international ratings, no matter where in Mexico they come from.

These kinds of deals conspired to tarnish the era of unbroken PRI rule. Corporations fought to keep taxes down to just 12 percent of GDP, one of the lowest rates in the world, ultimately leading to government debt crises in the 1980s and 1990s and the landmark defeat of the PRI in the election of 2000. The incoming president, Vicente Fox of the National Action Party, tried to reform the oligopoly culture but failed, largely because there is still widespread support for oligopolies, at least in the state sector. Polls still show that an overwhelming majority of Mexicans are hostile to privatization and believe that the government should control the economy. By 2006, when Fox left office, 90 percent of the national legislators came from unions, farm groups, and other organizations with long-standing ties to the PRI. Fox failed to curtail their power because they still held power.

Mexico is not a modern capitalist democracy in which political parties battle it out to determine what's best for the country. It's a premodern political economy in which special interests vie for access to the political boss and shares of the pie. This is particularly true in the oil patch. The PRI still considers its 1938 decision to take over the oil industry a landmark victory for the nation, and has so far resisted all suggestions from current president Felipe Calderón that selling part of Pemex could bring some market logic to bear on Mexican oil fields. The public-sector union in the oil industry refuses to open the industry to outsiders, for fear of losing influence over the profits. Pemex has nearly 150,000 workers, including more than 11,000 who do no work—their jobs no longer exist—but they can't be fired because of unreformed privileges of the labor law, according to Mexico scholar Carlos Elizondo Mayer-Serra.

The Pemex monopoly is so inefficient that the country gains little from spiking oil prices. Investment is low, and search and discovery efforts are minimal. Mexico is a declining exporter of oil, with production falling from a high of 3.4 million barrels per day in 2004 to 2.6 million barrels per day last year. It is earning a lot less from oil than it did five years ago, and still faces the downside risk of higher oil prices, which have a major negative impact on Mexico's major export: cars, to the United States. At the same time, because of limited refining capacity, gasoline imports are rising. The end result is that rising oil prices add little if anything to Mexico's growth.

The Worried Tycoons

The list of top Mexican billionaires reflects this stagnation. It has seen virtually no turnover in recent years. The same few families have gotten wealthier, and to maintain their extraordinary pricing power, they fight attempts to open the economy to outside competition, which leads in turn to stickier inflation.

Not that Mexican magnates are exactly comfortable. The tycoons who rank among Mexico's top-ten billionaires have an average wealth of well over $10 billion, among the highest in the emerging world, but they don't necessarily flaunt it. Like Brazil, South Africa, and other emerging markets where crime and social resentment against the rich run high, and kidnapping-for-ransom is a major industry, the super-rich tend to lie low. They ride around in bulletproof cars, surrounded by bodyguards, while trying hard to make themselves inconspicuous. Mexican tycoon Carlos Slim is the world's richest man, but you wouldn't know it from his home in Mexico City, a six-bedroom house with a small swimming pool, all hidden behind high walls. By contrast, I've traveled into the badlands of crime-ridden Uttar Pradesh with one of India's top billionaires, who went protected only by the clothes on his back and felt perfectly safe. And to say Indian billionaires are comfortable with displays of their wealth is an understatement, given the billion-dollar home of the country's richest man, Mukesh Ambani. At four hundred thousand square feet and twenty-seven stories, it looms over the swankiest neighborhood of Mumbai. If this seems excessive, India is still a healthier social environment than Mexico, where the tycoons have as much money, and more fear.

It's not only the tycoons who live in fear. To a large extent the decades-long drug war in Mexico involves the bad guys firing on police or on one another, yet there are inevitable spillover effects. An increasing number of wealthy and entrepreneurial Mexicans are securing a special class of U.S. visa that allows them to flee Mexico by investing in American companies. I just heard the story of a businessman who operates a hospital in Ciudad Juárez, just across the border from El Paso, Texas, who would not allow his family to visit Colombia for fear of the drug violence there. Now the drug violence in Juárez has forced him to move to Texas, and he visits his hospital only when absolutely necessary, accompanied by machine gun–toting guards. Meanwhile the drug situation in Colombia has improved so dramatically that his family vacations in Medellín, which was known only five years ago as the murder capital of the world.

Mexico's drug war springs in some ways from the cartel-style business culture. It is perhaps unsurprising that, after the toppling of the Colombian drug-cartels a decade ago, the center of cartel power would shift to Mexico, a Petri dish for monopolies of all kinds. When President Calderón warned in 2010 that the Mexican drug cartels were "trying to impose a monopoly by force of arms, and even trying to create their own laws," he might have been describing the established Mexican oligopolies (minus the firearms). To a large extent the cartels have carved the northern border region into corridors leading to the United States, with each cartel sticking more or less to its own area. The exception is when a government offensive takes out a cartel leader, setting off a battle among his underlings and rivals for his vacated turf.

The drug business operates as a kind of parallel economy, with little impact on the regular economy. Calderón's 2006 decision to unleash the army against the drug cartels has escalated the fight, with the number of drug-related deaths rising from 2,500 in 2007 to 13,000 in 2010. But the stock prices of Mexican companies seem oblivious to all this violence, and continue to be more heavily influenced by American and global economic trends than by local wars and politics.

Mexico's Asian Side

As America goes, so goes Mexico. An increase of 1 percent in the U.S. economy produces a 1.2 percent rise in the Mexican economy, and a U.S. recession has an equal and opposite effect. To a striking extent, the economic profile of Mexico is more Asian than Latin, in its heavy reliance on manufactured exports to the United States rather than commodity exports to Asia. That means Mexico competes head-to-head with China, and by early in the last decade, China was eating Mexico's lunch. With higher productivity growth and much lower wages, China looked like a juggernaut bound to destroy the Mexican economy. Trade with the United States had revived the Mexican economy after the collapse of the peso in 1994, so Mexico saw its prime advantage under direct threat. Just like in other manufacturing powers such as the United States and Japan, the "China threat" to factory jobs became a subject of popular debate and high public angst in Mexico, but in no other Latin country.

The fear proved partly right: some Mexican industries such as textiles did lose out to China, but others did not. With wages in China now rising sharply, the pendulum could start to swing Mexico's way. In 2002 the average manufacturing wage in China was 240 percent lower than that in Mexico; the gap is now only about 13 percent. Proximity to the U.S. border and rising shipping costs are also tilting the advantage back toward Mexico. That's especially true for factories that make heavy goods like cars, or products that feed "just-in-time" U.S. supply chains (which aim to replace goods as they are sold off the shelves, in order to keep retailer inventory down and profit up). The peso is also still cheap compared to most emerging-market currencies, another plus for its exports. So if there is hope for Mexico, it is in its manufacturing sector.

For now Mexico lies low in the water. If the global crisis of 2008 exposed many nations for borrowing too much, it exposed Mexico for borrowing too little. While the average emerging market increased bank lending to businesses and individuals by 20 percentage points to 50 percent of GDP in the 2000s, Mexico increased it by just 3 percentage points to 24 percent of GDP. This is quite remarkable: capitalism can't function without credit, and in Mexico credit is expanding more slowly than anywhere else in Latin America. Ever since the 1994 peso crisis the mainstream Mexican banks have kept an incredibly tight leash on credit—the kind of sluggish spirit that is natural in an uncompetitive market. (This is part of the story of Japan's stagnation, where bank lending froze years ago.) In recent years one of the key drivers of growth elsewhere in Latin America was an aggressive and innovative push by banks to extend credit into previously unserved low-income neighborhoods. In Mexico the banks haven't bothered.

Typically, even though money was tight, exceptions were made for the big private monopolies. In the last decade many of them borrowed to help build their global presence, and all looked swell until the crisis of 2008 exposed the flaws. Some foreign operations proved too expensive. The peso crashed, and the special monopoly price of capital jumped through the roof. Some of the Mexican global giants have seen their stock price collapse, most notably the cement company CEMEX, while others have had to retreat to the home market.

The global financial crisis has started the process of eroding the defenses and privileges of the oligopolies. Under pressure, the tycoons began to violate the unwritten rule against attacking one another's home turf: smaller players began to compete with CEMEX for its long-standing customers. Smaller telecommunication companies began pushing harder for the government to challenge the high connection and termination fees that America Movil, the dominant telecommunication company owned by Carlos Slim, used to control that market. And government started to listen, passing an antitrust law in 2011 that imposes harsh punishment for anticompetitive practices, including stiff fines and possible jail time for top executives. Passage of the antitrust law was quickly followed by a $1 billion fine against America Movil over the termination fees. Slim has fought back, and could tie the case up in court for years. The bottom line is that the nascent signs of government willingness to take on oligopolies combined with the outbreak of intra-tycoon skirmishing could foretell a turn toward genuine competition. But there is a long road ahead, and the overall scorecard for President Calderón is unimpressive: his priorities coming into office included reforming the labor law, correcting dysfunctions in the energy sector, and addressing the government's problem of raising revenue. Even by 2011 he had achieved no meaningful progress on any of those fronts.

Mexico is not the only emerging market dominated by oligopolists. The Philippines provides another clear example, but in the Philippines I can see a roadmap for change, with the arrival of a new president bent on reform. The Philippines also has a much easier task, with a per capita income only about one-fourth that of Mexico. The international consensus is that the Mexican economy will continue to underperform in the years ahead. Mexico's own central bank projects a trend growth rate of only 2.5 percent, which is about half the potential of most emerging markets, or less.

Mexican voters are frustrated with the deteriorating security situation, the constant threat of getting fleeced by petty local officials and the police, and the weak economic track record. The political system responds slowly to popular anger, partly because many Mexicans just leave the country rather than press for change at home. Between 2006 and 2010, Mexico saw a net outward migration of 2.4 million, by far the largest exodus in the world. (China, with a total population twelve times larger, saw the second-largest net exodus, 1.7 million.) The political class needs to face more pressure before real change comes, because it was the politicians who gave birth to the oligopoly culture in the first place.

6

In Russia, There's Room
Only at the Top

I T IS COMMON to refer to many a developing nation as a "land of contrasts," but Russia is different, more extreme, a land of outright contradictions. The government heavily controls what is said on TV but not in
the papers. Russians have an average annual income of around $13,000
but are probably the only people this rich who live in fear of frequent
power outages. Many Muscovites drive around the capital in fancy German cars, but there is no organized taxi service. If you want a cab you
either call a radio car or flag down a freelancer in an unmarked car. A
major exporter of wheat, Russia has to import millions of tons of meat and
poultry for its domestic consumption. It's no wonder outsiders struggle to
figure out what's going on, and change their minds so often. Since it was
opened to the world in 1995, during the early post-Communist period,
the Russian stock market has finished most years among either the three
best-performing in the world or the three worst.

They say money talks and wealth whispers, but in Moscow wealth
dances on the bar. It is the world capital of oversized nouveau-riche
displays, unrivaled for its gaudiness: the wild parties on weekdays, the
high-end prostitutes wallpapering luxury-hotel lobbies, the ten-thousand-
dollar champagne bottles. I see plenty of excess in other emerging-market
capitals, but this one takes it to a new level: I know Moscow businessmen
who go mushroom picking on weekends—by helicopter. There are signs

They say money talks and wealth whispers,
but in Moscow wealth dances on the bar.

of such limitless consumption at the top that local historians say it feels as decadent as the last days of ancient Rome. Yet other than St. Petersburg, Peter the Great's canal-laced showcase in the north, the second cities of Russia are gray and grim, still Soviet in look and morality.

Traveling inside Russia is like traveling through time: Moscow and St. Petersburg are connected by an ultramodern high-speed rail system imported from Germany, but the average age of trains in the rest of the Russian railway fleet is twenty years, which means that nearly half of the rail cars date to the Soviet era. Traveling the 440 miles from Moscow to St. Petersburg takes less than four hours; traveling roughly the same distance from Moscow to Kazan, referred to as the "third capital" of Russia, is a thirteen-hour overnight journey. The government is investing so little—investment represents just 20 percent of GDP, less than half the level in China—that the cracks in the system are growing all too visible. While auto sales are increasing at a double-digit pace (and are particularly strong in the luxury class), roads in and around Moscow are falling apart, resulting in the worst traffic jams of any capital city in the world. Every big emerging market (except Brazil) modernized its major airports during the economic boom of the 2000s, but St. Petersburg's Pulkovo Airport remains hulking and decrepit, yet another relic of Soviet times.

These contradictions are not mere cultural peculiarities. They go to the heart of how things work today: the Kremlin allows entrepreneurs to thrive in retail, Internet, media, and other consumer areas, even as it continues to exert state control over strategic sectors, especially oil and gas. Though oil and gas officially account for a bit more than 20 percent of GDP, the World Bank has said the number is probably too low, for complex accounting reasons, and it certainly understates the critical role of oil, which now makes up about half of federal revenue, two-thirds of exports, and most of the economic dynamism: if oil prices were to fall 30 percent, the economic growth rate would almost certainly fall to zero. The result is one economy under two systems, one somewhat free and one authoritarian. In 2007 I saw these contradictions as a stage that Russia would work through on the way to emerging as a European economic power. Now it looks more like a semi-permanent condition.

Russia is an oil state that has lost its way. The country went through a chaotic transition after the collapse of the Soviet Union in the early 1990s, with the economy struggling to regain its footing, with war breaking out in Chechnya, and with President Boris Yeltsin fueling national instability with his personal instability. He was drinking hard and constantly firing his top ministers, and running up the national debt. One of the biggest economic failures of the Yeltsin administration was the botched privatization of state industries. The process devolved into a fire sale of valuable companies to well-connected oligarchs. After all the chaos, the country needed stability, and the arrival of Vladimir Putin as president in 2000 would provide it. The political freedoms that had begun to emerge under Yeltsin largely evaporated, but from a purely economic point of view, Putin set up Russia for a decade of flowering prosperity.

While many incoming emerging-market populists have frightened Wall Street, Putin was more of a mystery at the start. His early career as a KGB agent, coupled with a steely-eyed persona, raised concerns about a return to old Soviet ways, perhaps even to Cold War conflict. The thin information on his rapid rise through the back rooms of the St. Petersburg city government opened up all kinds of speculation about his intentions. At just forty-seven years old he was young enough to rule for a long time. But for eight years at least, Putin provided the basics that Russia needed. He cut a deal that allowed the oligarchs to hold on to their companies so long as they stayed out of politics; he appeared to welcome outside investors; and he quickly brought Russia's debt under control.

Putin brought a healthy paranoia and caution to Russia's attitude about oil wealth. In the early 2000s, when the price of oil breached thirty dollars a barrel, Putin and his top economic aides were deeply afraid it would fall back to twenty dollars, as oil and gas already accounted for 50 percent of Russian exports and 30 percent of federal revenue. Traumatized by memories of the drop in oil prices of the 1990s, their planning focused on what to do if oil prices dropped. They saved oil profits in a rainy-day account called the oil stabilization fund, and by 2007 that fund held more than $225 billion.

In the early years Putin pushed some key reforms: consolidating banks, cutting the red tape required to start companies, and reducing personal income tax rates to just 13 percent, all of which helped stimulate a consumer boom. As oil prices rose, the money flowed. The streets of Moscow started to feel European, in the spread of café society and brand-name European retailers. The spectacularly ugly homegrown Ladas made way for Mercedes and BMWs. The latest fashion trends from Milan and Paris replaced an otherwise hard-to-kick 1970s look. The typical Russian now has more than one mobile phone, while just 70 percent of Chinese own one. Since the late 1990s the average Russian income has risen from $1,500 to $13,000, more than twice China's. All this activity fulfilled the aspirations of many Russians to regain their Cold War status as a major global player.

In 2007 I described Putin, who was already wildly popular, as one of the few emerging-market leaders who understood the connection between economic outcomes and political success. At the time it looked like Russia's economy was beginning to diversify beyond petroleum: non-oil sectors including media, consumer goods, and retail were booming. While growing state control in strategic sectors such as oil, gas, and mining, and the jailing of oil tycoon Mikhail Khodorkovsky on questionable charges, were scaring off many outside investors, those willing to look past the Khodorkovsky case were making a killing. In retrospect it was an unbelievable run.

Russia witnessed one of the most powerful domestic-demand booms in any emerging market. The stocks of banking, media, and consumer companies were on a tear—even as stock prices of Russian oil and gas companies drifted aimlessly, burdened by a "Russia discount" assigned to any firm thought to be targeted for Kremlin control. While these companies might be sitting on oil fields worth untold billions, it was obvious that they were run for the benefit of the Russian treasury, or self-dealing insiders, not minority shareholders. Between 2003 and 2007 economic growth averaged nearly 8 percent, and though the economies in China and India were growing faster, Russian companies were more profitable, because the Kremlin's heavy hand in the economy scared off a lot of foreign competition.

When Putin Lost the Thread

By late 2007, however, the Russian economic scene was beginning to change. As oil prices rose, so did hubris. The price of Russian crude surged by more than 200 percent between early 2006 and mid-2008 to $140 a barrel. Putin's government abandoned earlier fears and began to believe that prices were destined to keep rising as demand from China and other big emerging markets increased. The cautious approach to government spending was discarded, and Moscow displayed a growing willingness to purchase the good graces of the people: far from cutting pensions, as many countries were doing, Russia hiked them in 2007, and since then the ratio of pension payments to real wages has risen from 25 percent to 40 percent. More than half of all Russians now depend on the state for a living, 40 percent as recipients of social benefits and 12 percent as government employees (the comparable figure in the United States is 28 percent). The state share of the economy is approaching a massive 50 percent, and Russia is one of only two countries, alongside China, where state-owned companies account for more than half of the total value of the stock market (the figure for Russia is 56 percent).

During the global crisis of 2008, Russia was one of the hardest-hit countries in the world. The economy contracted by 10 percent, and the growth rate has since dropped by half from its pre-crisis high of 7.2 percent. To cushion the blow, the government siphoned off the oil stabilization fund, which shrank from $225 billion at the end of 2008 to $114 billion at the end of 2010. Russia needed an oil price of more than one hundred dollars per barrel just to balance the budget (and still does). When prices dropped to as low as fifty dollars in 2009, the Kremlin's finances fell into the red. The surplus Putin had built earlier in the decade has morphed into a budget deficit equal to 4 percent of GDP in 2010.

Furthermore, in a slow recovery, inflation should not be an issue, but it is a growing problem in Russia, where the inflation rate averaged 7.8 percent over the past two years, compared to an emerging-market average of 4.5 percent. Only India, which is growing much faster than Russia, and Egypt, roiled by the Arab Spring revolts, had higher inflation. This combination of slow growth and rising prices suggests that the potential growth rate is falling sharply: like Brazil, Russia has been putting so little into new plants, roads, and equipment that its workers are less and less productive.

The bottom line is that Russia was an amazing comeback story until 2008, when the financial crisis revealed that Russia lacks the institutional strength and political will to implement serious reforms that would sustain strong growth, especially now that it has become a relatively large economy. The challenge of growing from a per capita income of $13,000 is very different from that of growing from $1,500 a decade ago. Since 2008 businesses outside the oil patch, such as the local auto manufacturers and the real estate sector, have fared poorly, and growth of the consumer and retail sectors has stalled. Russia needs a new source of income beyond oil. It is now struggling to generate 4 percent economic growth, and falling behind its peers in the race to catch up with the West.

Putin was probably the man to save Russia from chaos in 1999, when the economy was in crisis and the war in Chechnya was raging, but it is now far from clear that he has the right vision to take the country to the next level of economic development. And he plans to stay on as the country's leader. Putin moved from the presidency to the prime minister's office in 2008, and is running again for the presidency in 2012. He could hold that office for two terms, until 2024, extending his reign at the top to a quarter century.

A rule of the road: be alert to the moment when rulers have outlived their usefulness. No matter what the system of government, it is a worrying sign when leaders try to extend their hold on power, as they tend to develop an authoritarian streak over time and their focus shifts to protecting vested interests or they simply run out of progressive ideas. In an established democracy, such leaders will be eased out by their own party, even if they were seen as dynamic forces of reform. Britain has done this twice in recent decades, to Margaret Thatcher on the right and Tony Blair on the left. The worst case of stale heads of state, however, is in the former Soviet republics, from Belarus to Turkmenistan and Kazakhstan, which are full of leaders who have abolished term limits or anointed themselves president for life. In recent years, the general success of emerging markets has helped convince many leaders in Africa and Latin America that they personally are the source of their nation's success. From Cameroon and Nigeria to Bolivia and Venezuela, incompetent or corrupt leaders have fought successfully for the right to extend the deadline on their terms in power. A related dodge is stepping down in favor of your spouse. This is how Nestor and Cristina Kirchner extended their hold on Argentina, which has been so badly run it was demoted from the list of nations Wall Street tracks as "emerging markets" and into the lower class of "frontier markets," where the rule of law is thin and enforcement of the existing rules even thinner.

Russia is now a leading example of this stale leadership circle. Putin's disapproval rating has doubled since 2008 to 40 percent as of late 2011, and the decline has accelerated following his announcement that he plans to stand for president again in 2012. Had he decided to ride away into the sunset in 2008, following his second presidential term, he could have gone down as one of the most successful Russian leaders in postwar history, but now that legacy is at serious risk.

The Missing Middle

There is no middle ground in Russia. The proportion of small and medium-sized enterprises is lower in Russia than in any other major emerging market. Small, dynamic, and entrepreneurial firms like these were crucial to the emergence of Japan, Taiwan, and South Korea, but they hardly exist in Russia. It is an economy of well-protected state behemoths and mom-and-pop shops you will never hear of.

In development economics there is an old saying: a rich country makes rich things. South Korea and Taiwan produce many hi-tech products and South Korea built global consumer brands, ranging from Samsung to Hyundai. Russia has—nothing. The Moscow stock exchange lists not one large global manufacturing company. For a country that sent the first man to space and has produced twenty-seven Nobel Prize winners in economics and the sciences, this is a sad outcome. Russian companies are not serious international players even in signature national products like vodka. Not one of the top-five global vodka brands today is Russian.

Another simple but often overlooked gap is in geography. Russia is one of the twenty least-densely populated countries in the world, and there are really only five cities that have the critical mass of people and income to draw in global brands. Consider the challenge that Magnit, Russia's largest retailer by number of stores (more than four thousand outlets), has set for itself. Starting out in the mid-1990s with food convenience shops, and branching out to "hypermarkets" that sell "everything a family needs," Magnit has been opening stores at an extraordinary pace of up to one every eight hours, aiming for 40 to 50 percent annual revenue growth. But with only eight hundred cities in the country, and only twelve with more than a million people, Magnit looks for locations in towns with as few as five thousand residents. Analysts say it sometimes ends up slapping its sign on buildings that aren't much more than shacks. To supply this sprawling network is an extraordinary logistical challenge, running refrigerated food trucks to thousands of locations across five thousand miles of territory.

Russian wealth and power are concentrated increasingly in Moscow, and the government exerts ever-greater control over business. Russia is now home to 100 billionaires, trailing only China (115) and the United States (which has 412). There are 69 billionaires living in Moscow alone—the largest concentration for any city in the world. Even though its economy ($1.8 trillion) and stock market (totaling $785 billion) are about one-fourth the size of China's, Russia's billionaires possess almost twice as much total wealth as their Chinese counterparts, and face far less competition. The 2011 Forbes list of billionaires shows that eight of the country's top-ten billionaires were also on the list in 2006, and many are in fact holdovers from the same group that acquired major companies at knockout prices in Yeltsin's 1990s fire sale.

Of course such low turnover should be expected since nearly 80 percent of Russia's billionaires are involved in the commodity industries, particularly oil and gas. In those businesses government patronage often determines success, and if connected tycoons treat their patrons right, they can sustain these profitable contacts for many years. Outside of the oil and materials industries, Russia is generating modest wealth at best. And below the billionaires, there is a missing class of the very rich: though Russia ranks third for the number of billionaires, it does not even make the Boston Consulting Group's top-fifteen list for having the most millionaires. China is ranked second for the number of billionaires and third for millionaires, with 1.1 million.

Many outsiders try to play the investment game in Russia by just following the big tycoons. They try to figure out how much oil money is flowing into which pockets, and then bet on the tycoons who are most closely aligned with the current political regime. In one 2011 note to clients, a Citibank analyst tried to show where the "rents"—disparaging jargon for monopoly profits—are going in Russia, meaning how much goes back to the voters, how much is put back into the economy, and how much is "captured by oligarchs." It then advised clients to "stick with oligarchs who are successful at accessing rental flows," and picked a few companies it saw as well positioned.

This is a classic mistake to make in emerging markets. Following a tycoon sounds like a clever exploitation of inside knowledge but it is hugely risky because as soon as the regime falls—which can happen very suddenly —the chosen oligarch can see his wealth evaporate overnight. This has happened repeatedly to investors betting on magnates and companies with close ties to powerful leaders, ranging from Thaksin Shinawatra in Thailand (driven out in a 2006 coup) to Hosni Mubarak in Egypt (felled in the popular revolt of 2011).

Another missing chunk of the Russian economy is banking. Compared to Europe, Russia has no truly modern banks at all. The system is dominated by one big bank, and very few Russians invest at home, so it's tough to get loans of any kind. The mortgage market is virtually nonexistent, representing about 3 percent of GDP, the lowest of any emerging market. Most Russians pay cash to buy a house. Small enterprises pay interest rates of 15 to 20 percent on business loans. Russians borrow so little that the total value of loans, as a share of GDP, is similar to the totals in far poorer countries such as Egypt. The financial sector resembles that of frontier markets such as Nigeria rather than of any other major developing country.

So as the crisis of 2008 was approaching, many tycoons had turned to foreign banks for credit. The Kremlin was basically unaware that many Russian corporations were deeply in debt. Even one of the big state-owned oil companies had to borrow from Chinese state banks, in exchange for future oil deliveries. Second-tier state companies were in deeper trouble, and as the crisis gained speed, foreign creditors and investors started to pull out fast. To stem the outflow, and prevent a collapse of the ruble, Russia was the only major country during the recession of 2008 that was forced to let interest rates rise, with short-term rates spiking to 29 percent from 6 percent.

Russia is missing a financial sector in part because it is the only major country that has seen its currency wiped out twice in the last two decades. The ruble was devalued in 1991 after the fall of the Soviet Union and again in the crisis of 1998. During the Great Recession, Russia was also the only major emerging market to experience a classic banking crisis—in which the central bank was forced to inject cheap debt into struggling banks to save them. That put Russia in a class alongside Kazakhstan, Nigeria, and the Ukraine. When foreign funding suddenly dried up in the crisis of 2008, Moscow's stock exchange panicked and fell by 74 percent over two months—the hardest-hit market in the world.

The tycoons, many of whom had put up stock as collateral for foreign loans, were nearly wiped out. To rescue them, the Kremlin drew down foreign-exchange reserves and tapped the rainy-day oil fund. The best-connected tycoons survived (which is why the list of top billionaires shows little change) but in diminished form. The upshot has been a big step backward in the form of more state control, with no more revenue.

The Kremlin has used the bailout process to encourage distressed business owners in sectors like mining to hand over stock to people with ties to the governing party, United Russia. During the crisis, mining oligarchs were forced to pledge huge blocks of shares to secure bankruptcy-preventing loans from state agencies. The government has never called in this collateral, so while the Kremlin gained considerable leverage over favored businessmen, Russia's treasury actually gained nothing. The word among Moscow businessmen is that the Kremlin has firmly encouraged these oligarchs to fund projects worth hundreds of millions of dollars in the southern city of Sochi, which is hosting the 2014 Winter Olympic Games. Now the first question posed to many Russian firms during meetings with foreign investors is, "What does the government want from you?"

There is an ongoing criminalization of politics, and a deepening of ties between government and business. Russian companies in practically every sector have a job category that I've seen rarely in other parts of the world: staff to deal with bribe-seeking public officials. This is hardly a recipe for efficiency, and the more profitable a small company becomes, the more frequent the visits. Many Russians just give up and leave the country, which is one reason why the small-business sector is so weak.

Even well-connected oligarchs have lost confidence in their country. Money was flowing into Russia from 2004 to 2008, but that flow reversed in 2009. Net foreign direct investment was negative $9.5 billion in 2010, meaning Russians were investing much more in factories and businesses abroad than foreigners were investing in Russia. In fact this is probably the only major emerging market suffering a large and accelerating outflow of private capital: based on Russian central bank estimates, the outflow hit $80 billion in 2011, up from $42 billion in 2006. This pace suggests that the tycoons are increasingly worried about slow growth and the decay of the business climate at home.

Sometimes it's clear where this money is going—one Russian magnate recently made real estate headlines by paying $78 million for a mansion in Silicon Valley. Sometimes it's murky. One of the anomalies in the books kept by Russian companies is that high profits are not always reflected in cash flow, suggesting that the cash has been diverted to debatable purchases. I suspect it is no coincidence that realtors in the South of France say that many of the top-end villas in Cap Ferrat and Monte Carlo—those in the $200 million to $400 million range—have been purchased by Russian oligarchs and big state companies as retreats for the top brass.

The Russian business climate is equally maddening for foreigners. World Bank surveys rank Russia 120th out of 183 countries for the ease of doing business. Russia is the only major country in the world that still requires business travelers and tourists to file an official request with the Russian foreign ministry ahead of a trip to the Russian embassy to fill out a visa application. This hardly makes for a business-friendly environment, particularly for a country that aspires to see Moscow become a global financial center.

You Need to Read between the Lines of Good News in Russia

Nevertheless, some signs suggest that Putin and his team recognize the need for change. At a conference in Moscow in late 2010, Putin asked the organizers to invite a foreign investor to give him a frank assessment of Russia's economy. I made the presentation to Putin, under the full glare of national television cameras and top cabinet ministers, arguing that Russia would find it hard to grow at anywhere near the levels of the past decade because commodity prices were unlikely to maintain the galloping pace of recent years; there was little else to the Russia story beside commodities; and the government's role in the economy was excessive for a middle-income country. Putin seemed to be all ears, taking notes and responding that the Russian government would withdraw from some nonstrategic industries.

However, there's a certain hollowness even to positive signs in Russia. Since my encounter with Putin, the Russian government has announced an accelerated privatization plan for state-owned companies. But in Russia "privatization" means only that the government sells down its ownership from 60 to 51 percent. The government owns less stock but still controls the company.

The way the Kremlin is dealing with perhaps the worst aging problem in the emerging world offers another example of how even good news has a way of disappointing in the end. Russia's working-age population will fall by about 870,000 people per year between 2010 and 2015. That's a loss of close to 1 percent of the working population each year, double the European average, and the only example of demographic decay among the largest emerging markets. In the same 2010–2015 period the working-age population in India will rise nearly 2 percent per year, and in China 0.5 percent (after which China's labor force, too, will begin to decline).

The one clear solution to the graying-population problem is immigration—letting in more young families from abroad—but it's a solution Russia resisted for nearly two decades after the fall of the Soviet Union. Perhaps embittered by the quick scramble for independence among its former republics, Russia shut the door behind them after they left. In 2007, however, Moscow instituted new policies that have made it one of the few large nations in which immigrants are flowing in, not out. Of the ten most-populous nations, only Russia and the United States have net positive immigration flow. (China, India, Brazil, and South Africa all have a net negative immigration flow.) In 2011 Russia was expected to take in forty thousand immigrants, mainly from the former Soviet satellites in Central Asia.

This immigration flow is a plus, but a minor one. It's a good thing immigrants are coming, but forty thousand is a tiny number in a population of 140 million, and it doesn't begin to balance out Russia's severe aging problem. In addition, because most of the immigrants are Russians or Russian speakers, effectively repatriating after a long absence, this apparent opening to the world ends up looking more like yet another turn inward.

This pattern—signs of reform exposed by their backstory as ineffectual, even empty gestures—appears again and again. President Dmitry

Medvedev has been the leading force behind the development of the city of Skolkovo, about five hundred miles west of Moscow, as an incubator for start-up technology companies. That sounds suitably modern and forward thinking—but insiders see it largely as a way to protect Russian entrepreneurs from rapacious bureaucrats by giving them a direct line to the Kremlin. Investors in big Russian retailers were pleased when the Kremlin recently decided to close an open-air market in Moscow because it was evidently a cesspool of health, safety, and tax-code violations, and a long-standing symbol of black-market practices that legitimate public companies find it hard to compete with. But dig a little further: CEOs of the legitimate retailers did not in fact see this as a step toward a more open and law-abiding economy, but as retaliation against the owner of the open-air market, who had apparently refused to partner with high Kremlin officials in a hotel project in Chechnya.

The reformers in the government are burned out after fighting so many battles with the statists. For many years now there has been a level of open warfare in the Kremlin—palace intrigues for all to see—that is absolutely unique to Russia. This is not a healthy kind of transparency. The constant jockeying for position seems an end in itself and ultimately prevents Russia from moving forward.

That Putin still enjoyed considerable popularity up until late 2011 reflects what one of Medvedev's top aides described to me, just one year earlier, as Russia's "czarist mentality." By that he meant a national embrace of paternal authoritarian figures, and a thin commitment to democracy and free markets. This is hardly a new read on Russia, but it was interesting to hear it from a key player and force for reform within the Kremlin. Where does all this leave Russia? Of all the major emerging markets, Russia was the last to recoup the output lost during the recession of 2008, with the economy returning to its pre-crisis peak only by the end of 2011. To regain its momentum, Russia needs not only a new non-oil economic model. It needs a new non-czarist mindset.

7

The Sweet Spot of Europe

A MAJOR HAZARD FOR INVESTORS traversing Central and Eastern Europe is letting the heart rule the head, because it's easy to fall for the charms of Budapest and Dubrovnik. They are beautiful places to visit, but not necessarily great places to invest.

And then there is Warsaw, which has a face no visitor could love. About 85 percent of the city was destroyed in World War II, including the Old Town and the Royal Castle. What the Communist authorities built in its place is gray and dreary, and while the Poles tried to re-create Old Town, the result has a Disneyesque faux-fourteenth-century feel, and the Poles know it. The building that dominates the skyline is the Palace of Culture and Science, built in "Stalin style" and said to be a present from the dictator himself to the resentful Poles, who joke that the palace offers the best views of Warsaw because it is the only place in the city from where it can't be seen.

The Poles may have the last laugh, though. Alongside the Czech Republic, another liberated Soviet satellite, Poland is in a much stronger position than Russia is. The Czech economy has been growing at a fast clip for a decade, and now, with an average income of just over $20,000, the republic is well on the way to recovering its prewar status as one of the leading industrial nations. Meanwhile Poland, its average per capita income growing steadily from a lower base of just over $14,000, could join

Poland is the far side of the moon from Russia—
staid, predictable, with a Warsaw business
community that throws no wild parties. Even the
new architecture has a kind of dullness to it.

Korea and Taiwan as a rare developing nation that grows out of poverty, through the middle-income ranks, and joins the class of rich nations.

The reasons are different from the resentments, rivalries, and fears that drove economic competition in Asia. They have to do with the positive attraction of the European Union, the sixty-year-old experiment in continental partnership that has opened Europe's national borders to a free internal flow of people, money, and goods. It's been fashionable for years to criticize old Europe for stagnation and cushy welfare-state complacency, and it is now widely viewed as a failing experiment, owing to the debt crises threatening Greece, Portugal, Italy, and Spain. World markets are bubbling with speculation that stricken nations like Greece may drop the euro, rather than comply with the tough conditions EU leaders want to impose for a bailout, and that somehow the Eurozone itself may break up.

But off to the east, a very different story is playing out. There is a culling of the flock as Hungary, the economic star of the 1990s, sinks into an odd political nostalgia for its imperial past and scrambles to dodge any serious reckoning with its debts. In sharp contrast, Poland and the Czech Republic are largely debt free and catching up to the richer nations of Western Europe, while other countries, including Romania, are already suffering a painful post-crisis restructuring, with mass layoffs and wage cuts that could leave them much more competitive as a result. For all the abuse it takes as a political and economic model, the European Union is still a powerful growth engine, at least for those new and aspiring members who take the rules of the union seriously.

The Twin Stars of the East

It is often the case that fear fires reform, and that is part of the story in the Czech Republic and Poland. After the collapse of the Soviet Union in 1990, many of its former satellites would have done just about anything to avoid getting sucked back into Moscow's orbit, and to solidify a place in the West. The leaders in Prague and Warsaw have been putting reforms in place for more than a decade, not so much by studying what has worked in Europe, but by working to fulfill the requirements to join the EU and adopt the common currency of the Eurozone, in order to gain access to the new markets and the generous funding the EU offers newcomers. True to form, Europe has been focused less on the demands of dynamic growth than on ensuring stability as newcomers join. The EU membership criteria are centered on building institutions—which simply means a functioning parliament; apolitical courts; honest government bureaucracies including the police; free press and media; and so on.

Poland and the Czech Republic, along with Hungary and seven other nations, were well on their way to meet the EU membership criteria when they joined the union in 2004, and at that time they also vowed to work toward meeting the additional requirements of Eurozone membership, which sets very specific targets for government deficits (less than 3 percent of GDP), government debt (60 percent of GDP or less), and other economic basics from inflation to long-term interest rates.

Fortunately for the newcomers, strong institutions and freedom from excessive debt are powerful catalysts for growth, and become more important as a nation becomes richer. That's why relatively rich emerging markets such as the Czech Republic and Poland are breakout nations, even when many of their neighbors seem to be pedaling backward. After the launch of the euro in 1999, there were plenty of EU members that adopted the new currency but did not play by the rules, flouting the guidelines on debt and restraint in government spending, which led to the major debt crisis in Europe today. Not just Greece and Portugal but also some of the founding members, like France, have been violating the budget rules and running deficits well above 3 percent of GDP for years—which is coming back to haunt them. Unlike Poland and the Czech Republic, nations from the Baltics and Balkans and much of Central Europe, including Hungary, Romania, Bulgaria, and Ukraine, went into the global crisis of 2008 with deep government deficits and heavy household debts, and have struggled mightily in its aftermath.

The breakup of the pack has been dramatic: Eastern Europe is home to nations that were slammed unusually hard in the crisis, while some others sailed through. Poland is the only economy in Europe that did not contract in 2008 and 2009, and today it has the most vibrant labor market in Europe, creating jobs at a pace so rapid that many immigrant Poles are returning from the United Kingdom and other hard-hit nations to find work at home. The Czech Republic did contract by 4 percent during the crisis, but it recovered early and quickly, and is viewed as a safe haven from the debt fears echoing out of troubled parts of Europe. These economies are stable magnets for capital inflows and over the past decade, Poland and the Czech Republic received net flows of foreign direct investment (meaning investment in factories and other hard assets) worth 2 to 4 percent of their GDP every year, most of it from Western Europe.

At the height of the economic turmoil in late 2008 and early 2009, there was much fear in Europe and the United States that the crisis would disintegrate into a full-blown depression, comparable to the disaster of 1930s America, when the breadline became the symbol of the country. The richer nations pulled out all the stops to avoid a depression—spending billions in public funds to stimulate the economy, dropping interest rates to zero to encourage lending. But the smaller nations of Eastern Europe, the Baltics, and the Balkans did not have the money to spend. This is the one region that saw a painfully hard landing, just short of a depression in some nations.

During the early years of the Great Depression the U.S. economy shrank by one-fourth, and one in four Americans went unemployed. In 2009 alone, Hungary saw industrial production fall 17 percent. Unemployment in the Baltics and the Balkans shot up by as much as 15 percentage points; in Lithuania the unemployment rate hit 18 percent, and in Latvia it was 20 percent. Romania, which whipsawed from economic growth of 6 percent in 2007 to a decline of 7 percent in 2009, was one of the first countries to need bailouts from the International Monetary Fund and the EU to make its interest payments during the crisis. If the public mood of these nations never plunged into the depths of despair that gripped America during the Depression years of the 1930s, it is probably because they were accustomed to hard times in the not-so-distant past, during the Soviet era.

The story of why the nations of Eastern Europe are following such different paths out of the crisis is rooted in part in the politics of the post-Communist era. The Iron Curtain was more porous in some nations than in others, and the Soviets gave more freedom to some leaders than to others. In Hungary the leadership carved out the most liberal of the Soviet satellite systems, which came to be known as "Goulash Communism" because the Hungarians could afford meat for their stews when others could not. The relatively loose reins allowed Hungarians a bit more freedom than most to speak, travel, and do business in the West. The Hungarians enjoyed the highest standard of living in the East. They felt they were the most Western and European nation in the region, and so they grew the most comfortable with their own leaders.

The Czechs had the opposite experience, enduring the strictest Communist government outside that of East Germany—thoroughly corrupt and incompetent—and saw their standard of living fall from one of the highest in the world in the 1920s to a state of gray stagnation. The Poles, meanwhile, were somewhere in between. When the Berlin Wall finally fell in 1989, the Czechs drove the Communists out of politics or any position of real responsibility, and along with the Poles leaped to embrace Europe and the West, becoming star pupils not only of the European Union but also of the IMF and the World Bank, which preached much the same mix of market freedom and budget discipline.

Poland has long been a regional trendsetter—in fact it was the first satellite state to break from the Soviet orbit. In recent years it has developed a strong education system that produces a talented workforce; a growing cadre of small to medium-sized companies that are competitive across Europe; well-run banks far stronger than those of its old nemesis, Russia; and good-quality consumer companies. The central bank is genuinely independent of political interference. In many ways these rising stars in the East look more solid than their Western models.

With a population of thirty-eight million, Poland is the only nation in Eastern Europe with a domestic market large enough to generate economic growth, regardless of troubles in the rest of the world. Things are so much better right now that not only are Poles bringing their money home, they're bringing themselves with it. Over the last decade, after the EU opened up service industries to cross-border competition, the "Polish plumber" became a symbol of West European fears of a great inrush of cheap labor from the East. Now the Polish plumber is heading home. While Poland lost 150,000 jobs during the recession, it has since added them all back plus 100,000 more, and the unemployment rate—which had fallen steadily before the crisis—is falling again.

The Czech Republic mirrors this story, only in a smaller population, with much more exposure to the global economy, and a far more exciting and cosmopolitan capital in Prague. On the surface Prague is no more beautiful or charming than Budapest, but given all the political weirdness of Hungary, it is Prague that is increasingly seen as the jewel and gateway of Eastern Europe   the very role Budapest aspires to.

Unlike Poland's economy, the Czech economy contracted during the crisis because it sells many of its exports to Germany, which was hard hit. But its foreign debts were manageable, in large part owing to its solid domestic banks and well-managed government. The core of Czech banking and bureaucracy is so sound that the economy has grown steadily through long years of political turmoil, with weak coalition governments ever since the Velvet Revolution overthrew the Communist regime in 1989. A victory by center-right parties in the 2010 elections raised the prospect of a strong legislative majority for the first time, but at this point Czech society has such sturdy permanent institutions that it can thrive even with weak elected governments.

These former Soviet satellites also have a much greater chance than Russia does to emerge as impact players in global industrial competition. A rich country needs to make rich things to keep growing, and Russia doesn't have even one globally competitive manufacturing plant. Poland and the Czech Republic by contrast have many, particularly in the car industry. The Czechs are the only nation in the East that have preserved their own auto brand, Skoda, now an arm of Volkswagen but still independent in terms of design and engineering.

While the story of Russia over the last two decades is a story of larger-than-life personalities—Gorbachev, Yeltsin, Putin—the story of Poland and the Czech Republic is one of maturing systems unencumbered by preening autocrats. Poland is the far side of the moon from Russia—staid, predictable, and with a Warsaw business community not known for throwing wild parties, even on weekends. Even the new architecture in Poland has a kind of dullness to it. This is a very healthy sign for future growth as it suggests money is not being frittered away.

Despite relatively high incomes, Poland and the Czech Republic have not yet priced themselves out of global competition. Compared with Moscow or Rio, it's much easier to find a reasonably priced hotel in Warsaw or even in the tourist hot spot, Prague, mainly because of the inexpensive exchange rates. The inflation-adjusted value of the Polish zloty has remained flat for a decade. The cost of a luxury apartment in Warsaw has been roughly doubling every five years, yet at four hundred dollars per square foot, it is still way below the levels seen in other emerging-market cities, such as São Paulo, where high-end homes fetch close to eight hundred dollars per square foot. Central European labor costs are only 27 percent of those in Western Europe, and even adjusted for the fact that Central European workers are less well trained and equipped—productivity is 40 percent lower—the labor in Central Europe is still less than half as expensive as in Western Europe.

The Hungarian Exception

While Poland and the Czech Republic were racing to forget the Communist past, Hungary was lost in it. Hungarian politics became a contest between former Communists and the anti-Communist opposition, which built its appeal around nationalist calls to revive Hungary as the star of the East, a nostalgic vision that harks back to the Austro-Hungarian Empire. No Hungarian party represented the forward-looking pragmatism of the Czech consensus that the first job was to control the budget and build the institutional basis of a free-market economy. Instead, by 2000, Hungary had devolved into the most bitter ideological battleground in the region, with the most liberal Left and the most nationalist Right scrambling to undo each other and vie for the hearts of "the people" through generous public spending.

Though Hungary started the last decade as perhaps the most successful economy in post-Soviet Eastern Europe, attracting the highest flows of foreign investment, it was done in by a series of governments—Left and Right—that promised to control the budget but didn't. Hungary became an ignominious exception to the general trend of growing financial responsibility in emerging markets. Physically and culturally Hungary straddles the imaginary border between northern and southern Europe, and the widespread sense in investment circles is that the southern tendency to live high and spend freely was a big reason why it went astray. In its age-old competition with its sister imperial city, Vienna, fabulous Budapest matched every public monument the Austrians built—only more lavishly, from the main coffeehouse to the Opera.

The Hungarian leadership has come to be seen in investment circles as odd and lost. The conservative Fidesz Party of Prime Minister Viktor Orbán is inclined to blame the country's problems on foreigners, and is disturbingly close to the far-right supporters of Jobbik, or the Movement for a Better Hungary, who have been known to march around Budapest in SS-style uniforms. Orbán has provoked neighboring states by granting Hungarian passports to Hungarians who now live in Romania and Slovakia, a kind of throwback attempt to reassemble the "greater Hungary" of its imperial days. Orbán won the last election in a landslide, and he rewarded supporters with a new law that forces foreign banks to accept huge losses on mortgage loans doled out to Hungarians at the height of the boom. Wall Street insiders are calling it the Hungarian "bank robbery law," and it is not the way to reestablish the country's credibility and attract much-needed foreign investment.

The conflict between Budapest and global markets dates to 2000, when the government launched the loan scheme that would prove to be the unraveling of Hungary. The government offered subsidized mortgages with few restrictions on who could take them or how much they could borrow, and it soon started to spin out of control. When the government tried to dial back and cut the maximum loan by two-thirds to $22,000, Hungarians wouldn't take no for an answer and started to look elsewhere for credit, and not only for houses.

Enter the big European banks, which at the time were chasing business all over the region in hot pursuit of what they believed were responsible future members of the Eurozone. They offered low-interest loans in Swiss francs and euros at a 2 percent rate (the Hungarians had been happy to borrow forint at 8 percent), triggering a debt explosion. By late 2007, the lion's share (90 percent) of new mortgages in Hungary were being granted in Swiss francs and euros, setting the country up for collapse when the crisis hit and foreign banks started pulling out.

The Czechs and Poles were offered the same deal but did not really bite. The Poles did take out some foreign-currency loans, but in much smaller amounts than the Hungarians did. The Czechs, who had comparably low interest rates at home, did not partake at all. One reason is that their governments were not turbocharging easy money with bad policy by heavily subsidizing home mortgages. The other reason may go back to cultural differences, the devil-may-care southern side of the Hungarian lifestyle. Whatever the case, foreigners won't touch Hungary now; their favored target after the fall of the Soviet system has seen investment fall for eleven quarters in a row since the crisis of 2008.

The economic lead Hungary held in Eastern Europe a decade ago is gone, and among the region's principal economies it now has the least competitive currency, the highest interest rates, and the worst unemployment problem. Between 2000 and 2010 the race to jack up welfare benefits increased the public debt from 50 percent of GDP to 80 percent, requiring the government to hike taxes sharply in order to meet the debt payments. As taxes got heavier and welfare benefits became more attractive, Hungarians had less and less incentive to work, gutting the labor force: today only 55 percent of adults are working, the lowest rate in Europe other than Malta, where women by tradition do not work. Both Hungary and the Czech Republic have populations of 10 million, but Hungary's workforce is just 3.8 million compared with 4.9 million in the Czech Republic. The point here is not to trash Hungary, only to dramatize how bold the responsible but boring choices made by the Czech Republic and Poland really were.

A rule of the road: watch for steady momentum behind economic and political reform, particularly in good times. Nations typically implement reforms only when their backs are against the wall. Even in China, which pushed reforms harder and longer than most, the kinds of changes that the leadership contemplates today are not the kinds of reforms that improve productivity and set economies free to grow without triggering inflation; they are the expensive quality-of-life reforms in which richer countries indulge, like extending the scope of the welfare state. The same shift is now taking place across many of the major emerging markets, including India and Brazil. Reform feeds growth that breeds complacency, and reduces the incentive to reform further. Poland and the Czech Republic are exceptions.

The Sweet Spot

These two nations now occupy a unique sweet spot in the global economy: the period after a nation joins the EU but before it joins the Eurozone. It is the point at which the nation has created the stable banking and financial institutions required for membership, attracting huge new flows of investment from its fellow EU members, and becoming eligible for generous EU transfer payments to help it catch up to the average per capita income level of EU economies. The assumption always was that once a nation joined the EU, taking the next step to adopt the common currency would provide yet another boost. Eurozone membership, and the budget discipline that membership encourages (but cannot enforce), would make these small, post-Communist states look more stable and reliable, better able to repay loans, and therefore eligible for lower interest rates.

This has largely happened, but it has proved to be a double-edged sword. Once a country adopts the euro, it enters a danger zone where the cost of capital becomes too cheap, and supposedly smart investors start making all kinds of mistakes. In the case of Portugal and Spain, it now looks as if the euro (and the low interest rates that came with it) set them up for the real estate bubbles that burst in the 2008 crisis. Among Slovaks, who embraced the euro in 2009 just before the Greek crisis, a public backlash has broken out against the fact that Slovakia must now stand alongside far richer Eurozone members like Germany and bail out somewhat richer Eurozone members like Greece.

Meanwhile Poland and the Czech Republic are enjoying the sweet spot, and could continue to do so for many years to come. They are taking full advantage of their EU right to free movement of people and goods within the union: Polish and Czech exports to the rest of the EU have risen rapidly, and both benefit from EU subsidies and transfers ranging from income support for individuals to funds for building roads or buying machinery for private firms. Between 2007 and 2010, the EU sent transfers to Poland worth 10 percent of the country's GDP, or more than $1,200 per person. However, this kind of money does not help if it is not used wisely. Romania, for example, also has a huge pot of EU money, but because of incompetence and corruption, little of it has been spent, putting future transfers at risk even when so much obvious work remains to be done, including rebuilding one of the worst road networks on the continent, a system that has hardly any multilane highways.

The sweet spot provided some insulation from the contagion that swept out of Greece in 2010. As questions arose about Greece's ability to pay its mounting debts, investors first began dumping Greek bonds, and then they started to abandon the euro because it is the Greek currency. The value of the euro started to fall, raising questions about the ability of other Eurozone nations to pay back debt. For a brief period Poland and the Czech Republic were swept up in the contagion, before the markets started to realize that they did not have mounting difficulty paying their debts; indeed they never accumulated large debts in the first place. Hungary, in the sweet spot but deep in debt, remained a target.

Most of the new EU nations are now happy to stay in the union but are not sure about becoming part of the Eurozone. Far from rushing to go all the way and adopt the euro, they are delaying that day of reckoning in any way they can. The Czechs have already postponed their entry date numerous times as public sentiment turns against joining early. Czech President Vaclav Klaus has called the euro "a failure" and said his country would seek to opt out. In Poland recent opinion surveys show that for the first time, a solid majority (60 percent) is against adopting the euro. It's an open secret that in December 2010, Chancellor Angela Merkel of Germany called Poland and the Czech Republic and invited them to join the Eurozone early because she wanted more fiscally conservative allies in the running European battle over how to handle spendthrift members. The Poles and the Czechs both said thanks but no thanks. Hungary did not get an invitation.

A big reason for the turn against the euro is the realization that adopting the common currency is like putting on policy handcuffs. In a crisis, nations that can't let their currencies fall in value will face what economists call "internal devaluation": because the currency cannot adjust, wages have to fall sharply to allow the country to remain competitive, or exports will collapse. That's what happened to small members of the Eurozone in 2009. Faced with a choice between a falling currency and slashing wages and jobs, any nation would pick the currency drop. As soon as the crisis started gathering momentum in 2008, the Polish zloty and the Czech koruna were free to fall. Exports picked up immediately, dampening rather than magnifying the suddenness and severity of the downturn.

Where Hayek Lives

Not all of the neighbors were so well positioned. Among the nations of the Baltics, the Balkans, and the smaller economies of Central Europe, only Slovenia had joined the Eurozone by the time the crisis hit in 2008. But many of these countries had deep ties to the euro anyway: like Hungary they had borrowed heavily in euros or Swiss francs, or they had pegged the value of their currencies to the euro. Because of their foreign debts they did not have the option of borrowing even more to spend their way out of recession, which was the route John Maynard Keynes had recommended as the answer to the Great Depression, and the route virtually every rich country has followed in hard times since the 1930s. Instead, these states on the periphery of Europe have suffered the dreaded internal devaluation too.

If there is a silver lining to this story, it is that some of the hardest-hit countries may now be poised for a creative economic boom. In the early years of the Depression the United States was effectively acting on the theories not of Keynes but of the then lesser known Austrian economist Friedrich Hayek, who counseled that the job of government in the face of a downturn was to stay out of the way and let market forces liquidate the deadbeats and deadwood in the economy. The result was a severe U.S. contraction and 25 percent unemployment rate, but by 1950 the economy had nearly doubled in size compared with the 1929 peak. The pain had unleashed a boom, just as Hayek said it would. Contrast that to Japan, which responded to its severe recession in 1990 with every possible stimulus and bailout known to Keynesians (and then some), and today has an economy only 20 percent larger than it was in 1990.

Today Hayek's approach lives on in one region of the world: the troubled states of Central and Eastern Europe. Already there are signs of a Hayekian recovery, meaning a rapid rise from the depths, at least in some nations. Bulgaria may be going the way of Hungary, where the ruling party is still dodging the tough Austrian solution and promising voters that "No one will be worse off!" But Estonia and Lithuania made sharp wage and spending cuts early on, and are already bouncing back as exports and employment recover. Romania, with a per capita income of only $8,000, has a government that now seems to get it. Bucharest is tackling a deficit that hit 9 percent of GDP (second highest in Europe after Greece) before the crisis. Its private companies are going through a painful downsizing—the total number of jobs is down 14 percent, and the average manufacturing wage in Romania is only four euros an hour, versus eighteen euros in Greece. That's a tough situation, but it also means that big European manufacturers are now looking at a more competitive Romania as a possible site to build factories. The hard landing could even put Romania in a position to emerge, alongside Poland and the Czech Republic, as a future star of Europe.

8

The Monophonic
Voice of Turkey

THROUGH THE WINDOWS of Istanbul's first Four Seasons Hotel in the Sultanahmet neighborhood the wails of the *adhan*, the Muslim call to prayer, ring five times a day. With muezzins singing out from atop the minarets of the Old City's many mosques, chiming in at split-second intervals, there is a stereophonic quality to the choir. But move down the hill into the neighborhood of nightspots and modern hotels hugging the shores of the Bosporus, and the sounds of the *adhan* vanish. Here the name on everyone's lips, the monophonic voice of Turkey, belongs to a powerful and charismatic orator whose base of support lies outside the power centers of the capital, old or new. He is Recep Tayyip Erdoğan, the prime minister nearing his second decade in power who is firmly reshaping Turkey into a straightforwardly Muslim country.

Erdoğan leads a classic counterrevolution, a movement to restore order and tranquility after a period of great upheaval. In the 1980s the late Václav Havel, at that time only a dissident Czech writer, put the call to counterrevolution well; he wrote that people living under Communism yearned for a "normal life," free from the Communist call to "permanent revolution," the unceasing efforts to turn themselves into model socialists. The Velvet Revolution of 1989 overthrew Communism, made Havel president, and freed Czechs just to be themselves. They've been a huge success ever since. The transformation now under way in Turkey is very

Here the name on everyone's lips belongs
to a charismatic orator, Recep Tayyip
Erdoğan, whose base of support lies outside
the power centers of the capital.

similar. For eighty years Turks lived under a regime that constantly pressured them to be more modern, more European, to suppress any sign of Muslim or Eastern roots. A nation in which 99 percent of the population identifies itself as Muslim was not allowed to be itself in public or private.

Erdoğan brought Turkey the chance to be comfortable in its own skin. A system that reserved the most desirable positions for people who subscribed to secular European ideals is giving way to a system that allows upward mobility to practicing Muslims as well. The government, the courts, the military, the police, the schools, the commanding heights of the private sector—all the power centers once cornered by the secular elite have been opening up to Muslims. This freedom is in turn releasing the economy to grow through all its natural channels, no longer focusing only on trade ties to Europe—as it has in recent decades—but also on the Muslim (and non-Muslim) nations of the Middle East, Central Asia, and Africa.

Unleashing growth is often about lifting rules that don't make economic sense, and Turkey is now growing by deregulating Islam itself, promoting new business empires to rise up in the pious Muslim heartland of Anatolia, and allowing Turkey to resume the commercial position it held as a bridge between Europe and Asia under the Ottoman Empire, which lasted more than six centuries, from 1299 to 1923, and extended from modern-day Hungary in Central Europe to Libya in North Africa and Iran in the Middle East. The result of this revival is that no other country with an average income in the $10,000 to $15,000 class—a large group that includes Brazil, Russia, and Mexico—has better prospects of being a breakout nation.

The Moderate Muslim Takeover

Erdoğan's counterrevolution is not complete. The roots of the conflict between secular and Muslim parties in Turkey run too deep to be forgotten in a generation. The country's modern incarnation was founded on the rubble of the Ottoman Empire after World War I, with a commitment to radical modernization under soldier-statesman Kemal Atatürk. The thorough defeat of Ottoman armies had demonstrated the utter backwardness of Turkish technology, and Atatürk set out to create a Turkey that could

compete with Europe. As a war hero who led Turkish resistance to the
Allied occupation after World War I, Atatürk had become a living legend, which gave him the clout to impose his alien, modernist creed on a
conservative Muslim nation. Wrenching change was the order of the day;
Atatürk scrapped the Arabic alphabet for Latin letters in 1929, rendering
99 percent of the population functionally illiterate overnight, in the name
of catapulting them into the European mainstream.

Atatürk spoke of "fighting religion," and the state he created soon
came to see itself as what some scholars have called a government for the
people in spite of the people. Dedicated to protecting Turks from Islam,
Atatürk's party ruled unchallenged through World War II, then opened
elections to splinter parties that also subscribed to his ideals, while ban-
ning Islamist parties for threatening those ideals. The coups that rocked
Turkey in 1960, 1971, and 1980 involved the secular army overthrowing
secular parties for corruption, chaos, or attempts to liberalize the system. The basic idea of government for the government was enshrined in
the constitution of 1982, following the 1980 coup, which established the
military and the courts as protectors of the secular state. The first three
articles define the country as a secular and Turkish-speaking democracy
bound to the ideology of Atatürk, and article 4 forbids even proposing
amendments to the first three articles. This was a government pushing
the Turkish people to embrace the liberal culture of Europe, which would
itself never fully embrace the illiberal taboos at the heart of the Turkish
constitution.

The 1982 constitution's authoritarian vision of the state gave birth
to intensely conspiratorial politics that haunt Turkey to this day. With
the secular elite running a Muslim nation, those in power came to see
Muslim parties plotting to topple them at every turn, and Islamist parties
came to see the elite conspiring to suppress them with every imaginable
tool of state power. Islamist parties arose and were quickly banned, often
for championing what appeared to be social issues—like allowing Islamist
women to wear headscarves in public offices—but were in fact seen by
the secular elites as fundamental threats to their hold on all the top jobs
in the country, and to their aspiration for Turkey to evolve into a modern
European society. Necmettin Erbakan, the leading Islamist politician of

the postwar era, saw four of his parties banned before he finally became the first Islamist prime minister in 1996, but not for long. His Refah Party was tied in with deeply conservative circles that talked up far-fetched visions of an Islamic military alliance to mirror NATO, an Islamic currency, and a reestablishment of the caliphate under Islamic law. This was way too much for the secular elites to handle, and in 1997 Erbakan got a letter from the military asking him to step down for anti-secular activities, which he did.

But the secular system was on its last legs. Since World War II modern Turkey has had, on average, one new government every nine months. All were run by parties of the urban elite in the rich coastal cities of the Istanbul-Ankara-Izmir triangle, but they were scared and squabbling, at best leading fragile coalition governments. Chronic political instability led to consistent spending overruns and economic chaos, in particular the killer combination of high interest rates, high inflation, and slow growth. It was not possible for the leading secular parties to produce the type of leader who can turn around an emerging market—the kind who understands the connection between good economics and good politics and has mass appeal to sell reforms—because the secular parties had no base among the religiously conservative masses.

Every nation eventually has its definitive crisis, and Turkey's started in 2000. The secular coalition that replaced Erbakan was highly unstable, as usual, and by 2001 the government was mired in infighting over cynical attempts by the leading party to keep a dying prime minister in office, sparking a speculative attack on the Turkish lira that mushroomed into a full-blown banking and currency crisis. With inflation running at more than 70 percent, and interest rates spiking to 6,200 percent in late 2001, the lira lost half its value almost overnight, and the country was saved from financial collapse only by a bailout from the IMF that ultimately totaled more than $20 billion.

Turkish voters were fed up, setting off a political earthquake. In 2002 they overwhelmingly rejected both the leading secular parties and the traditional Islamic parties, turning to a party that had broken away from the Refah Party and offered a much more moderate vision of Islam, intent on joining the European Union and working closely with the United States through NATO. This was the AK Party. It had no record in national office, but its leader, Erdoğan, had gained a reputation for running a competent and clean local government as mayor of Istanbul—indeed "AK" is a synonym for "clean" in Turkish. Winning 32 percent of the vote in a fair election, nearly three times more than the next-strongest party, the AKP was in solid position to reshape Turkey.

The AKP's arrival in power aroused the usual paranoid warnings from the secular elite of an "Islamic takeover," but from the beginning it has used the voters' mandate to sort out the basics. Since it took over, government debt has fallen from 90 percent of GDP to 40 percent, and private-sector debt is now at 45 percent of GDP, relatively low for a country in Turkey's income bracket. Most significantly, by 2004 inflation had fallen into the single digits for the first time in thirty years, after averaging 75 percent in the 1980s and more than 50 percent in the 1990s. As a result, interest rates fell dramatically and helped lift economic growth. Under Erdoğan, GDP growth has averaged 5 percent, up from 4 percent between 1980 and 2000, and the average per capita income in Turkey has risen from $3,500 to $10,500. Far from pushing an Islamic takeover, the AKP moved carefully on contentious social issues, like the right to wear headscarves in public, and instead focused on accelerating Turkey's campaign to join the European Union, selling membership as another route to expand Turkey's markets and increase economic stability.

Stability has made Turkey a model for Islamic countries across the Middle East and helped Turkish businesses focus on the long term. During the decades of rapid inflation, Turkish businessmen say, it was impossible for them even to consider obtaining international long-term financing, because those lending models don't work when inflation is in the high double digits. Local bank assets were heavily invested in high-yielding government paper, which meant there was no need for them to make loans. Ambitious projects were never entertained because no one could think beyond six months. Now, Turkey is pursuing crucial infrastructure projects including high-speed train routes, nuclear energy plants, and Canal Istanbul, an alternative route to the Bosporus, currently the sole connection between the Black and Mediterranean seas. The more comfortable Turks are with the future, the more secure Erdoğan becomes. In

2011 Erdoğan won a third term in office, making him the longest-lasting leader in modern Turkish history. The drawn-out era of revolving-door government is over at least for now.

The Turkish Putin?

Today in Turkey the clash between Islam and secular forces is giving way to a new point of dramatic tension: that the victorious forces of moderate Islam will push their success too far and create an authoritarian regime. My sense is that like so many other regimes Turkey is subconsciously internalizing the lesson of China: a leader who gets the economy right can get away with almost anything in politics. Erdoğan has gotten the economy right, and his political tone and tactics are getting tougher.

In its first term the AKP was pushing reforms based on minority rights and religious freedom, all in line with EU demands. After a big reelection victory in 2007, a somewhat different AKP emerged, still pursuing European reform but now clearly more confident at home, intimidating opponents and running critical media out of business. Erdoğan is advancing a constitution that grants the president more power, and has hinted that he might run for this newly muscular office himself.

The last leader on the edge of Europe who sought to extend his reign by simply switching offices was Vladimir Putin. There is a lot of talk in Ankara about how Erdoğan is following Putin's lead, leveraging the popularity that flowed from a decade of economic success to grasp for more power, both in constitutional changes and in crackdowns on rivals and critics. In the last election the AKP printed huge posters proclaiming "Erdoğan 2023," the year of modern Turkey's centennial. From an economic point of view, however, the real problem with Putin is not his power grabs, but that he has lost respect for fiscal discipline and became increasingly reliant on high oil prices to fund outsized government spending. That's not happening in Erdoğan's Turkey, which has no commodity exports to get hooked on, and where government debt is still falling as a share of GDP.

Putin has effectively gutted organized political opposition, and faces no real adversarial party in the legislature. He runs a kleptocratic economy in which ambitious rivals will no doubt seize any opening to bring him down. Turkey, with genuine power bases in the legislature, judiciary, and military that can still counterbalance the president, is a much more stable democracy than Russia. It's true, as critics emphasize, that Erdoğan has threatened with Putinesque bluntness to "eliminate" opponents of his constitutional reforms, but those reforms would also change the pro-government constitution to be more respectful of individual rights, and to balance the enormous power of the military and the courts.

Erdoğan's language and tone are also not out of step in the midst of a counterrevolution. As recently as 2007 the secular elite in politics and the military were openly calling for a "national reflex" to expel the "foreign" AKP from power. The secular movement was publishing highly popular books claiming Erdoğan and his fellow AKP leader, President Abdullah Gül, were Jewish or linking them to secret international networks. To an admirable degree the AKP did not respond in kind and continued to talk mainly about EU membership, taming inflation, and attracting foreign trade and investment. It was only after the big 2007 election victory that the AKP government started using tax charges against its enemies and arresting critical journalists. These are the same tactics Putin has used, but they are also similar to the methods earlier military governments in Turkey had used against religious parties. Calling Erdoğan a new Putin misses the very Turkish context of the battle he is waging.

I suspect Erdoğan would prefer to be seen as a Turkish avatar of Lee Kuan Yew, the legendary father figure of independent Singapore. In the early 1960s Singapore was a stagnating outpost of the British Empire, and Lee saw a merger with a common market of neighboring Malay provinces as a solution to the city-state's economic woes. But the merger failed, owing to ethnic and racial tensions reminiscent of the current tensions between Turkey and Europe, and Malaysia tossed Singapore out on its own. Lee used these trying circumstances to justify the imposition of authoritarian rule dedicated to economic development, and he executed the model with strategic brilliance, becoming famous worldwide as a leader to whom neighboring states turned for guidance in moments of crisis. In a small way Erdoğan has begun to carve out a similar role: spurned by Europe, he is leading Turkey to an independent regional role, with an increasingly firm hand at home.

Too Fast, Too Late

Before China's emergence as a rising power, nations like Turkey thought that to advance economically, they had to adopt Western liberal democratic values. The success of an authoritarian and centrally directed form of capitalism in China has dented those convictions and opened the door to experimentation. Erdoğan is clearly ambitious to complete his basic project—freeing moderate Islam to be itself in Turkey—and he understands that strong economic growth has provided him the political power to promote that goal. The risk is that to achieve his grand aim he may now be pushing too hard to grow too fast, by continuing to invest public funds heavily and to keep interest rates low during a new boom. (Though the central bank is supposed to have independent control of interest rates, in countries like Turkey, signals from the top political leader are tough for the bankers to ignore.) The growth targets that made sense in 2002, when Erdoğan took power, no longer make sense now that Turkey's per capita income is over $10,000.

Today confidence in Istanbul is sky high because of the economy's admirable performance after the Great Recession of 2008. For the first time, Turkey got hit by a crisis not because it was collapsing, but because the world was collapsing around it. All the work Turkey did after 2002 to get its books in order paid off as foreign investors returned quickly when the crisis abated. Turkey is the poorest member of the Organisation for Economic Co-operation and Development (OECD), the club of industrialized nations, and suffered the sharpest contraction in 2008, as GDP growth fell by more than 10 percent, but it also enjoyed one of the fastest recoveries. By early 2011 Turkey's economy was indeed putting up China-type numbers, briefly growing at an 11 percent annual pace, the fastest in the world.

Still, Turkey is no China. The boom in China was built on huge savings that funded investment and loan growth. In contrast, Turkey's savings are very low—particularly for a young and relatively rich population—at only about 20 percent of GDP, compared to nearly 50 percent in China. That means Turkey has to borrow from abroad to fund exploding growth in credit that in late 2010 and early 2011 was rising at a pace of 30 to 40 percent a year. Borrowing heavily abroad is not the way to grow fast at

Turkey's income level, because the money flooding into Turkey is mainly short-term investment in stocks and other financial assets, which can be pulled out quickly in a crisis. This recurring threat of a spiking deficit in the current account—the broad measure of trade that includes income from foreign investments and loans—has long been the Achilles' heel of the Turkish economy. China, as a big exporter and creditor to other countries, has a huge current-account surplus.

This vulnerability to foreign debt would not be so threatening but for the fact that, unlike China, Turkey was for many years a weak competitor in global export markets, so its export revenues were unreliable. Turkey was still following a 1960s-style import-substitution strategy—trying to promote Turkish industry by shutting out foreign imports—as late as 1994, more than a decade after China started opening to the outside world. As a result Turkish businesses enjoyed clubby profits at home but faced retaliatory barriers abroad; in 1994 the top-five-hundred Turkish companies were earning a pittance, barely 8 percent, from exports.

The competitiveness problem is easing under the AKP. Reducing interest rates helped to bring down the value of the lira, making Turkish exports less expensive, but that drop in the currency's value came only in 2011. It was the AKP's effort to free up trade and expand into new regions that pushed trade as a share of GDP up from 40 percent in 2002 to a much more normal 50 percent, and manufacturing has edged up slightly to account for 24 percent of the economy. Ford and Fiat have decided to move European operations to Turkey, and double their research and development there, where employing an engineer costs roughly 25 percent of the European average. Turkish consumer appliance manufacturers like Arcelik and Vestel are competitive across Europe, and dominate the large home market.

None of this has crunched the overall trade deficit, in part because Turkey has to import every industrial commodity—from oil to copper. Top foreign advisers have urged Turkey to run the economy counter-cyclically—in other words to save aggressively in good times to be able to fund more of their growth without foreign borrowing. One way to save more would be to ease up on public spending when the economy is going strong, but AKP officials brush off the suggestion, saying they still have many schools and roads to build, to become more competitive.

The danger in an economy like this is overheating. Turkey has been compared to a sports car—touch the accelerator and it takes off—because the eager young population is largely free of personal debt (household debt is just 15 percent of GDP) and the consumer market is "underpenetrated," meaning Turks are still relatively unlikely to own a dishwasher, a mobile phone, or an automobile (just over one in ten owns a car, compared to one in four Poles). The implication is that when the government stimulates the economy—through public spending or low interest rates—growth takes off quickly. In recent years, Turkey has pushed for growth all the time, as if it were chasing China.

Questioning the Appeal of Europe

Ever since the emergence of the AKP, Europe has been asking itself who "lost" Turkey, as if it were a shock to see a pious Muslim nation choose leaders who reflect the views of the national majority and who want to carve out a commercial position that matches their geographic position— perched between Europe and Asia. It is true that Turkey under the AKP is shifting its commercial orientation eastward, but that is in part a practical response to economic trouble in the West.

Turks no longer see acceptance into the European Union as a chance to enter a promised land, because that land is mired in debt crises of its own. Opinion in Turkey is shifting against the European Union, but so is opinion in Eastern European nations, as they watch how nations in the Eurozone are forced to share the pain of the debt-afflicted members. In 2010 a major Ankara daily heralded the benefits of EU membership in an April Fool's Day headline that read, "Turkey Bails Out Greece."

Why push to join a failing club, particularly if the club doesn't want you? Since the leaders and the people of France and Germany have made increasingly clear that they are hostile to Turkish membership in the EU, it's hardly surprising that Turkish popular support for pushing the bid has fallen, from 73 percent in 2004 to just under 50 percent now. The Turkish deputy prime minister, Ali Babacan, told me that Turkey still seeks European guidance on reform, but it's all about "cherry-picking" the best of the EU's standards, and these days those tend to be more political than economic in nature.

The United States is no longer quite the economic magnet it once was, either. Following the crisis of 2008, the relative retreat of the United States opened up opportunities to expand influence where American businesses are afraid to go, particularly remote parts of Africa and the Middle East. Turkish companies first cut back, as their Western business dried up, then moved quickly to diversify into new markets in Asia, Russia, North Africa, and the Middle East. Turkey, for example, now has the second-largest global construction industry, after China, much of it in nations on its borders. Ten years ago just 7 percent of Turkish exports went to the Middle East. Now that share is 20 percent. A decade ago Iraq was not even on the list of top export markets for Turkey, and today it is number four. In the wake of the 2009 U.S. withdrawal from Najaf, the nerve center of the Iraqi Shiite rebellion against the American occupation, Turkish entrepreneurs came rolling in, and now do a booming business in construction. One Turkish businessman, who travels to Najaf in his Hummer, says he sees similar opportunities all over the region. At the simplest level, Turkish businessmen say, this move toward the East is an obvious strategy, exploiting their natural linguistic, cultural, and even transport advantages in the region.

In the same way that the entrepreneurial creativity of Seoul has generated a "Korean Wave" of fascination with Korean music, movies, and soap operas across Asia, so too the cosmopolitan energy of Istanbul is producing a tide of new TV shows and pop-music acts that are attracting customers from across the Middle East. Pop art often flows from raw economic dynamism, and both Korea and Turkey have it. Turkey is capitalizing on the popularity of its TV shows by drawing visitors from across the region to tour the sites where these shows are made. Only four or five years ago I saw hardly any Arab tourists in Istanbul, but now they travel there by the busload, and seem drawn to the city as a "Paris of the Middle East," a symbol of what Islam can achieve. Between 2005 and 2010, the number of tourists arriving from Israel fell 72 percent, while the number from Turkey's Arab neighbors rose between 121 percent (Jordan) and 246 percent (the United Arab Emirates).

The Rising Power of Anatolia

Not surprisingly the Erdoğan government is cultivating these new trade links to fellow Muslim nations mainly through businesses in Anatolia, the heartland of political Islam in Turkey and the base of the AKP's support. President Gül has led high-profile tours throughout the Middle East, Africa, and Central Asia, including Turkmenistan and Kazakhstan. He typically travels with a few-dozen CEOs in tow, all representing the new Anatolian business class with close ties to the AKP. A leading light of this group is Ahmet Çalik, who recently joined the Forbes list of global billionaires on the strength of his growing investments in areas ranging from textiles in Turkmenistan to construction all over the Middle East.

Observers in the West often wonder whether this new Anatolian political and business elite represents the kind of fundamentalist threat that has emerged in recent years from many Middle Eastern countries. That threat arises when powerful forces believe that Islamic law is universal law, governing all facets of life from private choices to politics. There is almost no support for this worldview in Turkey where—even under the AKP—the state enforces a single, moderate interpretation of Islam in schools and through the Religious Affairs Directorate. The vast majority of Turks, some 60 percent, see religion as a strictly personal matter, and another 30 percent think religion should have a moral influence on politics, but in a way that is compatible with modern democracy and economic development. This group has been compared to mainstream political Christianity in the United States, which also doesn't try to impose biblical law on society. Today 90 percent of Turks would fall in the mainstream in the United States in terms of how they view the role of religion in politics. Only 10 percent would feel comfortable in Iran or Saudi Arabia, where religious police enforce public morality and Sharia law is the order of the day. There is certainly no talk of imposing Sharia law in Turkey.

Until recently, before the AKP started placing more of its people in law enforcement, devout Muslims in Turkey were more likely to be targets of the police. In 2008 a state prosecutor attempted to ban President Gül from politics, under the constitutional injunction against anti-secular activities, citing as one piece of evidence the fact that Gül's wife wears a headscarf in public. This is absurd. It is one thing for a nation like France, a birthplace of the liberal republic, to ban headscarves in a society with no Islamic roots. It is quite another for a Muslim nation to do so. Moreover Erdoğan and Gül do not insist on similar shows of piety from other top AKP officials, so it's hardly government policy.

The moderate nature of Islam in Turkey has long roots. For many decades visitors from other Islamic nations have been stunned by what they saw happening on the Bosporus, the late-night partying, the unveiled women with cigarettes dangling from their fingers like old-time Hollywood starlets. The scene if anything has grown more vibrant and smoky over time, including in the last decade under the AKP. The nightclubs on the Bosporus don't even get rolling until after midnight, and by the early morning the streets are so crowded with fancy cars that it is advisable for international visitors to take a boat back to their hotels.

I was recently at Anjelique, one of the nightspots on the waterfront, when the coast guard stopped by to order the club's management to turn down the music, which was so loud it would never be allowed in an equally well-populated Manhattan neighborhood. There were cracks among the revelers about how this was the work of some new AKP morality police, but to me it looked like routine enforcement of a reasonable noise ordinance, not religious intimidation. Certainly no one was scared. The club turned down the volume for about fifteen minutes, until after the coast guard vessel sailed away, and then the bass began thumping again. A colleague of mine considered the scene and said, "You can't put this back in the bottle."

Many AKP insiders in fact see Erdoğan as the man holding the line against conservatives who would tilt Turkey even more sharply toward conservative Islam and the Middle East. While Erdoğan is trying to share the wealth more broadly between Turkey's European and Asian halves, this is happening gradually. Among the top-one-hundred companies, the number of those that hail from outside the Istanbul-Ankara-Izmir triangle in western Turkey rose from sixteen in 2000 to thirty-nine in 2011. The number of Turkish cities that export more than $1 billion in goods each year has risen from four to fourteen, and many are Anatolian cities smiled upon by the AKP. The industrial city of Kayseri, Gül's hometown, is coming on as a manufacturer of furniture and plastics. Indeed one of the keys to Erdoğan's appeal is that he speaks like an inspiring street fighter from the gritty Kasimpasa neighborhood of Istanbul, not like one of the Western-educated statesmen who dominate the top ranks of the secular parties.

The big banks are shifting their attention to these new growth centers, and the share of new loans that go to Istanbul, Ankara, and Izmir is shrinking. Istanbul's share of the rapidly growing credit pie fell from 46 percent to 41 percent in just the last three years. Marketing experts say this spread of growth to the provinces is showing up in the distribution of wealth, with the top 20 percent of the population, still centered in Istanbul and Ankara, losing share in almost every category of spending, from health to education.

The urban poster child for Turkey's new Middle Eastern orientation is Gaziantep, a city of 1.3 million just an hour west of the Syrian border. One of the oldest, continuously occupied cities in the world, built around a sixth-century citadel and fortress, Gaziantep is also surrounded by modern malls and pistachio groves: it became an instant magnet for Syrian tourists and shoppers after visa restrictions were lifted in 2009. The number of shoppers arriving from Syria each weekend rose from five thousand to sixty thousand in 2010, before falling back when political revolts broke out in Syria in early 2011.

Despite the expansion of Anatolian business empires, more and more of the "white Turks"—the secular elites of the Istanbul-Ankara-Izmir triangle—are growing comfortable with Erdoğan. The stability he brings offers them a significant upside, because the old elite continues to dominate westward trade ties to Europe and the United States. The list of top Turkish business groups still includes the same small circle of family names that prevailed for decades, before the AKP came to power: Koç, Sabanci, and Dogus. And as the AKP pushes forward with free-market reforms, most recently in privatizing the state-controlled energy industries, the leading bids all come from this same cluster—the businesses with the resources and connections to pull off projects of this size. The Anatolian elite is rising at a speed fast enough to satisfy Anatolia, but not so fast as to upset Istanbul.

Still, the dominance by old family firms is not normal for a modern economy, and it offers further evidence that Erdoğan's counterrevolution remains incomplete. To a degree unparalleled even in nations where oligarchs are the supreme economic powers—nations like Russia—Turkish family empires continue to metastasize into more sprawling and less focused conglomerates, with banks owning glass companies, hoteliers buying into natural gas, and cement makers moving into retail. This kind of sprawl tends to dilute competitiveness and profits and is unthinkable in other emerging markets like South Africa, where companies face real pressure to deliver for shareholders.

The Turkish job market shows the same mix of the backward and the modern. In an attempt to create a modern European welfare state, Turkey has imposed unusually heavy burdens on employers. Among the OECD nations it has among the highest standards for minimum wages, social security benefits, and severance payments. These burdens grow with the number of employees, discouraging firms from increasing the official payroll—yet growth has been so fast lately that official employment is growing strong. The consumer market in this nation of seventy-nine million is vibrant, and Turkey is one country where the "demographic dividend" of a growing young population (average age, twenty-nine) is a real plus because the economy is starting to produce a lot of new jobs: between 2009 and 2011, Turkey generated 3.2 million new jobs, more than in the twenty-seven nations of the European Union, Russia, and South Africa combined.

That does not even include hiring in a black market so vast—estimates suggest as much as 20 percent of the economy—that Turkey has more or less given up on trying to impose broader taxes on corporate or personal income. Some 80 percent of the government's revenue comes from taxes on the few industries that are heavily regulated, such as the telecommunication, automobile, and gasoline sectors. As a result cars are more expensive in Turkey than anywhere in Europe, and gasoline is just as expensive as in the EU. "Sin taxes"—imposed on goods that Islam discourages—are another big source of revenue but the reasons here are more practical than religious: spirits are sold through state-regulated liquor stores that can't hide from the taxman. There's probably no other country that relies so heavily on indirect taxation of just a few target industries to fund the

gears of government. This is a rare system built to avoid, instead of confront, tax dodgers, and it's not likely to change soon because the Erdoğan
government is not inclined to create another point of confrontation with
the secular business elite. Asked recently whether he was afraid of new
tax hikes by the AKP, a top Turkish businessman responded, "They know
they can only push so far."

The Turkish Model

The AKP is reveling in the new respect that Turkey commands throughout the region, and unabashedly supported the democratic revolutions
that swept across the Arab dictatorships starting in early 2011. Westerners who see Erdoğan as somehow too Islamic—and focus on his clashes
with Israel over Palestine—look past the many fights he waged with the
West's main rivals in the region (Iran, Syria) and the high-profile visits he
paid in 2011 to the nations that overthrew dictators that year—Tunisia,
Libya, and Egypt.

Egypt is a particularly intriguing case, because more than any other
nation in the region it has the size, the history as a Middle Eastern power,
and the ambition to become another Turkey. Long before the outcome of
the struggle in Cairo was clear, Erdoğan called openly on dictator Hosni
Mubarak to step down. In March 2011 Gül went to Egypt and held court
at the Turkish embassy in Cairo, where all the players in the unfolding
drama of Egypt's popular revolt came to see him and seek his tacit bless-
ing. Even the conservative Muslim Brotherhood came to talk to Gül about
how to emulate Turkey's economic success.

Then in early fall Erdoğan himself was welcomed in Cairo by huge
crowds chanting "Egypt, Turkey. One Fist!" Erdoğan was greeted as a
symbol of how much a Muslim nation can achieve only one decade after
suffering the depths of economic and political crises. Today, Egypt indeed
looks much like Turkey did when Erdoğan first took power: a per capita
income of around $3,000, a large and young population of about seventy-
five million, no great wealth in natural resources but a strategic location
on a geopolitically critical waterway (in Egypt's case, the Suez Canal), a
political system that is just opening up to Islamic parties, and an inflation-
riddled economy awaiting a leader who knows how to jump-start growth.

During a meeting in September 2011, the Egyptian deputy prime minister Hazem El Beblawi told me, "The Turkish parallel gives us a lot of hope." He further added that Erdoğan's speech in Cairo, calling on Egypt to become a "secular nation" and to confine the role of Islam to private life, was inspirational stuff. "Do not be wary of secularism," Erdoğan had said. "To Egyptians who view secularism as removing religion from the state, or as an infidel state, I say you are mistaken. . . . It means respect to all religions. If this is implemented, the entire society will live in safety and atheists as well as the pious will be protected by rule of law."

For the leader of a party that sprang from decades of struggle against the secular autocracy of the Atatürk regime, this embrace of secular moderation is impressively levelheaded. It's the attitude of an inspiringly normal country, and bodes well for Turkey becoming a breakout nation as well.

9

On the Tiger Road

The Commodity Economy That Works

There is no visible sign left of the riot zone in Jakarta. The fires, set by Indonesians demanding the end of the Suharto regime and seeking revenge against all its allies, have long since burned out. The stick-built construction projects, abandoned half-finished and skeletal when the mobs came looking for Chinese businessmen, targeted as friends of the regime, have been completed. The children, sent abroad for schooling by Chinese parents scared for their safety, have long since returned. Semanggi Junction, where protesters halted army troop carriers trying to reach the burning buildings of Chinatown, is now the placid home of a lavish new mall and the Ritz-Carlton Hotel.

The Asian financial contagion that rolled out of Thailand in 1997 sparked protests across the region, but none nearly so angry or violent as the fiery street revolts that brought down Suharto, after thirty-two years in power. On Jalan Sudirman, the main drag and "money street" of the capital, money fled after 1998, and properties like the legendary Hotel Indonesia, where the 1982 hit *The Year of Living Dangerously* (with Mel Gibson) was filmed, fell into seedy disrepair. It has since been rehabilitated as the Hotel Indonesia Kempinski, where the breakfast room is adorned with photos of Suharto's predecessor, Sukarno, alongside John F. Kennedy and Marilyn Monroe.

With things looking up under a new leader, maybe
Manila will replace the World War II–vintage "Jeepney,"
which is still a staple of public transportation.

But the Suharto years are not forgotten. The overwhelming sense one gets in Jakarta today is of a nation governed by a desire never to go through that experience again. Indonesia was the country hardest hit by the crisis of 1997–1998, suffering a drop in GDP of around 20 percent during that period. That is why the protests were so violent. But because Indonesia also learned the deepest lessons, it was best positioned to thrive after the crisis of 2008. In fact by late 2011 Indonesia was one of the very few economies growing faster than it did during the global boom from 2003 to 2007, with growth accelerating from 5.5 percent during that period to over 6 percent.

Led by Indonesia, the nations of Southeast Asia are experiencing a reversal of the process that triggered the financial crisis of 1997–1998. Unlike the global meltdown of 2008, which originated in the United States, the Asian crisis began in Thailand with the fall in the value of the baht, and spread across the region, which is why it is still seen as the formative event of recent Southeast Asian history. The roots of the crisis are complex and hotly debated, and its causes and consequences varied from country to country, but one common factor was that in the early 1990s newly and incompletely deregulated banks in Southeast Asia started borrowing heavily from abroad to fund increasingly speculative borrowing at home, often by politically well-connected "cronies" with close ties to the banks. The bank borrowing was fueled by the fact that many of the Asian currencies were "pegged" to the dollar, which was rising in value and taking the baht, the ringgit, and the won up with it against rival currencies such as the Chinese yuan and the Mexican peso. When Southeast Asia's exports began to falter in 1996, and its high-flying stock and property markets started to wobble, locals started to flee and foreign lenders withdrew abruptly. The result was a snowballing crisis in which the flight of capital put downward pressure on the currencies, which made it more difficult for the banks to repay foreign debt, further stoking capital flight.

The damage was catastrophic—much worse than what the West suffered in 2008. The value of the Korean won and the Thai baht fell by half, and the Indonesian rupiah by 80 percent. Regional stock markets plummeted by as much as 90 percent, turning Malaysian and Thai billionaires into millionaires. The incomes of millions of ordinary citizens dropped below the poverty line, fueling revolts that toppled leaders in Thailand, in South Korea, and most dramatically in Indonesia. The contagion swept across global markets, dropping oil prices to ten dollars a barrel and precipitating a domino-effect collapse of the ruble in Russia, though fears that the economies of Europe and the United States would be derailed, too, proved overblown. At the time the East Asian economies were just not big enough to bring down the West. Though the recovery came quite quickly, the fall was so sharp that most of Southeast Asia was still poorer, in per capita dollar terms, in 2005 than in 1998, and none of these nations have yet recovered their old position as market darlings in the West. That status would shift quickly to others, including China and India.

Today, however, many big businessmen in Southeast Asia say the tables are starting to turn against China. One catalyst of the Asian crisis was China's 1994 decision to battle a severe downturn by sharply devaluing the yuan, and then holding it there for the next decade. That single move, perhaps more than any other, undercut the competitiveness of exports from Southeast Asia, which could not respond to the Chinese devaluation because their currencies were pegged to the dollar. Now, however, all the Southeast Asian currencies are floating and relatively cheap, while China has been allowing the yuan to rise slowly, and Chinese wages are increasing quickly, making manufactured exports from Southeast Asia much more competitive in global markets.

The cost of hiring a factory worker in China has risen significantly, to an average of $450 per month in 2010 from less than $200 in 2005. In 2010, labor costs in China were almost twice as high as those in Thailand, roughly three times higher than those in the Philippines, and four times higher than in Indonesia. Businessmen in Thailand and Indonesia are saying it is like the 1990s played in reverse, and they can feel themselves gaining momentum in competition with the Chinese. As global markets start to recognize that the cost advantages are tilting back in favor of Southeast Asia, money could flow into countries such as Indonesia as fast as it flew out in the late 1990s.

While Beijing's leaders are feted as economic wizards for dodging the global downturn of 2008, the Indonesian president Susilo Bambang

Yudhoyono, widely known as SBY, managed the same trick—without the massive spending binge China employed. Indonesia got through the crisis largely unscathed, with less debt than when it started, and rewarded SBY with reelection in 2009. He ran on promises to pursue economic recovery and signaled his seriousness by picking a respected technocrat over the favorite sons of allied parties as his running mate. SBY is the first leader in Indonesia to serve two terms since the fall of the Suharto dictatorship in 1998, and he is bringing the stability and the flexibility the country needs to sustain a new phase of rapid growth.

Indonesia is now by far the best-run large commodity economy. A large population and a wealth of natural resources—once viewed as a curse, a source of easy money that sapped a nation's will to produce and excel—are now seen as providing a competitive advantage, benefiting countries such as Brazil and Russia. Indonesia is the only Asian economy blessed in both respects: As the world's fourth-most-populous nation, the country has a large enough domestic market to generate demand even when global demand is weak. It also has vast untapped reserves of crude oil, coal, palm oil, and nickel.

Indonesia is one of the few emerging markets where leaders have come to accept the new normal and are not taking dangerous (big spending, easy money) steps in an attempt to return to the unusually high growth rates of the last decade. As a result Indonesia has less of a post-crisis debt problem than any other big emerging market. It has not blown through the profits of the commodity boom of the last decade, as Russia and Brazil ultimately did, and has the savings to increase investment in the economy. In fact it is the only Southeast Asian country in which investment as a share of GDP, now 32 percent, has surpassed its pre-1998 high. Investment so far has been primarily in the commodity sector but is spreading to other, more productive parts of the economy. What Indonesia has not reinvested it has saved, paying down public debt, which has fallen from 97 percent of GDP in 1998 to 27 percent now.

Indonesia knows its own weaknesses: 55 percent of its export earnings come from commodities, leaving it highly vulnerable to swings in commodity prices. The president of one of Indonesia's largest banks recently told me the cautionary tale of how Indonesia flourished in the 1950s, when exports of rubber and tin took off as the United States built up strategic reserves at the start of the Cold War. Once those drivers stalled, the price of commodities collapsed, and Indonesia got slammed. The experience seems to have ingrained in Indonesians a farsighted commitment to learn from past disasters. Furthermore total exports account for just 25 percent of the economy, making Indonesia one of the few East Asian nations that is not trying to export its way to prosperity, despite a global slowdown.

Sensible Caution, Efficient Corruption

Indonesian banks and corporations now operate with a caution uncommon in most emerging markets. Most of the big-business figures who were prominent in the late 1990s are still around, including the Salim, Riady, and Bakrie family business empires, all highly diversified with interests ranging from mining to motorcycles to instant noodles. They seem to have reinvented themselves out of necessity. Hit hard in 1998, many had to claw their way back from some form of bankruptcy, or buy their companies back from the government repo man. As the growth in investment shows, however, big Indonesian business is exercising a sensible caution, neither too eager nor too afraid to take on risk and make things happen. It is not the paralyzing kind of caution that is currently stunting domestic investment in Brazil.

Indonesia under Suharto had become a case study in why conglomerates should not be allowed to own banks—because combining lender and debtor under one roof is a debt crisis waiting to happen. As a result, many big Indonesian conglomerates are out of the bank business and are working hard to build clean balance sheets and professional corporate governance. The newly independent banks are very careful about whom they make loans to, and companies are very careful about where they invest. Since many of these tycoons were struggling to regain control of their companies for many years after Suharto's fall, memories are fresh, and vigilance is still high. Tycoon Anthony Salim, who was forced to give up one of Indonesia's largest private banks and other holdings in the credit meltdown of 1998, today tells investors that survivors of the crash no longer see wealth in terms of assets obtained on credit; now the definition of wealth is "cash flows, cash flows, cash flows."

Although Indonesia still scores very poorly on global surveys of corruption, there's a growing realization (at least in the region) that the country has a lot of good, clean companies now. Indian entrepreneurs say it's a lot easier to open a cement plant in Indonesia than back at home, thanks to "efficient corruption" of the kind businessmen often encounter in China. They may have to pay someone off, but it's relatively quick and easy to figure out whom. And once they get to the right person—or find the right government partner—the payoff is not just pocketed, the job gets done. Some investors even note with approval that to cut through Jakarta traffic, there is a number to call to hire a police motorbike escort, which will clear the way for a price of around a hundred dollars. During downtown rush hour—when traffic rules say there must be at least three people per vehicle—mother-and-child teams can be hired off the sidewalk to fill the requirement. A dubious service, yes, but locals say it works, providing the mothers with a reasonable living.

To outsiders, Indonesia is an easy place to do business, sometimes almost too easy. While India and China are starting to challenge new projects on environmental or social grounds—a desire to protect indigenous people, for instance—Indonesia is still pretty much an environmental anything-goes zone. Foreign direct investment in Indonesia is reasonably strong, at $10 billion a year in a $650 billion economy. Indian and Chinese investors are all over Indonesia, looking for coal, palm oil, and other investments, and not only because regulations are loose. One reason why Indonesian coal is so attractive is because much of it is close to the surface, and therefore easy to access.

SBY's landmark presidency has gotten relatively little attention around the world, in large part because he perfectly expresses the nation's sober post-Suharto ethos. A former general with an overwhelmingly popular mandate, he has mystified some observers by failing to use his clout to force reforms through the legislature. One of the big debates in Jakarta as of late 2011 was why SBY was not pushing more aggressively to gain passage of a land acquisition bill that would speed the pace of development. The most credible answer seems to be that SBY does not want to remind anyone of Suharto by ramming through business deals. He wants to build institutional credibility. There's not much flash or drama—just a steady move in the direction of greater stability.

The Rise of Second Cities

A rule of the road: check the size and growth of the second city, compared to the first city. In any big country the second-largest city usually has a population that is at least one-third to one-half the population of the largest city. This ratio reflects regional balance in the economy, and it holds true for many of the nations that were breakout stories in recent decades: São Paulo and Rio de Janeiro in Brazil, Seoul and Busan in Korea, Moscow and St. Petersburg in Russia, as well as Taipei and Kaohsiung in Taiwan. It's a red flag if a country is stuck in violation of this rule, but it's a good sign if a capital-centric nation is moving toward greater balance. It's even better if the country is producing new cities with populations of one million or more, which suggests that growth is lifting all regions—not favoring the elite in the capital city. Indonesia fits both criteria: the second city of Surabaya, with a population of 2.8 million, has roughly one-third the population of Jakarta, and there are four other cities with almost two million people or more, and eight with nearly one million or more.

Indonesia is emerging as a uniquely successful case of archipelago capitalism. While power struggles between the central government and provincial officials and tycoons threaten the ability of both India and China to manage growth, SBY is turning the conflicts of the world's most fractured population—245 million people representing dozens of ethnic groups and languages spread out over seventeen thousand islands—to his advantage by allowing more local autonomy. Suharto (and Sukarno before him) had worked hard to unite Indonesia under a nationalist "pancasila" philosophy that demanded consensus and harmony, and this philosophy was used to justify the often violent suppression of ethnic and regional differences. Under Suharto, the capital city of Jakarta was the focus of all political and business attention, but now a lot of new cities are opening up. SBY was one of the movers behind a key 2001 law that began the decentralization process, and as president he has given second cities confidence that they will be left free to flourish. As a result, SBY not only won a legitimate 70 percent of the vote in 2009 but also won broadly in twenty-nine out of thirty-three provinces, in part owing to the expanding economic freedoms he is granting the regions.

Decentralization is also creating a vibrant new business culture outside of Java, the province that hosts the capital city of Jakarta. In the last years of the Suharto era the bank system controlled by his cronies was funneling credit back to companies owned by the same circle, based mostly in Jakarta, which received 66 percent of the loans issued in 1995. Since then that share has dropped steadily, to 33 percent today. The same decline in crony control is clear in the central government, which accounted for 73 percent of all public spending in the late Suharto years, but accounts for only 48 percent today.

The rise of provincial power has brought a surge in construction and investment. Growth in cement consumption is now much faster in the outlying provinces than in Java, and in the last five years foreign investment has risen 23 percent in the provinces, compared to 10 percent in Java. This is further greasing the wheels of efficient corruption, businessmen say, because local authorities are starting to compete for the growing pot of investment dollars by lowering the price of bribes and tips. Since bribes collected locally are spent locally, the decentralization of corruption tilts the upside of even ill-gotten gains away from Jakarta.

Employment and minimum wages are rising much faster in the hinterlands too, attracting a flood of internal migration. The number of households is growing nearly two times faster outside Java than inside. As of 2010 the fastest-growing province in the country was no longer Java; it was Sulawesi, the third most populous, located at the center of the Indonesian archipelago. This shift represents a kind of punctuation mark, an end to the Java-centric Suharto era.

What Curse of Oil?

Indonesia is one of the few commodity-driven economies where you don't get the sense that a lot of people are living way beyond their means. Jakarta has few of the nouveau-riche excesses of Moscow, and prices are a small fraction of what one encounters in Rio. Indonesia has much lower structural inflation than Russia (6 percent, compared to 10), and because it is investing (rather than consuming) more than both Russia and Brazil, it should be able to grow at a faster pace in the years ahead. (Indonesia's investment rate of 32 percent of GDP compares to 20 percent in Russia and 19 percent in Brazil.) It's a commodity economy that works.

The Philippines Is No Longer a Joke

There was a time when the Philippines was seen as an Asian trendsetter, and fashionable young Malays would sport the barong, the formal embroidered shirt favored by Filipinos, to look cool. But that was back in the 1960s, when the Philippines had the second-highest per capita income in Asia, behind only Japan. The nation's fortunes have shifted dramatically since then. By the 1970s South Korea and Taiwan had passed the Philippines in per capita income terms. Malaysia and Thailand followed in the 1980s and China in the 1990s. Then in 2009, in a moment the Manila elite thought it would never see, Indonesia's boom made Indonesians richer than Filipinos for the first time in modern history.

When I visited Manila in early 2010, returning for the first time in twelve years, the Philippines was still the undisputed laggard of Asia, a nation mired in chronic incompetence. My overwhelming impression was of how little had changed. The contrast to the frenetic progress of China and India could not have been starker. The same handful of family-owned conglomerates still dominated local markets, running everything from malls and banks to airlines and breweries, with no new players to be found. Forget high-speed trains: "Jeepneys," which trace their origin back to World War II, remained the preferred mode of public transportation. While nearly all other major Asian cities boasted fancy new airports, most international visitors to Manila had to trudge through a graying terminal commissioned in the 1980s.

The failure of the Philippines is typically attributed to chronic political instability since the fall of the dictator Ferdinand Marcos in 1986, but that explanation is not enough. Thailand has been even more unstable, but its economy outperformed the Philippine economy through the 1990s. In the last seventy-five years Thailand has seen eighteen coup attempts and seventeen new constitutions; the Philippines has had around a half-dozen coup attempts and one constitution. The difference is that at least until the 2000s, Thailand's unstable leaders made better economic choices—from controlling debt and restraining crony capitalism to making the country more attractive to foreign investment, as Japanese car companies turned Thailand into their Asian factory-away-from-home.

Now, at long last, the Philippines looks poised to resume a period of strong growth. The new president, Benigno "Noynoy" Aquino III, probably has just enough support, and looks likely to generate just enough reform momentum, to get the job done. The Aquino name is still virtually synonymous with the promise of change: Benigno III's legendary father, Benigno junior, was the opposition leader whose assassination by Marcos supporters sparked the People Power Revolution that brought his mother, Corazon Aquino, to office in 1986. Benigno III was originally dismissed in foreign circles as an unimpressive fifty-one-year-old bachelor who had lived most of his life with his mother and had not made much of a mark in a low-profile career as a Philippine senator. However, Filipinos saw him as an honest figure who could deliver on the Aquino mandate for change, and they were desperate after nine years of drift and decay under outgoing president Gloria Macapagal Arroyo. Following his mother Corazon's death in 2010, Noynoy Aquino won the presidency on a wave of public sympathy. His victory margin was unprecedented, and his task daunting at a time when it seemed like the whole country was in disrepair. At a conference in Manila in December 2010, put on to attract foreign investors to new infrastructure projects shortly after Aquino took office, the electricity went out in the middle of a speech by the minister in charge of power.

Aquino is delegating power to competent technocrats and seems to understand what needs to be done to get the lights back on. To begin with he needs to revive investment in perhaps the only Asian nation that consumes way too much of its income—consumption accounts for an outrageous 80 percent of GDP, 10 percentage points higher than in the United States, and over 40 percentage points more than in China. That leaves little savings to invest in building up the nation's industrial backbone. In a telling sign of the long investment drought, the Philippines now uses no more cement than it did twenty years ago, even though population has risen from seventy million to ninety million.

The old caricature was that Asians are culturally more inclined to save money than Americans, but in this respect, the Philippines is far more American than Asian, perhaps in part a legacy of the fact that the Philippines was once a U.S. colony. The savings problem tends to spill over into debt and deficit trouble, but Aquino is starting to take this on too. By 2011, the administration was ahead of its own aggressive debt-busting schedule, which aims to bring the budget gap down from 4 percent of GDP in 2010 to 2 percent by 2013.

Aquino also needs to create an environment in which businessmen are confident enough to invest—which in return requires tamping down corruption, taking on the family tycoons who still dominate the economy, and enforcing contracts fairly. All those goals are combined in Aquino's first big initiative: an invitation to private investors from all over the world to join in open bidding on a series of public-private projects to rebuild the highways around central Manila, begin a commuter rail network, and upgrade its dilapidated airport.

Indeed the Manila international airport is a prime example of how cronyism and ineptitude has retarded economic growth. Recently voted one of the worst airports in the world, Manila has three terminals, but only the 1980s terminal is fully open to international airlines. The second terminal dates to the 1990s and is used by a local tycoon who doesn't want to share it with foreign airlines; the third was finished in 2002 but did not open until 2008, and then only to local airlines because of ongoing construction contract disputes that still scare foreign airlines away. Many investors saw the saga of the international airport that is open mainly to locals as a classic case of Third World incompetence. It's a big reason why foreign direct investment has been so low and why the Philippines has not been able to exploit its tourism potential. Even though the country boasts some of the world's most beautiful beaches spread across thousands of islands, it can muster only three million tourists a year, far fewer than the five million who visit the single Indonesian island of Bali.

In recent meetings with investors Aquino showed up casually dressed and smiling and did not make any tall promises: he emphasized his intention to keep his government clean, was attentive but not hostage to investors, and focused on giving talented Filipino expats a reason to come work at home. This is a critical priority. More than ten million Filipinos have left the country since the early 1980s for better prospects abroad and are now scattered across the world, from the United States and Japan to Britain and Germany, to Saudi Arabia and the United Arab Emirates. The cash they send home has been growing by double digits for the last decade, and now accounts for 10 percent of GDP, making these remittances the strongest growth sector in the Philippines. Many investment banks see this as a strength—remittances do help the balance of payments—but to have so many locals seeking work abroad is a major embarrassment, and it has created a subculture of entitlement among Filipinos who live off remittance checks rather than jobs. The stereotype of the Filipino expat is the maid in Hong Kong, but many also hold corporate and middle-class jobs. The country needs some of that talent to return home.

Indonesia's relative success over the past few years shows what the Philippines could become: it takes only a modicum of political stability and some basic economic sense. The Philippines has the world's fifth-richest store of natural resources, including oil, copper, nickel, gold, and silver. It has a large and young workforce—half of the population is under twenty-one, and two-thirds of them live in cities. That's a very high urbanization rate for a nation with an average income of only $2,500, and because the concentration of people and business drives growth, it's a big economic plus.

The Philippines also has some basic advantages over Indonesia—including a well-educated English-speaking population. For three decades it squandered those advantages, but there are signs of a turn-around, the most dramatic being the rise of the Philippines as a rival to India in "business process outsourcing"—the industry that provides the operators who answer calls for customer service at almost any major global company. Call centers did not exist in the Philippines a decade ago, and now it's a $9 billion industry employing 350,000 people. These centers are starting to open outside metro Manila and pop up all over the islands of the Philippines, to the point that some analysts think it may turn into another successful case of Southeast Asian archipelago capitalism. It could be made to happen, if the third Aquino can get the people-power revolution right.

Thailand's Code Red

There is no more dominant capital in Asia than Bangkok, where the ten million residents outnumber the population of the next-largest city in Thailand by more than 10 to 1. Normally, as a country grows richer, it develops more balance between the capital and the second cities. So for a nation of Thailand's wealth (the average income is around $5,000) to have not even one other city with more than a million people is astonishing. The residents of Bangkok account for 15 percent of the national population, and take home 40 percent of the national income. This lopsided picture is the bigger story behind the country's recent political chaos.

A running battle between the poor rural "red shirts" and Bangkok-centric, middle- and upper-income "yellow shirts" has defined Thai politics for the last decade, and is a direct result of the overwhelming power of the megalopolis and its elite. Even though Thai incomes are twice those of Indonesians or Filipinos, 70 percent of the Thai population lives in the countryside, compared to about 50 percent in Indonesia and 33 percent in the Philippines. Normally populations get richer as they move to the cities, so those numbers suggest there are serious political and cultural obstacles keeping Thais on the farm. Agriculture accounts for only 7 percent of GDP but almost 40 percent of the workforce, which sets the stage for the conflict between the rural voting bloc and the Bangkok elite.

When I visited Thailand in March 2006, the country was witnessing a unique, elitist uprising of the yellow shirts, a shifting coalition of big and small businessmen, royalists, and army officers. They were angered by then prime minister Thaksin Shinawatra's alleged abuses of power and his pandering to red-shirt voters. A former telecommunications tycoon, Thaksin had positioned himself as a champion of the rural poor and was first elected prime minister in 2001. He delivered aggressively with a populist menu of state support for his countryside constituency, including no-strings grants to rural villages, one-dollar hospital visits for the poor, and much more. The yellow shirts saw Thaksin as a pitchfork pointed at the heart of Bangkok's long-standing dominance, and in September

2006 they took action. An army coup—the eighteenth to rattle Thailand in seventy-five years—drove Thaksin into exile, prompting an escalating series of retaliatory protests by the red shirts. Over the next five years, four different yellow-shirt prime ministers tried to reestablish control, offering even more generous rural subsidies than Thaksin had, but none had any credibility with the rural majority, so nothing got done. Every time I visited Bangkok, the red shirts were stirring—shutting the airport down for a week in 2009, fighting police in battles that left more than one hundred Thais dead during the spring of 2011.

Given the constant threat of street fighting, businesses were unwilling to make new investments. The economy, sluggish since the Asian crisis of 1998, continued to idle along, which only added to the political tension. As elections approached in July 2011, the thinking in Bangkok was that if the red shirts prevailed, the military would intervene again, setting off another cycle of confrontation. Thailand—the 1990s darling of global investors—had become a financial no-fly zone. A colleague of mine described the staples of the stagnant Thai economy as "rice, tapioca, and massage," and he wasn't entirely joking.

No one saw the new regime coming. Just a month before the 2011 elections, Yingluck Shinawatra, Thaksin's younger sister, wasn't even on the political radar. A businesswoman and major player in Thaksin's party, she had insisted she would not be a prime-ministerial candidate. When she decided to run, all one of her rivals could think to say was, "She's very good looking." Shinawatra stormed out of nowhere to win a victory so convincing that even the military did not dare overturn the results, even though she was widely seen as a proxy for her brother.

The new prime minister offers some hope of a turn in Thailand, as she looks to lift up the rural population. International investors are not too excited by the government agenda, with its focus on doling out more support for the red-shirt constituencies rather than sharpening productivity and growth. But there won't be any progress in the country with the vast majority allowed only a tentative influence on power, subject to military whim. Now that democracy appears to have worked, the military has stepped down, and it's possible that a new leader can produce enough stability to address the basic fault lines of the economy.

Exporting to Excess

One of the lessons of the Great Recession was that what goes up must come down—Thailand, though, never went up. While all its peers were big winners in the great global boom of 2003 to 2007, Thailand slipped into what felt like a recession, as growth downshifted from 6 percent to less than 5 percent. Much of the problem was that the running street battles brought commercial life to a halt, creating a second major imbalance in the economy. Alongside the growing rural-urban divide, Thailand's domestic market was going flat. As consumption went slack, exports came to play a larger and larger role in the economy. In fact, though domestic investment was falling sharply, the heavy investment in new roads and factories before 1998 had put Thailand in a strong position for an export boom. Car exports from the (mainly Japanese) plants along the eastern seaboard have surged from insignificant numbers before 1998 to more than a million vehicles a year, making Thailand the biggest auto exporter in Asia after South Korea and Japan.

This apparent strength would be exposed as a vulnerability by the crisis of 2008. Remember, it's all about balance, and a strength taken too far can become a liability. Many nations seem to think that more exports are always better, but in Asia, economies from Taiwan to Thailand are suffering from too much dependence on exports. The mere mention of Asia conjures images of booming growth, a surging middle class flocking to new malls, and buzzing entrepreneurial energy. The reality is that the consumer piece of that picture is missing in nations such as Thailand, Malaysia, and Taiwan. At the peak of its power in the mid-1990s, Thailand with its population of sixty million was one of the world's top consumers of luxury goods, such as Mercedes-Benz cars, Volvo trucks, and Johnnie Walker Scotch, but those days are gone. By the 2000s, the Thai consumer was in sharp retreat.

Japan, the original Asian export powerhouse, was able to break through the middle-income barrier in the 1970s and 1980s because it created the right conditions for domestic investment and consumption to take off, and exports as a share of Japanese GDP averaged only 10 percent during that period. In Thailand, exports as a share of GDP have risen from 20 percent in 1980 and 35 percent in 1998 to 72 percent today, even though per capita income is still $5,000 compared with $35,000 in Japan. This is way out of whack, and it has led to trouble. When the 2008 crisis hit, and demand from the United States and Europe started to collapse, export-dependent nations like Thailand and Malaysia (where exports also account for about 70 percent of GDP) saw much sharper downturns than the Philippines and Indonesia (exports for both represent less than 30 percent of GDP).

One of the more unusual signs of stagnation is that Thailand has failed to enjoy the standard payoff when women work. Thailand has a very large population of working women, which normally translates into a higher level of economic development. It stands to reason that the more people there are earning incomes, the richer the society will be. But Thailand's high rate of female labor-force participation (66 percent) has produced no boost in growth. This is perhaps particularly surprising given that in Thailand the groom's family must pay a dowry to the bride, and not the other way around as in many Asian cultures. The male dowry would seem to suggest a society that traditionally puts a high value on the earning power of women. One reason why women have little impact on national growth in Thailand may be that they land mainly in low-end or temporary jobs, with little chance to make an impact on productivity. Another possibility is that when national politics are this big a mess, the gender politics of the workplace can't provide much of a boost.

By now Thai leaders should have taken steps to rebalance the economy to rely more on domestic investment, but instead they just kept doing what they were doing. Thaksin tried all manner of subsidies and supports to boost rural incomes, and he did make a big dent in rural poverty, but those handouts are no substitute for new businesses creating real jobs. Neither he nor his successors were able to create the conditions that would have drawn new investment to the heartland.

What Thailand needs is a transformation similar to the one that has unfolded in Turkey under the AK Party. Founded a decade ago, the AK Party led its own red shirt–style movement of relatively low-income and rural voters to election victories over an entrenched elite, but with one big difference: while Thaksin alienated the urban elite with heavy-handed policies, the AK Party avoided a confrontation. It began by providing the macroeconomic stability needed to help revive investment. As the economy picked up speed, the AK Party was able to satisfy its rural base by steering some of the new investment to previously neglected provinces, thereby rebalancing an economy once dominated by Istanbul, Ankara, and Izmir. And it was able to start winning over some of the urban elite as well.

It's not yet clear whether the current Thai government has the vision to provide that kind of strong leadership, or the maturity to avoid provoking another coup. Having cleaned up their debts since the crisis of 1998, Thai corporations have the money to invest; all they need for now is political stability and confidence. If the domestic market revives, guided by a red-shirt government, it's possible that Thailand may also see the emergence of real second cities in the years ahead. And that might even give Thailand a shot at becoming a breakout nation this decade.

The Acronym Nation

Mahathir Mohammed, one of the world's longest-serving leaders when he stepped down as Malaysian prime minister in 2003, has been blogging lately. He's been complaining that the soft authoritarian regime he created is now too tough on bloggers like him. For the tenth anniversary of 9/11, he repeated the charge that the U.S. government orchestrated the attack to give itself an excuse for making war on Muslims. It would be easy to dismiss all this as the ramblings of a bitter retiree, except that Mahathir's views still shape a tiger economy that lost its claws in the crisis of 1997–1998 and has yet to grow them back.

What Really Happened after 1998

At the height of the crisis Mahathir defied the great Western powers and appeared for a time to win. He blamed the malicious conniving of foreign speculators for triggering the crisis, and the harsh belt-tightening imposed by the IMF for making it worse. He broke from the Asian pack, many of whom were willing to listen to the IMF's advice to cut spending and rewrite the banking rules to make them more open, more Western. Mahathir instead slapped on currency controls to keep the foreign speculators from fleeing, and ramped up spending to restart the economy. It worked for a time—Mahathir looked like a hero to some—but now the verdict of history is in.

Malaysia's economy slowed dramatically after the Asian crisis. The annual growth rate fell by nearly half, to 5 percent or less, about the same rate at which the economies of Thailand and the Philippines settled. However, not all 5 percent growth rates are created equal, and Malaysian growth is of lower quality than its neighbors'. There is a widespread sense in Kuala Lumpur that the economy has been growing because of extensive government spending and fortunate circumstances—rising global commodity prices have been a huge boost to its rubber and palm oil exports—not from smart choices.

The spending launched by Mahathir to battle the Asian crisis is still flowing. While its neighbors started to clean up the red ink and cronyism, Malaysia went from running a surplus to running a deficit every year since 1998. Fueled by revenues from rising commodity prices, government spending rose from 20 percent of GDP in 1998 to 28 percent now—one of the highest levels in East Asia. Malaysia is the only Asian nation where government debt has risen as a share of GDP—from 20 percent to 50 percent over the last decade. Its large young workforce—60 percent of the population is under twenty-five—should be a competitive advantage, but so many are either not working or not employable that Malaysia has to import labor. The economy looks increasingly statist, slow-footed, uncompetitive, and the leadership adrift. The dramatic changes introduced in Indonesia, including the reform of the big conglomerates, the decline of public debt, and the shift of power to the provinces, have no parallel in Malaysia.

It is as if Malaysia were sliding backward. Instead of pushing itself to become more competitive in more advanced fields, Malaysia has been relying more and more on exports from its palm oil and rubber tree plantations, which were the core of its economy in the eighteenth century. Malaysia's share of global commodity exports is rising, but its share of global manufacturing exports has fallen by 26 percent in the last decade. Twenty years ago Malaysia's main exports were consumer electronics, which were assembled from components produced in other Asian countries for big global brands, and that is still the core of what remains of Malaysian manufacturing. But its manufacturing trade surplus has fallen sharply in the last decade, while China, Korea, Taiwan, and Singapore have all seen sharp increases.

The competitor that Malaysia seems to obsess about most is tiny Singapore. The rivalry goes back to the postcolonial period, when the British were pulling out, trying to figure out how to draw borders across a region with a Malay majority and a large Chinese minority. For a brief period the majority-Chinese enclave of Singapore joined in a federation with Malaysia, where Malays and other native people known as *Bumiputeras* comprised a 60 percent majority (with Chinese making up 25 percent of the population and Indians 7 percent). But ethnic tensions busted up the union. Mahathir was a critical player, charging that the Chinese business elites in Singapore were keeping the poor Malays down. Cast off on its own with few resources, the city-state of Singapore nonetheless became a remarkable success as a regional financial capital under the leadership of Lee Kuan Yew. Since 1965, its per capita income has grown seventy-one times, to $37,000, while Malaysia's has grown twenty times, to $8,000. When the overall size of Singapore's economy surpassed Malaysia's in 2011, there was bitterness in Kuala Lumpur: Mahathir commented that Singapore had gotten where it is by focusing only on growth, not on "a fair distribution of wealth between races as we have in Malaysia."

Malaysia's problems go beyond race and old rivalries. Every nation in Southeast Asia has seen protests against the Chinese business class at some point in the postcolonial period, but only Malaysia keeps the fires burning as a matter of public policy. Even before Mahathir took power in 1981, Malaysia had created a program of affirmative action to give *Bumiputeras* greater ownership stakes in companies. Mahathir built that program into a sprawling system of racial quotas and subsidies for all walks of life, from schools to government posts. Even today the 60 percent Malay majority feels they do not have a fair share of the economic pie, but the 30 percent Chinese minority feels just as marginalized, trying to compete against favored Malay tycoons. Where everyone's a victim, it's a wonder anyone ever had the confidence to invest in the economy.

The racially charged political environment has made it difficult to open doors, to dial back the privileges for *Bumiputeras*. Feeling shut out, foreign and local investors started to move their money abroad. As opportunities dried up, talented Malaysians began to move abroad too, and the brain drain made Malaysia even less attractive to investors.

Malaysia is the only Asian nation in which foreign direct investment is falling: the total flow of investment dollars went negative in early 2006 and is still flowing out fast, at a rate of −2.5 percent of GDP in the last quarter of 2011. One important thing economists look for in an emerging market is a strong "investment cycle," which shows that businesses have the confidence to spend money on new factories, new office buildings, new enterprises. In Malaysia money from local and Japanese investors fueled the rise of heavy industry through the 1990s, and rising exports drove up the rate of growth in the economy to a peak of about 9 percent before the Asian crisis. Then came the bust, and after 1997 private investment fell from 40 percent of GDP to 20 percent. This is the biggest difference with other Southeast Asian markets such as Indonesia: Malaysia has fallen off the investment map.

The Truth about Those "Evil" Speculators

The tragic thing is that Malaysia's turn inward likely springs from a misreading of the role those "evil" foreign speculators played in the crisis of 1998. In the worst crises of the emerging markets, from Mexico in the 1980s to East Asia in the 1990s, politicians were always quick to blame the sudden draining of the national accounts on feckless foreigners and their "hot money." Mahathir took this argument to its low point when he blamed the 1998 collapse of the ringgit on a worldwide conspiracy of Jewish financiers, but the basic idea that rich foreigners are always the first to run in a crisis is widely accepted. The truth is that the first to flee are most often the well-positioned insiders. That's why there is now a small industry devoted to tracking the trades of corporate insiders, and the same principle applies to countries. A rule of the road: watch the locals, they are always the first to know; they will be bringing money home to a breakout nation and fleeing one in trouble.

When financial crisis looms, money tends to flee in three phases. The first to go are large local investors, who in many emerging markets

must move money through underground channels because of rules lim-
iting capital flows. The use of back channels means that this flight of
money will not show up in the standard national accounting categories,
but often produces a marked rise in the catchall category called "errors
and omissions" in the balance-of-payments statements. Another common
dodge is that companies, from small businesses to state-owned giants,
will start under-reporting exports and over-reporting imports, as cover for
the money flowing out to banks and investments abroad. It is generally
the case that the best-connected tycoons will have the best information
on troubles at the treasury, and will lead the pack heading for the door.

Foreign creditors are the second pack to go—at that point the flow of
short-term interbank loans from foreign banks starts to slow or reverse.
The surge of short-term credit in the boom, and the reverse in the bust,
are easy to spot in specialized industry reports—but these sources are not
widely followed in the press. In the case of Malaysia none of the available
data are transparent enough to nail down exactly who left when in 1998.

Normally the last to go are the foreign investors in the local stock
market, which is widely tracked in real time. They are also the easiest
to spot, which is one reason why they attract so much blame from angry
locals. The rules in many emerging markets now require foreign investors
to report their holdings more fully than locals do. There is no crisis in
Malaysia right now, but it is not a vote of confidence that both locals and
foreigners are pulling money out of the country.

Grand but Unfinished Plans

Malaysia has an addiction to central planning that critics have likened to
the Soviet model but that probably owes more to the watery British socialism of the early postwar era. Malaysia's first five-year plan dates to 1955,
two years before independence, and its government has been planning
with gusto ever since.

Officials greet visitors with a blizzard of acronyms, describing their
many schemes to recapture growth, and as a whole they get the problems
pretty much right. With manufacturing flagging, and corporations moving abroad, they understand the need to regain competitiveness, restart
investment, raise the skill level of the workforce, even to make the ubiq-

uitous affirmative action system more transparent and market friendly. These goals are all built into the NEM (new economic model), which was unveiled in March 2010 and aims to double Malaysia's per capita income by 2020. The NEM includes both an ETP (economic transformation program) and a GTP (government transformation program), which have targeted dozens of NKEAs (national key economic areas) for reform, and launched no fewer than 131 EPPs (entry point projects) to fix those targets. The army of civil servants devoted to writing these acronyms seems to reflect a culture of micromanaging that goes back to Mahathir, who never saw an issue too small to comment on. Only now the culture lacks a single strongman to get things done.

The issue in Malaysia is execution: the country has become famous for presenting grand schemes that don't get built, for announcing new "growth corridors" that appear only on paper. Many of these plans look very old economy; current prime minister Najib Razak, for example, has plans for an "Iskandar region growth agenda," which is essentially a rebranded version of plans first hatched by Mahathir twenty years ago as the "South Johor economic corridor." Nothing happened, which is why, for instance, the Eighth Malaysian Plan ended in 2005 with 80 percent of the funds unspent.

To be fair, some of these plans do yield results: one success was a financial master plan that has done a lot to strengthen and consolidate a sprawling and corrupt banking system over the last decade. Others have yielded partial results: Mahathir's Multimedia Supercorridor—stretching thirty-one miles from downtown Kuala Lumpur to the international airport—has fallen well short of his vision that it would become a new Silicon Valley. As of 2009 Malaysian papers were reporting that many of the new tenants were government agencies. Lately, and encouragingly, it has been booking major multinationals to use its space for data centers— still not the core of a modern innovation economy.

Over the years Mahathir faced a series of confrontations with key centers of power in Malaysia: the provincial royalty, the courts, and the civil service. He emerged victorious each time, creating new institutions that were loyal to him, but they now stand as obstacles in the way of his successors, Abdullah Badawi and Najib. Both created new agencies to try to control the old, and thus added a new layer of acronyms. Najib's is called the Performance Management and Delivery Unit (PEMANDU). Staffed by private-sector consultants on contract and led by a turnaround specialist, its mission is to narrow the number of targets the government is shooting at, and to make sure it scores some hits. The fewer new acronyms they produce, the more likely they are to succeed. Malaysia needs to move on and rebuild the institutions damaged during the later stages of Mahathir's rule. Nearly a decade after his retirement, Mahathir should not be casting such a long shadow on the country.

10

The Gold Medalist

WHEN I WANT TO TAKE THE PULSE of the global economy, I look for vital signs not in London, not in Frankfurt, not in Tokyo, not even in Mumbai. I look in Seoul. South Korea is one of the first major countries to report economic data, and the numbers are fast, accurate, and reliable. More than that, South Korean companies are major players in a broad selection of industries, from cars to chemicals, and they are very open to outsiders: foreigners own more than one-third of Korean stocks, among the highest shares in the world. As a result the KOSPI index, the Korean equivalent of the S&P 500, provides a highly accurate picture of global trends. Whether the big story is Silicon Valley and technology, as it was in 2000, or China and the large emerging markets, as has been the case over the past decade, South Korea is always at the heart of the action. Little wonder then that in some financial circles the index from Seoul goes by the moniker "Dr. Kospi."

South Korea's rare ability to stay at the cutting edge of fast-changing industries has put it in a class by itself. South Korea and Taiwan are the gold medalists of the global economic race, the only two nations in recorded economic history to achieve five straight decades of growth above 5 percent. Both nations are former colonies of Japan that built their success by copying essentials of the Japanese system. They invest heavily in research and development and work to contain the kind of income

*Clever Korean branding: the pop idol Rain—performing
above in Guangzhou, China—has given himself a one-word
stage name that can be understood almost everywhere.*

inequality that can produce popular resistance to rapid growth. Both are
at a turning point as their economics mature; with per capita incomes
of more than $20,000, growth is naturally slowing. Korea, however, has
a much better chance than Taiwan of catching up with Japan, whose
income level has stagnated at $35,000 for many years.

Though economists have long talked about South Korea and Taiwan
as a pair, because they grew at such similar speeds for so long, their
basic differences are glaring and growing. South Korea, with a GDP of
$1.1 trillion and a population of forty-eight million, is twice the size of
Taiwan ($505 billion and twenty-three million) and is pulling away as
a competitive force: in 2006 the total value of the South Korean stock
market surpassed Taiwan's for the first time, and it is now considerably
larger, at $1 trillion versus $700 billion. Intriguingly, the family dynasties that still dominate the top-thirty Korean companies, and that were
widely seen as the heart of a severe "crony capitalism" problem at the
depths of the Asian financial crisis in 1998, have reformed so dramatically that they are now a core strength for the local economy. Hyundai,
spoofed a decade ago for its authoritarian management style, impen-
etrable bookkeeping, and laughably bad cars, is now a world-beater. Taiwan, meanwhile, sticks to the narrow niche of banging out goods sold
under the "made in" label of other countries. And while both gold medalists are the richer halves of divided nations, Taiwan has little to gain
from the distant prospect of reunification with the much-larger Chinese
mainland, while South Korea is already preparing to adopt the well-
disciplined workforce of North Korea, which could fail at any moment.
Of the two gold medalists South Korea has the better chance to be a
breakout nation, in the sense of continuing to grow faster than most
people would expect.

South Korea is coming out of Japan's shadow and redefining the
limits of what is possible for a manufacturing powerhouse. These are
both intensely conformist societies in which popular opinion tends to
cement behind the status quo, but in South Korea the definition of the
status quo can change in a flash. When crisis hits, Japan scrambles to
defend the existing economic system, while South Korea mobilizes to rip
it down and rebuild. The contrast could not have been more striking in

the crises of the 1990s, when Japan struggled for years to keep bankrupt companies alive, and South Korea quickly cleaned house. South Korea has become a model of change; Japan, a symbol of the status quo. As the KOSPI index became a mirror of world markets in recent decades, Japan's Nikkei index fell into a long swoon largely impervious to global trends. It is symptomatic of these shifting fortunes that today the richest man in Japan is an ethnic Korean, the billionaire entrepreneur Masayoshi Son.

No Service Please, We're Korean

My sense of what's happening on the Korean peninsula has changed dramatically since the great global boom of 2003–2007, when the Korean "miracle" appeared to be running out of steam. Like most Asian nations, South Korea had grown since World War II by manufacturing low- or moderate-priced goods for sale to rich nations, and this strategy seemed to be reaching its limits. Seoul had negotiated earlier development steps—like the shift from light to heavy manufacturing, textiles to steel—with great speed and skill. Starting with Park Chung Hee, the general who took over in a 1961 coup and led the nation until his assassination in 1979, a series of autocratic Korean presidents proved remarkably adept at running a command economy, building national industrial behemoths like Samsung and Hyundai. South Korea became a global leader in steel, petrochemicals, and shipbuilding. By 2003 South Korea had become a vibrant democracy, but the basic economic model had not changed: manufacturing accounted for such a large share of the economy, and South Korea already held such a sizable share of global manufacturing exports, that there simply didn't appear to be much room to grow.

The next natural development step was long overdue, and Seoul knew it. That would have been to start nurturing a stronger domestic consumer market, to balance exports, and building service industries like finance, tourism, and retail stores. But for mystifying reasons, Seoul has never been able to develop a service sector with the deftness it brings to manufacturing. The government can't seem to resist interfering in service industries, which even today in South Korea have a productivity growth rate about

half as high as that of manufacturing, largely because of meddlesome government regulations and guidance. After the tech bubble burst in 2001,
Seoul tried to foster a consumer revolution by encouraging the spread
of credit cards, but it got a household debt crisis instead. Many Koreans
maxed out on multiple cards at the first opportunity. Today spending by
individuals continues to shrink as a share of GDP, from 75 percent in
1970s to 53 percent, almost 20 percentage points below the average for
countries in South Korea's income class. Households are still digging their
way out from under those huge credit card bills, and household debt as
a share of the economy is 146 percent, one of the highest levels in the
world. Indeed the South Korean consumer is now suffering from a case of
"boomophobia," a fear of debt that often afflicts nations recovering from
a boom-bust cycle.

But I now see another, very different side of South Korea despite the
stunted development of the consumer market and the service industries.
At a certain point, when an apparently unconventional approach is working, you have to rethink the conventions, not the approach. South Korea
continues to export its way to prosperity by way of manufacturing, against
increasingly harsh odds. The export-led growth model was relatively simple to execute back in the 1960s because there were only three major
players—Japan, Taiwan, and South Korea—but now Thailand, Malaysia,
Indonesia, China, India, Vietnam, Bangladesh, and others have joined
the competition. Yet South Korea has managed to outplay everyone at this
game, particularly Japan and Taiwan, its rivals for the most prestigious
and profitable niches in manufacturing.

A rule of the road: don't get hung up on rules. In the past, when manufacturing accounted for 25 to 30 percent of GDP, the manufacturing story
typically reached its natural limits and the economy started to shift focus
to services. Normally this transformation comes relatively early in the
growth game, at a per capita income as low as $10,000. This was the case
in the United States, Japan, and even Germany, which is still a manufacturing powerhouse. South Korea is now fifteen years past the $10,000
income level, indeed it has more than doubled that level, and yet Korea's
manufacturing sector is still expanding steadily. So perhaps it is carving
out a rare exception to the normal evolutionary path.

The "Germany of Asia"

In a testament to Korea's unique industrial prowess, manufacturing now forms 31 percent of the economy, up from 26 percent just five years ago. Korea is also moving beyond its traditional strengths in cars and steel to emerge as a global player in new growth industries such as industrial machinery, robotics, aerospace, biotech, rechargeable batteries, and material science. The result is GDP growth of over 4 percent—no mean achievement for a nation as rich as South Korea. People are starting to talk about South Korea as the "Germany of Asia"—the regional gold standard for high-end manufacturing, a position heretofore held by Japan.

The big breakthrough came in the mid-1990s when South Korean manufacturers started to challenge the global dominance of big Western brands. Until then developing nations had limited their ambitions to making goods sold under a brand based in Europe or the United States, and skeptics doubted whether they could ever master the marketing arts required to give a foreign name genuine brand cachet in the West or Japan. No Third World company had ever gotten a real grip on the street slang or comic timing it takes to pull off cutting-edge advertising in New York or Tokyo, and when companies like Samsung started spending heavily to promote their own brand internationally, many analysts saw this as a waste of money for a country whose real strengths could be only cost and efficiency. Taiwan was praised for sticking to its knitting—making laptops and other consumer technology products sold by Dell, HP, and other big Western producers.

South Korea has proved that critique wrong. While a few emerging nations, led by Mexico and South Africa, have produced strong multinational companies, with very few exceptions they are actually regional companies competitive on their home continents in fields like telecommunications, media, and brewing. South Korea alone has produced genuinely global brands built on high-end manufacturing led by three of its original giants, Samsung, Hyundai, and LG, which together now account for 16 percent of South Korean GDP. They are making breakthroughs not only in the United States and Europe, but also in emerging markets ranging from Asia to Latin America. South Korea is the only manufacturing exporter to have gained market share in China over the last decade, while all the other big manufacturing powers—including Japan, Taiwan, the United States, and Europe—have lost export share to countries that sell mainly raw materials, like Indonesia, Russia, and Brazil.

This relentless push into emerging markets is making it possible for South Korea to redefine what is possible in global manufacturing. Five years ago, when analysts considered the prospects for South Korean companies they looked at a traditional range of potential markets, predominantly in the West and Japan. Now that range has opened to the entire world. It's happened incredibly fast: in 2003 two-thirds of South Korean exports went to developed nations; in 2011 two-thirds went to developing nations. Last year South Korea exported more to China—from mining equipment to steel and cosmetics—than to the United States, the EU, and Japan combined. And in this case the West was particularly slow to see how quickly the rules of the economic regime were changing, how fast Korea was going global, even at a time when "globalization" was still a favorite buzzword.

Contrast South Korea with Japan, and its achievement is even more impressive. Japan, the original export-manufacturing juggernaut, now earns just over 10 percent of its GDP from exports, which is less than it did a decade ago. The rising value of the yen, particularly against both the euro and the Korean won, has rendered Japanese exports steadily more expensive and less competitive over the last two decades. Meanwhile South Korea's exports continue to grow at a strong double-digit pace, more than twice as fast as the overall economy, and now account for 53 percent of GDP, up about 20 percentage points in just ten years. In the last decade South Korea has become one of the most open major economies in the world, with total trade equal to 100 percent of GDP, and it has maintained its share of the global economy at 2 percent, while Japan has seen its share fall by nearly half, to 7 percent. In global economic competition everything is relative, and relative to Japan, South Korea is an overwhelming winner.

A Conservative Society That Mobilizes in the Face of Crisis

The cultural response to crisis plays a big role: Japan's effort to bail out failing companies in the early 1990s led to increased government ownership in the economy and falling productivity. In the crisis of 1998, when exploding foreign debts led to a collapse of Asian currencies, South Korea was forced to run hat in hand to the International Monetary Fund for a record $58 billion bailout package—and it looked like it would take many years for the Koreans to pay it back. At home the sense of humiliation at the need for an IMF loan and its tough conditions touched off anti-globalization street rallies in Seoul but also inspired a national campaign to turn the economy around fast. While the citizens of other crisis-hit countries (including Taiwan) moved their wealth to the Cayman Islands for protection, Koreans began mobilizing to pay the national debt, waiting in long lines to donate their gold jewelry to the cause. Roughly 40 percent of the biggest Korean companies were allowed to go under, including well-known multinationals like Daewoo, and many more were sold off to new owners. After a purgatory year South Korea was soon back in the thick of global events as South Korean tech stocks rose sharply in the dotcom-driven bacchanalia of 1999 and 2000. By mid-2001 the IMF debt was repaid.

It is this embrace of creative destruction that separates South Korea from both Taiwan and Japan. The great national housecleaning set up Korean conglomerates to take on the world. After 1998 the big Korean corporations brought in more professional managers to oversee day-to-day operations, but with the founding families still in charge the long-term strategic decisions were no less bold. Since 2000 these companies have moved aggressively to build plants in China, where they are producing cars, petrochemicals, and consumer-technology products like mobile handsets. That's a major reason why Korean manufacturers have maintained a cost advantage over Japanese competitors. Since 2004 South Korea's share of the global market for IT products including cell phones and LCD TV screens has roughly doubled to 30 percent. That gain has come mainly at the expense of Japan, as Korean companies beat their Japanese rivals in the race to establish premier brands in big emerging markets. Asked why Japanese companies have allowed themselves to fall behind Korean rivals, a Japanese economist recently told me, "No sense of urgency." Japan is comfortable with its average income of $35,000.

South Korea is now outhustling Japan even in the research and development game, a critical measure of commitment to innovation and change in any country. In the early 1970s, President Park set out explicitly to copy

Japan's R&D strategy, which was led by the government. Today the South Korean government is only peripherally involved, and the big private companies have taken over. They have their own research think tanks, employing a vast army of researchers, and they have boosted spending as a percentage of GDP from an already high level of 2.6 percent a decade ago to 3.7 percent by 2009, the year South Korea passed Japan. Much of the Korean R&D spending goes into technology and automobiles, which explains the extraordinary breakthrough that cars from Hyundai and Kia have made in the U.S. and global markets.

Father Dictates Best

The rise of China has produced hot debate over whether democratic or authoritarian systems are more likely to stimulate growth. My sense is that what matters is not so much the political system as the motivation and vision of the leaders, but on the corporate level the global rise of family-owned and intensely patriarchal companies like Samsung and Hyundai adds weight to the argument that autocratic systems can be very effective. To many emerging countries, building a globally competitive "national car" was once seen as the ultimate symbol of arrival on the world stage, and several (Malaysia, Yugoslavia, Russia) have tried and failed in recent decades. China and India are attempting now with the Chery and the Tata. So far, only South Korea has beaten the odds, and it achieved this singular feat with very strong hands at the wheel.

Hyundai's risky 1986 decision to enter the North American market—with cars then technologically inferior to Japanese and European rivals—has been attributed to the "bulldozer leadership" style of the group's charismatic founder, Chung Ju Young. The first year brought surprise success—owing in no small part to the fact that many Americans thought Hyundai Motors was a new subsidiary of Honda, a mistake encouraged by the similarity between the company logos. Soon, however, a combination of quality problems and disputes between Korean and American managers led to a decade of weak sales and to late-night TV jokes about Hyundai being a Korean version of the Yugo, an infamous flop out of 1970s Yugoslavia. Even ten years later Toyota executives still dismissed Korean rivals as competition only for used Toyotas.

Instead of retreating, Hyundai decided to push deeper into the U.S. market under the leadership of the founder's eldest surviving son, Chung Mong Koo. Aiming to build a reputation for cars that are reliable and affordable, Chung pushed hard on quality control and in 1998 decided to offer a ten-year warranty, twice as long as any then available from other manufacturers. The U.S. media said the offer was "crazy," and Hyundai's American managers would later attribute this bold stroke to Chung's iron hand. In a more democratic corporate culture the risk of the ten-year warranty likely would have killed the idea, but it proved critical to changing Hyundai's image.

These moves were coming amid chaos in the Korean car industry, as the Asian crisis forced weaker players to fold. Daewoo was sold to GM. The small auto division of Samsung—widely seen as a vanity project of the founder's family—was sold to Renault. Kia was taken over by Hyundai, the one Korean car company to survive the crisis. Hyundai took the failure of its rivals as an opportunity to expand and poured money into the effort to get the look, feel, and new-car smell just right.

The U.S. skeptics had another field day when Hyundai opened its first U.S. plant in 2005 at a time when car sales were flagging. Did the Koreans really think they could succeed with a plant in Alabama when headlines were forecasting the "Death of Detroit"? The Alabama plant—unencumbered by the union rules that drive up costs in Detroit—is now one of the most efficient in the United States, and Hyundai's leaders have said this plant was essential in creating the perception that Hyundai stands not just for reliability but for "American-made" reliability, dampening the risks of trade frictions. By 2011 Hyundai and Kia were two of the fastest-growing brands in the United States, well reviewed, highly ranked for quality, and stealing market share from Toyota and other Japanese brands in the mass market for (new) family cars.

The year before, Hyundai had also achieved its strategic goal of becoming one of the world's top-five car companies, giving South Korea 8 percent of the global car market, up from 4 percent in 2004. While the Japanese carmakers have been slow to move into emerging markets, Hyundai has been quick to identify and pursue opportunities to build small cars in India, as a base for sales not only in India but also in Africa.

It has hired a former GM designer, and for its Kia subsidiary a former Audi designer, with an eye toward creating models that work in emerging markets all over the globe, including China.

The Korean experience backs up the argument that the strongest corporate model is family owned but publicly traded and professionally managed. The family gives the company an inherent focus on the long run, while selling stock on the open market forces the family to keep the books clean, to put experts in charge of day-to-day operations, and to keep the loopy cousins out of corner offices. The rising South Korean brands are strong case studies, but far from the only good examples. McKinsey studies showed that family firms beat global stock market returns by an average of 3 percent a year between 1997 and 2009 and came out of the 2008 crisis in much better shape than nonfamily rivals, with less debt, more cash, and higher R&D investment throughout the downturn. The international media focus far less on the basic strengths of family firms than on the frequent scandals, which is understandable. Looking inside the closets of the rich and powerful can be irresistible, and there is dirt to be found. On a trip to India Warren Buffett was recently asked what he thought of family-run companies and he responded, "They're great, until the families start fighting."

The big South Korean conglomerates are now run by a very powerful second or third generation: men who inherited the job but arrived with extremely strong personal qualities and credentials. However, second-generation leaders were also at the helm of some of the big conglomerates that failed in 1998, and the jury is still out on the third generation. For the next five to ten years, the key Korean companies appear to be in good hands. After that, who knows if they'll start fighting?

Why Taiwan Is No Korea

South Korea's unique success in building global brands—the stories of Samsung and LG are as striking as Hyundai's—also offers a big edge over Taiwan, its only real rival as a growth gold medalist. The difference in approach was night and day. From early on Taiwan was willing to work with Japan, while South Korea just wanted to beat Japan. Rather than confront larger Japanese rivals, the Taiwanese did manufacturing jobs for them on contract, often using their close cultural ties and proximity to the vast labor force of China. Taiwanese became by far the largest investors in factories in China, many of which are a short hop across the Taiwan Strait in Fujian Province, and for decades this was enough to produce steady rapid growth.

The problem, which has become increasingly clear in the last five years, is the narrowness of Taiwan's niche: its share of the global market for laptops has risen from 30 to 80 percent over the last decade, yet its companies have no pricing power because Western brands can easily turn to contract manufacturers elsewhere, or just play the five big producers in Taiwan off one another. And as China begins to lose some of its competitive edge, particularly in labor costs, so too does Taiwan. Its share of global exports has fallen sharply in the last decade, by about 20 percent, while South Korea's has increased by roughly the same measure. For years, Taipei has talked about ways to build its own global brands, with hardly any so far to show for it.

The Taipei stock market consists mainly of small companies that make parts for PCs that run Windows and Intel products, a niche so narrow that the Taipei stock market has been out of favor and underperforming ever since the tech bubble burst in 2000. No one looks to Taipei the way they look to Dr. Kospi, as a window on global trends. Instead of investing at home, for most of the last decade rich Taiwanese have been moving money abroad at a brisk pace, about $2 billion a month, investing in rival emerging markets like China and India, or in California real estate. One result of this persistent outflow is that every time world markets go bust, Taiwan investors always seem to turn up holding a share of the losing hand, a trend witnessed most recently with the fall of Lehman Brothers in 2008.

Since the early postwar years Taiwan has been much more open to outsiders than South Korea has been. (Seoul is wide open to foreigners who want to invest in the stock markets, but not those who want to control or work in Korean companies.) This is due in part to their very different experiences under the Japanese empire, which began expanding south in the late nineteenth century and seized Taiwan as its first overseas possession in 1895. Japan tried to turn Taiwan into a model colony, investing heavily in agriculture and building out an electric grid even into the countryside. The Japanese occupation of South Korea in 1910 was much more brutal, marked by constant local revolts and ending in 1945 with the rural areas still, literally, in the dark. So when Chinese Nationalists under Chiang Kai-shek fled to Taiwan and took over administration of the island at the end of World War II, they governed a less-traumatized population and were building up the economy from a higher base than their counterparts in South Korea.

South Korea emerged from the war ravaged, with vast tracts of the landscape and the cities devastated, but as a result it was more intent on building economic self-sufficiency than Taiwan was. Today South Korea is one of the top-five nations in terms of winning international patents and is rapidly expanding its share of new ones, while Taiwan is not even among the top twenty. Often Taiwanese manufacturers are content to buy essential advanced components from Japan rather than develop them at home. This dependence was made obvious after the massive earthquake that hit Japan in April 2011, which disrupted supply chains in Taiwan but did not affect South Korea nearly as much.

One gets the sense that the leadership in Taipei is starting to grasp at straws in its search for a new growth formula. Lately there has been talk about boosting tourism, and here Taiwan does have some potential upside if it can grab a reasonable share of the rising tide of tourism out of China. More than fifty million Chinese traveled abroad in 2010, and the number is growing at 20 percent annually, but this is unlikely to transform Taiwan when tourism accounts for less than 5 percent of GDP. It sometimes seems like every nation with a half-decent beach or a pretty mountain range is peddling tourism as a development plan, but the reality is that promoting tourism barely moves the needle in a reasonably large economy.

South Korea's economy is far more diversified than Taiwan's, and in more solid ways. Its brand names have pricing power, profits are strong, and they produce a wide range of goods. Though most famous for cars and consumer technology, the companies listed on KOSPI are quite evenly spread across many sectors. In fact the fastest-growing sector of South Korea's market over the last decade was not cars or technology but shipbuilding. Korea has long had a strong navy and history of building innovative ships; today the top-three global shipbuilders in terms of both size and technology are all South Korean.

Korean construction companies are also expanding fast. They developed expertise in factory engineering and construction during the government push in the 1970s and 1980s to build homegrown steel and petrochemical industries, and they are now putting that experience to use abroad. Though Korea has no oil, its construction firms got a big boost from the petroleum-price surge of recent years because they are global leaders in the construction of oil facilities. Korean construction and engineering firms are expanding into the Middle East, Central Asia, Africa, and Southeast Asia. This diversity is why KOSPI offers such an unusually accurate gauge of the global economy's vital signs.

South Korea's desire for self-sufficiency shows up in the corporate culture as well. Rather than buy businesses abroad, South Koreans mainly build their own, and in 2010 Korean direct investment in plants and businesses overseas hit $140 billion, up 300 percent since 2005. This expansion has been central to South Korea's ability to keep growing as a manufacturing power, but the country has also become highly efficient at home. Though South Korea has a significantly larger manufacturing sector than Taiwan, it employs a much smaller factory workforce (about 15 percent of the total labor force, compared to 25 percent in Taiwan). It also has one of the most dense robot populations in the world. That means South Korea is doing a lot more with fewer workers and is much more productive than Taiwan.

The bottom line is that South Korean corporate leaders were more visionary than their rivals in Taiwan, which is a bit surprising. Taiwan is arguably the more entrepreneurial and less insular culture. For one thing Taiwanese companies are more open to foreigners than Korean firms; it's much more common to see Indian programmers at a small Taiwanese company than at a Korean one. Taiwan is also a nation of small and medium-size companies, where firms don't get very big in part because employees are always leaving to start rival businesses. Today the top-thirty companies in South Korea account for 70 percent of the economy, and gigantism is not typically a model for creative innovation.

Most Koreans are happy to join a gargantuan company for life and wouldn't think of breaking away to compete with it. Yet the Korean preference for top-down control has not stifled creativity in new technology and emerging industries such as online gaming, biotechnology, and even in the arts. Since about 2000 Korea has been challenging Japan as a leader in the Asian pop-culture market, exporting soap operas, music, cosmetics, and apparel throughout the region. Korean TV dramas like *Dae Jang Geum*, the rags-to-riches story of a palace chef, have become the rage from Singapore to Beijing. Labeled *Hallyu*, the "Korean Wave," their surging popularity has transformed the Busan film festival into the biggest international cinema event in the region. Even Bollywood in India, long known for plagiarizing scripts from Hollywood, has been turning to Korean films for inspiration, with recent hits such as *Murder 2*, inspired by the Korean thriller *The Chaser*. K-pop now rivals J-pop at the top of the billboard charts even in Japan, the world's second-largest music market. In a duel of girl bands, both AKB48 of Japan and Girl's Generation of South Korea have become YouTube sensations, with roughly equal tens of millions of hits, but Girl's Generation is getting hits from throughout Asia as well as Europe and the Americas, while AKB48's hits come almost exclusively from Japan. The Korean gifts for music and storytelling also drive branding arms of its giant corporations, many of which have big in-house advertising departments in keeping with their preference for tight control of all facets of the manufacturing and selling process.

The Korea Discount

Because of lingering doubts about family-owned businesses and their willingness to change, global markets continue to impose a discount price on Korean stocks. Some efforts to clean up the murky accounting of family-run companies are still works in progress: it was not until early 2011 that South Korea introduced standardized quarterly consolidated financial statements—reporting that is a matter of course in developed economies. While some Korean companies still do business the old-fashioned way—greasing the palms of politicians for funding and contracts—corruption has diminished significantly in day-to-day business dealings and is now seen as a company risk, not a country risk.

Finally, some of the family-business owners are still seen as empire

builders, interested more in global market share than in generating profits for shareholders. South Korean giants are much less likely to pay out
dividends than Taiwan companies are—but that's also why they have so
much cash to spend on R&D and to reinvest for future growth. None of
this suggests that South Korea can build on its manufacturing success
forever, only that there is at least enough potential left in its global export
strategy to continue for a while longer.

The imbalances of the economy may yet undermine Korea. It is unde-
niably worrisome that large Korean companies see opportunities almost
exclusively abroad, and the stagnation of the service sector and the consumer market remain true anomalies in an economy of Korea's size. In
contrast to the triumph of Samsung and Hyundai, Korean banks and
telecommunication companies have not been able to succeed even at
home. The chairman of one of Korea's largest banks recently told me,
quite candidly, that the banks in general are very slow to keep up with
the innovative products and efficient services of their international peers.
That's why few of the forty largest Korean conglomerates borrow from
Korean banks. This also disadvantages small and medium-size Korean
companies, which don't have the same access to international lenders
that larger corporations do.

Sometimes it appears as if South Korea has a cultural blindness to
the value of services. As gracious and hospitable as any people anywhere,
Koreans seem to have a bias against paying for intangible products. For
all the innovation Seoul brings to manufacturing, the top hotel in Seoul,
the Shilla, has not seen a hot new competitor in two decades. When I
asked a local businessmen how this could be, he said Koreans don't like
to pay for services and prefer to just stay with friends or family when
they're in town.

The government has grown increasingly conscious of the political
risks of the manufacturing boom. South Korea is an intensely egalitarian society increasingly dominated by a few big manufacturing combines.
In its early years the country managed to grow while reducing inequality, first through land reforms that distributed property formerly held by
large landowners or the Japanese after World War II, and later through a
commitment to universal education that borders on fanaticism. From the

1950s to the 1980s South Korea had by far the highest levels of school enrollment among emerging nations, and today it also has the highest enrollment in basic education (and the third highest in higher education) of any nation, period. Spending on education has greatly outstripped spending on any other category, with the result that an unusually high percentage of Koreans have the credentials to enter the white-collar workforce. It's possible that these leveling trends helped to mobilize a consensus for radical change, as when South Koreans rallied to save the economy during the 1998 crisis.

But in recent years, as the conglomerates have grown more global and profitable, inequality has begun to inch upward. Koreans believe that wealth is more and more concentrated in the hands of the few big-business families that are succeeding in the global markets. Though conspicuous display abounds in the Korean middle class, the opposite ethos seems to govern the super-rich. None of the billionaires in Korea have a net worth of more than $10 billion, and their combined net worth as a share of the economy is just 4 percent, one of the lowest among emerging markets. If they are living a life of fabulous luxury, they are doing so with the utmost discretion.

How Unification Could Play Out in South Korea's Favor

Despite the growing differences, Taiwan and South Korea still share certain similarities. Their basic growth paths have been strikingly similar for the past five decades. They both have rapidly aging populations, which threaten to undermine the prospects for an Asian century. The fertility rates of South Korea, Japan, and Taiwan rank 218th, 219th, and 220th in the world, respectively, all clustered around 1.2 children per woman, well below the replacement rate of 2.1. With working-age populations on the verge of rapidly shrinking, tensions between workers and retirees are bound to increase.

South Korea and Taiwan also share an unusual status as the richer part of divided nations, a factor that played no small role in their relentless focus on economic growth. At the end of World War II, South Korea was divided from North Korea, and Taiwan separated from mainland China. For years both have faced the perceived threat of invasion—reason enough to stay vigilant in pursuit of economic and military strength. In the future, however, these divisions are more likely to play out in South Korea's favor. Taiwan has become overly dependent on cheap manufacturing labor in China, which is starting to lose its cost advantage, and the prospect of reunification with the mainland remains distant. For some years now many Korean leaders have assumed that the North was doomed to fail under the inept guidance of the late leader Kim Jong Il and his family, which is a big reason why Seoul has kept its government debt down to just 34 percent of GDP: it is preparing to absorb the high cost of rebuilding the North, which is increasingly viewed as an investment that could unleash more growth. In fact South Korean policy makers are so sure of the unification idea that when I recently asked a top national security adviser whether he had considered China's long-term strategic interest in keeping the Koreas divided, his response was that the lesson from history is that whenever China interfered in the Korean peninsula the cost of the invasion had often led to the downfall of its empire.

The defining feature of Korea's success over the past decade has been its ability to move out of Japan's long shadow as a manufacturing power. In a recent conversation Un Chan Chung, a former prime minister of South Korea, reminded me that his country is already the seventh-largest economy in the world, among nations with a population of more than fifty million and a per capita GDP of over $20,000. Given how rapidly we have seen political regime change transform Central Europe and now the Middle East, it is not unthinkable that South Korea could grow significantly larger in a single leap if a unified Korea emerges within the next five or ten years. Unification would add large coal reserves to an economy with no energy resources of its own, and a disciplined population of twenty-four million northerners to South Korea's already considerable labor muscle. Those who doubt how successfully the South can adopt the shut-in Communist society of the North should consider how quickly it is adapting to emerging trends all over the globe. That's why it now stands alone as the sole gold medalist.

11

The Endless Honeymoon

IN 2003 SOUTH AFRICA WAS GETTING READY to celebrate ten years of freedom since the end of white minority rule, but it was also suffering a case of guilt by association. Across the Limpopo River, Zimbabwe was disintegrating. Given both countries' histories of racial strife, many observers figured it was only a matter of time before South Africa, too, succumbed to violent demands that whites yield a share of the wealth to the millions of blacks who were still mired in poverty, without jobs or land of their own. That March I decided to go see for myself if these dark predictions had merit.

Arriving on a Sunday morning in Cape Town, my first stop was Robben Island, the infamous former penal colony where Nelson Mandela and other leaders of the black liberation movement were held for decades. Its squalid jail cells were the very symbol of apartheid-era oppression, but I found to my astonishment that many of the retired white prison guards were still living on the island with several former black prisoners, who were serving as guides to visitors like me. The ex-prisoners were living quietly alongside their ex-jailers, with no sign of imminent explosion. Robben Island was typical of the "forget the past and get on with the future" attitude I found among most South Africans during my travels from Port Elizabeth at the tip of the eastern Cape to Pretoria in the north.

*In South Africa the limits to racial integration outside
the office environment are clear in fine restaurants,
where it is hard to find blacks among the diners.*

For many years it struck me as remarkable that most black South
Africans were so determined to reconcile—the grace and statesmanship
for which Nelson Mandela became internationally famous appeared to
spring from a steadfast national character. Now, after many years without real progress, that statesmanship is starting to look like stagnation.
During the years of the economic boom from 2003 to 2007, South African growth did accelerate but only from 3 percent to 5 percent, much
slower than the emerging-market average, and it has since fallen back to

3 percent. The economy needs to grow at least twice that fast to solve its most basic flaw, a severe unemployment problem. Since the African National Congress (ANC) took power in 1994 the unemployment rate has remained at about 25 percent, a level that would almost certainly incite unrest in other nations. If anything, the economy looks likely to become less dynamic, not more: a working paper from the International Monetary Fund recently estimated South Africa's long-term GDP growth rate at just 2 percent, the most disappointing result for any major emerging market in recent times.

To this day South Africa is a developed market wrapped inside an emerging market. Because most white families have two cars, the overall ratio of cars to people is quite high, at 109 per 1,000 people, even though the ratio is much lower in the black population. In fact black South Africans are about as likely to own a car as Indians are, even though South Africa's average income level is five times higher than that in India. The amount held in pension funds is extremely large—more than $7,200 per person, compared to $267 in Russia, also mostly in white hands.

The economic justice that was a chief promise of Mandela and the ANC remains a distant hope. Among blacks the rate of joblessness remains abnormally high (30 percent), but for whites the figure is markedly lower (6 percent). Three out of four young blacks in rural areas have no job. Meanwhile urban professionals have no unemployment problem at all (0.4 percent). The income gap is just as wide today as it was when the ANC finally toppled the apartheid government nearly two decades ago; the standard measure of inequality, the Gini coefficient, is still stuck at 0.7 percent—one of the highest rates in the world. (At zero on the Gini scale, everyone has the same income, and at 1, just one person has all the income.) Few other countries, including Zimbabwe and Namibia, have a Gini coefficient of more than 0.6. Thus the surreal calm of South Africa grows more difficult to explain every year.

The Indian Honeymoon

The peace and quiet defies the momentum of an age when the Internet is accelerating the pace of social revolts, even in repressive dictatorships. Instead, South Africa is a real democracy with a progressive constitution, an independent judiciary, and free media. Despite the dominance of a single party, there is no censorship, no vote rigging, and no suppression of debate in the Parliament or press. The traditional democratic tools employed to hold leaders accountable are all in place, but they remain largely unused.

While it's common for liberation movements to enjoy a long honeymoon, the ANC has been living off the liberation dividend for close to two decades. The only similar situation I can think of is postcolonial India, where the Congress Party led the fight for independence and traded off that achievement to remain in power from 1950 until 1977, with limited economic gain to show for it. India's performance was so doggedly weak that economists looking for religious and cultural explanations came to call 3 percent the "Hindu rate of growth." In South Africa no one is looking to explain the "ANC rate of growth," which is also about 3 percent, much less protest against a system that produces so much stability and such modest progress.

The black majority is forever grateful to the ANC for overcoming the singular evil of apartheid, which deprived blacks of citizenship and confined them to inferior homelands with substandard housing, schools, hospitals, beaches—everything. It may take a new generation to adopt a critical view of ANC leadership. This too is reminiscent of India: after the demise of the repressive old regime the sense of relief endures, and it can take decades for a real opposition to materialize. Until some of its stronger leaders break away from the ANC (as internal opponents of the Congress Party ultimately did in India), they represent no challenge to the party's hold on the presidency.

So South Africa has stabilized at a remarkably low equilibrium, stuck in a kind of time warp. The legacies of the apartheid years still distort the system and stifle change. During the 1980s and 1990s, when the apartheid regime was under international sanctions, it developed one of the most top-heavy forms of capitalism on the planet, with much of the economy under state control and the rest in the hands of a few dominant cartels. The ANC not only has kept that basic structure but also has replaced the whites-only Nationalist Party with itself as the dominant ruling party, backed by its allies in perhaps the most powerful union movement in the developing world. None of these power centers—not the state, not the private companies, not the ANC or its union allies—seems to have much sense of urgency about ramping up growth. To the extent anyone in a position of political power has pushed major change, it's been about shifting wealth from private mine owners to the "people" in the form of state ownership, not about busting up all the power centers that stand in the way of a more competitive economy.

In politics there is no real national opposition to the ANC, an umbrella organization that houses the whole range of forces that opposed apartheid. Formally the organization is an alliance of the original African National Congress, the South African Communist Party, and the Congress of South African Trade Unions (COSATU). Informally this alliance includes everyone from free marketeers to European-style welfare statists, populists, and old-school socialists. Anyone who opposed white-only rule is welcome, and that's a broad cross section of the country. Indeed South Africa is the only nation in which the main trade union federation is part of the government, and the only Westernized nation where the Communists in government still openly call themselves Communist. Yet they are hardly shrill radicals. On a return visit in mid-2011 I found the Communists and the union leaders championing—of all things—local government procurement, in the hope that if the government buys more of its goods locally, employment will increase.

Even Helen Zille, the head of the leading opposition party, would agree that the threat to the long reign of the ANC is far from immediate. Her Democratic Alliance Party governs the province of Western Cape, with Cape Town as its capital, and she is the only non-ANC premier of any of South Africa's seven provinces. Zille has attracted growing support by providing basic government services like garbage collection and police protection that the ANC has largely failed to deliver. I found her regularly checking her Twitter account, fielding complaints ranging from trash on the streets to instances of drug abuse.

While Zille is a former antiapartheid activist, she and her party are seen as being "too white." After drawing just under one-fourth of the vote in the most recent nationwide elections, they have a long way to go before achieving their aim of becoming the national governing party. Zille sees no real chance of ousting the ANC at the next presidential election, in 2014, so her party is looking to 2019. By that time the ANC will have been in power for twenty-five years, nearly matching the record set by India's Congress Party for surviving off the liberation dividend.

Radicals for Responsibility

In recent years many emerging markets, including Brazil and Turkey, have seen leaders come to power on a wave of radical rhetoric, then become moderate once they are in office. South Africa has seen it three times, starting with Mandela. When he was released from jail in 1990, he immediately called for nationalizing the gold and diamond mines, as a way to quickly redistribute wealth to the black majority. The next year, he went to Davos, the annual discussion forum for the global elite, organized by the World Economic Forum, where he had a chance to hobnob with Western business and political leaders. When he returned he told his people that the international community would shun South Africa if they nationalized the mines, so they quietly watered down the idea.

Mandela strengthened democracy in South Africa when he stepped down after one term, rather than exploiting his popularity to build a personality cult, as leaders from Putin to Mugabe have done. The global markets quaked when he left, again fearing a move toward socialism under his firebrand successors, starting with Thabo Mbeki. A button-down minister with a stern moralizing streak, Mbeki took office in 1999 and quickly chose a finance minister, Trevor Manuel, who was popular with both the ANC rank and file and international investors. Under Mbeki the top central banker, Tito Mboweni, once a Leninist radical, also became very orthodox in practice at the bank. Mbeki was succeeded in 2009 by Jacob Zuma, a charismatic Zulu chief who came to power trailed by charges of rape and corruption, and talking about redistributing wealth to workers and blacks. Zuma scared global financiers even more than Mbeki had, but he has been just as moderate in office. Mandela, Mbeki, and Zuma proved the consensus wrong by focusing on the basics: controlling debt, stabilizing inflation, creating a base on which the nation could grow.

But moderation, while preferable to chaos, is no longer enough in the post-crisis global environment of less easy money and tougher competition. South Africa with a per capita income of $8,000 has a tougher growth challenge than poorer nations like China or India, and it has yet to deal with its fundamental problems. As with many emerging markets in recent times, it has gotten the basics of finance right—controlling government debt and inflation—but it has failed to create the conditions for dynamic competition, either in politics or in the economy.

The New South Africa Looks Too Much Like the Old One

The industries owned by the state in the late years of the apartheid regime under P. W. Botha are now owned by the ANC government, and are still poorly managed. The phone company, Telkom, is owned by the government—little surprise, then, that only 14 percent of South Africans have access to the Internet. The same goes for the electric utility, Eskom, which manages a grid plagued by rolling blackouts. The rail system is run by Transnet, which has been negotiating with private partners for five years to solve bottlenecks in the network that have prevented South Africa from raising iron ore exports even in the midst of a global boom in demand.

State ownership explains why the national flagship, South African Airways, has so little competition, and why there are no cheap flights to South Africa, which dampens tourism and business opportunities. Innovation, if it can be called that, often involves a clever entrepreneur attempting to offer an end run around some absurdity in the system: one new venture offers to connect companies directly to the national utility grids, in order to avoid the lofty prices and lousy maintenance offered by local government intermediaries.

This is all a throwback not to the socialism embraced by the anti-apartheid movement, but to the heavily regulated, 1970s-style capitalism practiced by the apartheid regime. The government can execute major projects—the World Cup soccer tournament in 2010 was widely deemed a success and delivered world-class sporting facilities—but South Africans have a growing list of complaints about the inefficiency of basic services. Many black South Africans in particular experience daily indignities ranging from absurdly long commutes to lack of water, blackouts, and slow or nonexistent Internet connections.

The Oddity of Great Wealth in a Slowly Emerging Market

Apartheid has left South Africa a relatively closed and protected economy. As in Mexico, the oligopolies that dominate many sectors, including finance, retail, and media, make steep profit margins and have the cash on hand to expand aggressively in their underserved region.

Before 1971 the world was still on the gold standard, creating a captive global market for South African mining firms. The fixed price of gold made a solid economic foundation for the apartheid system. When the gold standard ended, prices started to fluctuate wildly, playing havoc with the country's trade balance and the value of the rand. By then, however, the "mining houses" were so powerful that whenever gold prospects dimmed, they would buy up other sectors of the economy. By the end of the 1980s the big five South African conglomerates—Anglo, Sanlam, Mutual, Liberty, and Rembrandt—controlled 90 percent of the stock market.

When the international community started slapping sanctions on the apartheid regime in the mid-1980s, the Botha government turned more inward. By the time it collapsed, the business community was almost completely divorced from global market realities. There has been some movement under the ANC to bust up monopolies, but after their share of the market dropped to as low as 55 percent in 1998, the holdings of the top five conglomerates began to inch back upward. In the 1990s, the government "looked the other way as competition melted away," according to Alan Hirsch, a former top economic adviser to the president and author of the 2005 book *Season of Hope: Economic Reform under Mandela and Mbeki.*

These private-sector companies are heavily protected yet extremely well run (again much like Mexico), and they are the source of whatever global economic success South Africa enjoys. Though South Africa has the most sophisticated financial market in the emerging nations—the World Economic Forum ranks it the fifth most sophisticated in the world—much of the money is trapped at home, a legacy of capital controls imposed by the apartheid regime to prevent money from fleeing the country. Even though those rules have been gradually relaxed since the 1990s, the pool of domestic financial savings is still huge, with $750 billion in assets under management in the insurance, pension, and mutual-fund industry, which is a sum roughly two times the GDP of South Africa, suggesting there is a lot of accumulated wealth in the economy.

The tragedy is that the apartheid regime was so intent on keeping the black population down, it refused to deploy any of this readily available money in the black homelands, a decision that left the national networks of everything from schools to water lines in very bad shape. They remain so today because South African businesses have not invested much inside the country—the value of the capital stock (for example, heavy machinery and factory equipment) is actually falling as a share of GDP. That is one reason why productivity is declining too: South Africa has powerful private companies that still steer clear of South Africa.

How a Gold-Rich Nation Can Be Hurt by High Gold Prices

The unions are arguably even more powerful, and less helpful to growth. South Africa suffers an especially virulent case of "Dutch disease," which induces a resource-rich nation to suffer from its own riches. When the price of that resource goes up—be it natural gas in Holland, oil in Saudi Arabia, or gold and platinum in South Africa—it drives up the value of the local currency, undermining the price competitiveness of local manufacturing on the world stage. In South Africa the negative impact of an expensive currency is compounded by the demands of a powerful union movement run by former leaders of the struggle against apartheid. When the prices of gold and platinum have gone up, the union leaders have in turn demanded a greater share of the profits.

In most economies wages rise with increases in inflation or labor productivity, but not in South Africa. Here wages are rising faster than inflation and faster than productivity. The average wage hike was more than 9 percent in 2009 and 2010, even as inflation rose at around 3 percent, employment was stagnating, and labor productivity continued to lag behind that of almost all other emerging markets. By now both global and local markets have come to understand that when the gold price rises, the South African currency and wages will rise with it, and they punish South African companies accordingly. In the last decade, as the price of gold rose by more than 600 percent, the stock price of South Africa's leading gold companies actually declined. That's an incredibly counterintuitive outcome and contrasts with the impressive performance of gold shares in other parts of the world such as Australia, Canada, and the United States. Between 2005 and 2011, the price of shares in Barick Gold of the United States was up more than 50 percent, while Harmony Gold of South Africa was down 10 percent in dollar terms.

South Africa is deindustrializing at a point in its development when basic industry should still be growing. Despite the world's largest platinum and manganese reserves, along with abundant deposits of gold, iron ore, and coal, employment in the mining industry is falling. Mining now accounts for 3 percent of GDP, down from 14 percent in the 1980s, and South African manufacturing is hollowing out as well. The share of manufacturing has fallen from a peak of 17.4 percent of GDP in 2000 to 15.5 percent today, and South Africa's ability to create jobs is in decline as factories go idle. In the global crisis of 2008–2009, South Africa lost a million jobs, among the worst losses of any developing country, and it is not likely they are coming back anytime soon.

The South African union movement has yet to wake up to this new reality and remains more focused on strong wage growth for its own members rather than creating jobs for the broader working class. The union leaders came out of the antiapartheid struggle heavily focused on social justice, on "decent work at a decent wage," and they have tremendous power because of their long-standing ties to the ANC. The Zuma government is trying to change the union focus to just plain "jobs," but so far without much success. There is more strike activity now than when the ANC took power: last year South Africa lost 14.6 million workdays to strikes, compared with 4 million in 1994. The strikers are pushing for even higher wages despite increases that have greatly outpaced those of non-union workers in recent years. But the harder the unions push, the more corporations push back. One often hears South African corporate executives speaking openly about replacing jobs with technology. My team talks regularly to a company that is big in chemicals and explosives, and their focus is on building a new state-of-the-art plant that requires very few employees.

Tension is rising between the growing ranks of the unemployed and those who have secured protected union jobs under the ANC alliance—

the so-called black diamonds. Adcorp, South Africa's largest employment-services company and a leading authority on labor-market trends, calls this split a "new apartheid" and warns that, in the worst-case scenario, it could lead to an upheaval that pits the unemployed rural masses against the privileged urban job holders. Today the 2 million COSATU members are greatly outnumbered by the 6.4 million unemployed, the 3.7 million who do freelance work through labor contractors, and the 2 million-plus working in the informal economy.

To date, however, the unemployed are not organized, and they are rebelling only through channels that do not threaten the ANC. While there is scuttlebutt about corruption in powerful places, there is little visible sign of it. No leader is building a vast palace that would attract public protest and serve as the ramparts of his last stand in office. Yet there are mounting attacks on other targets, including white farmers in the countryside and the workers spilling over the border from Zimbabwe, fleeing the chaos of the Mugabe regime. Rates of alcoholism and of street crime are also extremely high: visitors are advised not to walk outside their Johannesburg hotels even in broad daylight, or stop at traffic lights at night, and it is impossible to meet anyone in the capital who has not been a violent-crime victim or known one.

Why the Unemployed Masses Are Not Angry at the ANC

The sprawling black market for labor may be siphoning off some of the discontent over the official unemployment rate. As many as one out of four workers has a job in the informal economy. At every traffic light and street corner, hawkers sell just about anything from jeans to sunglasses, or hire themselves out as day labor. Unlike surprised citizens in nations like Greece or Spain, where unemployment is climbing today, these South Africans have never experienced better economic times. A top official at the country's central bank told me that the outlook of this group helps explain the ANC's longevity: far from coalescing as an angry opposition, he said, most workers in the informal sector have "learned to live with what they have, and learned to live with quite little."

Another basic source of ANC political resilience is its welfare state. Under apartheid the state spent nine times more on whites than on blacks, but now that bias is gone and the government spends twice as much on blacks as on whites. Today South Africa is the only major country with more people receiving social grants than holding down jobs; there are sixteen million receiving social grants (a category that ranges from child and elder-care support to unemployment benefits), or six times more than there were in 1998. That's three recipients for every taxpayer, and welfare payments are the fastest-growing segment of the government budget. South Africa will soon spend more on welfare than on education—or, put another way, more on cushioning citizens from joblessness than preparing them for jobs.

When it first came to power, the ANC created a modicum of upward mobility for some black South Africans, helping to ease discontent, at least for a time. Normally a rising middle class is the natural by-product of an expanding economic pie, but in South Africa the growth was mainly the product of an affirmative-action program launched in the most fortuitous possible circumstances. The Black Economic Empowerment (BEE) set specific targets for all but the smallest companies to increase the role of black owners, managers, and workers, and tried to create a new class of black-owned companies as well. The program came into effect in 2003, the same year that the flood of easy money pouring out of the United States triggered a boom across all the emerging markets.

This growth environment greatly improved the chances of success for almost any social experiment, and in South Africa it helped usher in a degree of racial justice for the first time. The transformation was remarkable, as corporate meetings and boards once uniformly white and male became a rainbow of whites, blacks, people of mixed race, Asians, and, to an extent, women. But there are real limits to the degree of integration beyond the office environment. It is a telling sign that it is hard to find blacks dining at any of South Africa's fine restaurants. One black union leader whom I met recently called it a "cappuccino economy," with "white cream over a large black mass, sprinkled with some black chocolate on top."

The period of upward mobility has stalled. Most of the South Africans who were qualified for middle-class jobs have gotten them, and the rest lack the skills to compete in the global economy. Many new members of the middle class are now deep in debt, having borrowed heavily to enjoy the good life as the global tide of easy credit washed into South Africa during the 2003–2007 boom. The ratio of debt to disposable income is at 70 percent, one of the highest rates in the emerging markets; business confidence is declining; and the main engine of growth is the government, which accounts for a broadening share of the economy. The growing welfare state and rising debt may have shored up support for the ANC, but they are only making the economy less and less dynamic.

Why the Local Economy Doesn't Matter—to Some

The economic picture in South Africa does not matter all that much to its stock market because so much of its profits are earned outside the country. The top South African companies have smart managers, offer high dividends, and enjoy strong profits earned mainly in foreign countries. Among the top-sixty companies, 56 percent of their earnings come from offshore—one of the highest shares in the world.

A rule of the road: the sight of local companies "going global" is often celebrated in headlines as a national success, but the more accurate interpretation depends on the circumstances. Going global can be a sign of corporate strength or of national weakness. If more than 50 percent of a nation's corporate earnings are coming from abroad, it could be reason for concern. In Singapore, where businesses can't make all that much money at home because the population is so small, it is not alarming that more than 50 percent of earnings are made overseas. In nations with sizable domestic markets like Mexico and Russia, it can be read as a vote of no confidence in the local economy. South Africa is perhaps the leading example of this negative phenomenon.

For decades South Africa had turned its back on the rest of Africa. Back in the 1940s, when world leaders were negotiating the first international trade agreements, apartheid leaders objected to any attempt to categorize South Africa as an emerging nation, even if that meant favored treatment. They wanted to be seen as part of the white European world, and they steered investment abroad to white Anglo nations, mainly the United States and Australia. Then, as emerging markets got hot in the 1990s, South African investors started looking to China, Russia, and India, but still never to Africa. That has changed dramatically in the last decade: the new South Africa is searching for opportunity in its own backyard, expanding aggressively in fellow southern African countries such as Zambia, Mozambique, and Namibia, and then up the continent in Nigeria and Tanzania. The fact that South Africa's savvy multinationals are moving money away from home and into neighboring economies is a sure sign of where opportunity lies on the continent.

12

The Fourth World

THE UNUSUAL BEHAVIOR OF THE GLOBAL ECONOMY during the boom years from 2003 to 2007 sometimes brings to mind the quirky ideas of Rupert Sheldrake. In his 1981 book, *A New Science of Life*, Sheldrake explored the mysterious ways living things appear to connect, like the dog that seems to know his owner is coming home, or the experiment in which one hundred monkeys learn a new task, each one learning a bit faster than the last, as if the one-hundredth monkey was somehow tapping the knowledge of all those that came before. Sheldrake attributed these telepathic connections to "morphic resonance," the idea that living things can share information and memories through invisible clouds he called "morphic fields."

Despite Sheldrake's legitimate scientific credentials, his peers have roundly dismissed his theory as pseudoscience. When I look at the synchronized global market cycles of the past decade, I can't help but think of morphic fields and their alluring—but ultimately incorrect—explanation for curious phenomena. Major emerging markets that had always moved according to their own unique logic have in recent times been rising and falling in tandem, as if globalization itself had become a mystical life force. In the first half of 2011, the difference between the best and worst stock market returns in the ten biggest emerging economies was just 10 percent, a record low. In the 1990s, the typical spread was 100 percent

The rise of Nollywood, from virtually nothing two decades ago to Nigeria's second-biggest employer, shows how cheap new technology and some entrepreneurial zeal can spark a miniboom in the heart of Africa.

over a similar time period. Now many analysts and economists seem to think this "convergence" force is real and universal, and that all emerging markets will continue to grow rapidly, catching up with income levels in the West.

A closer look shows that globalization did not, in fact, resonate equally in all developing nations. There was and is a broad array of smaller countries that are not yet fully connected to global flows of trade and money. These nations comprise a chaotic Fourth World of "frontier markets" in which political leaders have yet to buy fully into the global market consensus, and where economic expansion and stock market growth are still more erratic than the norm. At a time when many investors are looking for major markets that do not follow all the others, the capacity of the frontier markets to chart an altogether different path makes them an object of fascination.

If smart thinking about the world depends on understanding how different the emerging nations are, that rule applies twice over in the Fourth World. "Frontier" is a term that has come into regular use only since about 2007, and it is defined several different ways, but the simplest way to think about these nations is that they are open to foreign investors but do not follow orthodox market rules. This state of semi-lawlessness makes them volatile and unpredictable, with economic growth rates that over 2010 ranged from a high of 20 percent in Ghana to a low of 2 percent in Serbia, compared to the much narrower range in big emerging markets, from 9 percent in China to 3 percent in South Africa. The frontier stock markets magnify those growth gaps, ranging in 2010 from a gain of 80 percent in Sri Lanka to a loss of 20 percent in Bulgaria, while the major emerging markets produced a maximum stock market gain of 20 percent in India and, at the other end of the spectrum, no gain in Brazil.

The boundaries of the Fourth World are defined not by poverty but by rule of law or the lack of it. The frontier is home to countries with average incomes under $1,500, like Ghana, but also the richest nation in the world, tiny Qatar, where the average income is now about $100,000. Only about fifty countries in the world are classified as developed or emerging, while around thirty-five are on the (constantly changing) frontier list* and nearly one hundred (including Paraguay, Senegal, and Turkmenistan) are beyond any category, off the maps of even the most intrepid market players.

The frontier nations occupy a world where insider trading can run rampant because it's officially tolerated, where financial data are spotty and often unreliable because the authorities don't always demand clarity from businesses, and where investors are at times advised to travel in the company of armed bodyguards. Research on the frontier is often less about number crunching than about pressing one's ear to the walls: when

---

* See appendix B for a full list of frontier markets.

one of my analysts recently asked a member of the crowd milling aimlessly around the Kuwait stock exchange what they were waiting for, the
reply was, "Rumors." The challenge of understanding reality in an environment like this is huge. The 2009 bursting of Dubai's huge debt bubble
came only days after the ruling sheikh had personally and passionately
assured investors that his emirate's troubles were overblown.

The "macromania" that seized observers of emerging markets over the
last decade, as major markets rose and fell in unison, did not extend to
the Fourth World, where every market tends to follow its own peculiar
rhythms, often at the whim of local leaders. Cambodia opened its stock
exchange in July 2011 for reasons that remain unclear: there were no companies ready to list, making it the only exchange in the world with zero
trading. Neighboring Laos opened its first stock market in early 2011, and
by mid-year had just two companies worth a total of $265,000.

Investors typically believe that thin pickings in a market limit choice
and are thus bad for business, but in the Fourth World it is not necessarily true that rich pickings will offer more attractive choices. Ukraine lists
more than five hundred companies, but this apparent abundance is the
unnatural result of a strategy Ukraine adopted from Russia, which is no
one else's model for how to run a stock exchange. In an attempt to create a vibrant market from scratch, Ukraine in 2008 simply required any
company with more than one hundred shareholders, and all banks, to sell
stock to the public.

Trying to use "forced listing" to manufacture a free-market culture
is obviously absurd, but it's pretty typical frontier-market behavior. For
Ukraine, the result was that many companies sold only a tiny portion of
their stock to the public in order to comply with the rules. The technical
term for this sold portion is the "free float," and in general the smaller the
share sold to the public, the less free the float. And the less free the float,
the less commitment a company's management has to the basic values of
a public company—like generating a profit and return for shareholders. In
fact many big Ukrainian companies have little commitment to these values and often won't even take calls from investors. Not surprisingly outsiders see the local Ukraine market as something of a joke, and Ukrainian
companies that want to be taken seriously go public in London or Warsaw.

This has real consequences: Ukraine was the hardest-hit nation in the crisis of 2008, with an economic contraction of 20 percent on a peak-to-trough basis, and a 90 percent drop in the value of its stock market.

The region most isolated from global market norms is the Middle East. Iraq, Iran, and Syria are still too closed to foreign investors to qualify even as frontier markets. The key frontier markets in the Middle East are the petro-monarchies of the Gulf region, and the largest of these by far, Saudi Arabia, is open only to investors from within the Gulf. That led to a spectacular stock market bubble in 2005, with Saudi Arabia's stock market becoming the biggest in the developing world—larger than China's or India's—based solely on oil-rich locals and neighbors. It was a good deal crazier than the dotcom insanity that gripped the United States at the turn of the millennium, and it popped soon enough, but when a bubble pops in the Gulf it does not make a sound. No one outside pays much attention because foreigners aren't allowed in.

We've seen how leaders in nations that attract a lot of foreign investment and trade have limited ability to defy convention, yielding the increasingly common phenomena of radical candidates moving toward the economic mainstream when they take office. By contrast on the frontier the pull of market orthodoxy exerts less force, and when things start to go badly, leaders on the frontier may simply close local stock markets, hoping the crisis will pass.

This is the financial policy equivalent of curling into a fetal position. It can temporarily halt a crash in stock prices, but almost always at the expense of an even worse crash when the market reopens, and to the lasting fury of buyers locked into bad trades. This is a recipe for chaos, especially when it's not even clear who is making the decision. At the height of the global crisis in 2008, the government of Nigeria announced that the stock exchange had closed owing to a technical glitch. When it reopened a few days later, no one was buying at any price, because no one believed the "technical glitch" story. Over the next year the market value dropped 76 percent.

Closing a market for an extended period is a quick ticket to demotion from emerging to frontier status. Pakistan was demoted in 2009 after it put tight limits on trading in its market for nearly four months, and Argentina was relegated to the frontier in 2009 after controls were slapped on the movement of capital in and out of the country. Inclusion in this club is no compliment to a nation like Argentina, a former economic star, but in the eyes of the big investment banks that keep the indexes, the only requirement for membership is a backward financial market. To avoid the frontier label some countries game the system: during its country-wide political revolt of 2011, Egypt closed its market for fifty-five days but reopened just in time to avoid demotion.

Of course there are the oddball nations such as Venezuela that went straight from a regular emerging market into oblivion rather than take a more leisurely spiral through the frontier ranks. Hugo Chávez got Venezuela booted off the lists for imposing caps on the movement of money in and out of the country, and keeps digging his nation deeper into disrepute, most recently by imposing a 95 percent tax on oil revenues above one hundred dollars a barrel shortly after oil prices hit that benchmark. Since much of the oil money was already earmarked to finance Chávez's various spending programs, the new tax was seen as a transparent bid to seize full discretionary control of oil profits in the run-up to the 2012 election.

Not surprisingly frontier markets often fail the basic task of a market, which in theory is to match buyers and sellers in an open forum that allows them to agree on fair prices. When rumors pass as information and rules make no sense, neither do prices. Investors who get in early and get a grip on what's going on can double or triple investments—but it's just as easy to lose everything.

The arbitrary management of arbitrary rules is hardly the main risk in the Fourth World. Traveling with armed guards in heavily armored cars is mandatory in some places. My team's security details in Pakistan offer useful tips—like where to sit in a hotel lobby: always choose a small chair, not a couch, so you can quickly pull the furniture over you in case of an explosion. One of our guards used this turtle tactic to emerge unscratched when the deadly 2010 bombing of a Karachi police station shattered the windows of a nearby Sheraton. In Nigeria business travelers have to be wary of the drivers at the airport holding name cards after a spate of cases in which bandits hijacked the pickup car en route to the airport, then used the name card to lure the arriving visitor into a back-alley mugging. Our travel documents to Nigeria now include a picture of the real driver.

There are also striking examples of nations with huge potential that are still largely closed to the outside world: Angola, the second-largest oil producer in Africa, with a $100 billion economy, is not considered a frontier market because it has no stock exchange. But that designation could change very quickly—Angola has been talking about opening a market for years. If it does it could get a huge investor response—domestic and foreign—on day one. The same goes for nations like Iran and Cuba, which are now deeply isolated, but neither so much as Mongolia was twenty years ago, when it opened its market to foreigners. Today the total value of Mongolia's stock market is $1 billion.

The frontier markets of the Fourth World are home to one billion of the world's six billion people, but they account for just 5 percent of global GDP and attract only 0.5 percent of global investment. An almost universal assumption holds that this gap will close over time—that the frontier will take a larger share of the global economic pie and take in more investment. In this case the conventional wisdom is likely to be borne out, though the fits and starts along the way will make it a volatile ride. The frontier is where the world is likely to see some of the most explosive growth over the next decade. These are countries where getting a few things right will make a huge difference. That's particularly true in nations that have recently suffered bouts of ethnic strife (like Kenya) or civil war (like Sri Lanka). Here just the absence of conflict can unleash growth.

Sri Lanka's Peace Dividend

I first visited Sri Lanka in 1997, shortly after a rebel bombing of the central bank headquarters had thrown the financial system into chaos. Military checkpoints made traveling around the capital city of Colombo rather punishing, but the overwhelming impression was of an utterly charming island and talented people trapped inside a seemingly endless civil war.

When I returned in 2011, the civil war had ended with surprising finality, and I took an extra day to go out and see the country, including the huge territory that had been behind the lines of the Tamil rebels

on my first trip. This should have been easy enough. For one thing, the
Tamil capital at Trincomalee is just 160 miles from Colombo—but the
new highways are still being built, and the best hotel in Colombo could
not provide a decent car. The helicopter on offer was a single-engine job of
the kind that routinely crashes in neighboring India. My accommodating
hosts arranged for the air force to take me up in a twin-engine helicopter.
I've taken helicopters in many emerging markets when the road network
is inefficient, normally a bad sign for the economy. But the aerial views
of the multiple expressways under construction, the lush green plantations of the interior, and the new resorts facing the turquoise waters that
drape the island helped convince me that Sri Lanka is no longer a land
in waiting.

In the 1960s Sri Lanka was billed as the next Asian growth miracle,
only to be stymied by a tryst with socialism that played a direct role in
igniting the civil war. Following independence in 1948, leaders of the
Sinhalese majority set out to correct the injustices of British colonial rule,
which had heavily favored the country's Tamil minority. Tamils had gotten the bulk of top jobs in the British administration, and in the early
years after independence Sinhalese nationalists aimed to put them back
in a minority role. The Sinhalese leaders soon evicted Tamils from official posts and in the 1960s and 1970s began to lavish more public jobs,
subsidies, and social benefits on their own kind, in the name of creating a
prosperous and egalitarian Sinhalese nation.

What they got instead was the Tamil rebellion. Launched in 1977, the
revolt would coalesce under the "Liberation Tigers" of Tamil Eelam, whose
pioneering brutality—in the use of child soldiers and suicide bombers—
would derail Sri Lanka's development for thirty years. During the war the
central government used sanctions to effectively cut off the rebel-held
region from the rest of the country and the world. With both the rebels
and the army punishing civilians suspected of aiding the enemy, trust—
the basis of any civilized financial system—broke down. Banks fled, and
Tamils put their savings in cash or gold. Security checkpoints restricted
the flow of goods, which drove up prices and cut off exports. The fields of
rice, red onions, green chilies, and tobacco were replaced by battle zones
and land mines. Farmers were reduced to growing food for themselves.

Offshore, the rebels deployed a navy known as the Sea Tigers, with three thousand men and women stalking the coast in fiberglass boats mounted with machine guns and grenade launchers. They harassed Sri Lanka's navy, sinking its smaller ships in suicide-boat attacks, and plundered passing civilian vessels. In 1980 these seas had provided 64 percent of the national catch of yellowfin tuna, skipjack, and shark, but that share fell to 26 percent after the Tiger threat grounded local fishermen. Beaches went undeveloped, and so did potential offshore oil fields.

During the war years Sri Lanka grew half as fast as Korea and Taiwan and became another country in the long line of emerging-market disappointments. In the 1960s Singapore's Lee Kuan Yew had visited Sri Lanka to study it as a leading model of development, but it was not long before Singapore had outpaced Sri Lanka.

Today it seems that Sri Lanka's time has come. As recently as 2007, the Tigers controlled large swaths of the North and East provinces, fielding men, women, and children in an army cultishly committed to a charismatic founder, Vellupillai Prabhakaran. It is conventional military wisdom that guerrilla armies can be contained or driven off but not destroyed; however, by mid-2009 the Sri Lankan Army had proved that wisdom wrong. In an all-out offensive the army cordoned off the Tigers in their stronghold on the northern Jaffna Peninsula, and in a feat rarely repeated in the age of mobile-phone cameras, it managed to seal the entire region from outside view. Then it pulled the cordon tight until Prabhakaran, his family, and most of the senior Tiger leaders were dead, along with untold thousands of civilians. The final stages of the war were highly controversial—charges of human-rights violations still fly against both sides—but the economic impact seems clear.

The civil war is over, the process of healing is under way, and there is every chance that Sri Lanka will again become a breakout nation. Despite slowing sharply during the war years, the economy continued to grow at an average pace of nearly 5 percent. The economy was running on one engine—the prosperous Western province where Colombo is located, and where the well-educated young population was producing strong growth in industries and services. The North and East Provinces, which account for 30 percent of Sri Lanka's land and 15 percent of its population, were

largely war zones. With the nation whole again, achieving a 7 to 8 percent growth rate over the next decade should be well within reach. Since
taking office in 2005 President Mahinda Rajapaksa has been consolidating power in ways that critics see as the start of a family dynasty; his
three brothers occupy key ministerial posts, and he recently capitalized
on his victory over the Tigers to win both a second term and a constitutional amendment allowing the president unlimited terms in office. For
now, however, he is deploying his growing powers to ends that suggest he
understands the fundamentals of growth, if not of democracy.

Though his country is still known by a name that evokes the bygone
influence of the Soviet Union—"Democratic Socialist Republic of Sri
Lanka"—Rajapaksa's regime is working to trim the fat left over from the
socialist experiments of the 1970s, including high taxes and government
debts that still equal 80 percent of GDP. It aims to raise Sri Lanka from
102nd to 30th in the World Bank rankings of nations by business climate before 2014. It is working to bring the vast swaths of formerly rebel-
held territory back into play, and to exploit the country's long-standing
strengths, including a highly literate population and an advantageous
location along key shipping routes to India and China.

Most economists tend to ignore war because their data sets don't capture it. The numbers may say a lot about prices and debt, but on the subject of what body counts or no-fly zones can do to growth they are usually
silent. Markets are especially bad at foreseeing the financial implications
of war—the most famous example, of course, is World War I, which took
most investors entirely by surprise, leaving many with heavy losses despite
the highly visible buildup of standing armies across Europe. Conversely,
markets are also quite weak at recognizing the benefits of peace. Well
documented by those who study it, mainly at agencies like the World
Bank and the UN, the "peace dividend" is real, and Sri Lanka is poised
to be a big beneficiary. The models that offer hope for Sri Lanka are
the high-growth economies that stalled with the outbreak of conflict but
returned to productivity when the fighting came to an end.

Members of this comeback club include Uganda and Mozambique,
both of which were growing at more than 5 percent a year before the outbreak of vicious postcolonial wars in the 1960s and 1970s. By the 1980s

Uganda became synonymous with the sadistic dictatorship of Idi Amin, and Mozambique earned the title of the world's poorest nation. Yet following decisive rebel victories—Uganda in 1986 and Mozambique in 1994—both countries have resumed impressively strong growth. Mozambique has been especially successful under the inspired leadership of Joaquim Chissano, who dumped socialism and voluntarily stepped down after his second term in office in 2004. The reforms pushed by Chissano and his successors drove growth to more than 7 percent in the last decade, partly by shifting money from military spending to address key economic priorities.

Another nominee for the comeback club is Iraq, which was the most successful economy in the Middle East from the 1950s through the 1970s, growing at a pace of up to 9 percent. Iraq was widely seen as a model for the region until 1979, when Saddam Hussein came to power and began launching disastrous bids for regional domination. The Iraqi economy collapsed in the 1980s during a war of attrition with Iran and began to recover only after Saddam was ousted by U.S. troops in 2003. Since then, as oil production began to recover, Iraq has posted growth of better than 5 percent on average, and was growing at an annual rate of more than 9 percent in late 2011.

The examples of Uganda, Mozambique, and Iraq suggest that it's possible to come back strong from a debilitating war, civil or otherwise, and Sri Lanka has a good chance to do so. A 2009 study by the U.S. Agency for International Development (USAID) of conflicts in sixty-two nations between 1974 and 1997 found that after a conflict ended, growth typically rebounded at a below-average pace in the first two to three years, but took off in years four to seven. Sri Lanka is already ahead of the curve, having posted growth of 8 percent in 2010, the first year after the peace.

To restart the economy in the former war zone, the government has established vocational training centers and low-interest loan programs, distributed boats and livestock, and begun building roads and bridges. Banks are returning, big retail chains are setting up shop, and domestic airlines are flying to Jaffna and Trincomalee again. The flood of state spending drove growth in North and East provinces up to 14 percent in 2009 and 2010, and forecasters are expecting the region to grow at above 13 percent for several more years, making it the fastest-growing area of the country.

The revival of the North and the East has had effects nationwide. On my helicopter trip I visited some of the newly renovated resorts, from the retro-chic Chaaya Blu in Trincomalee to the Cinnamon Lodge in Habarana, which lies in the "cultural triangle" formed by Sri Lanka's three ancient cities. It wasn't hard to imagine tourists, seduced by the country's raw appeal, coming in droves. While prices are not as dirt cheap as they were at the height of the war, they are still very low—$150 for a high-end hotel room—which means the Sri Lankan currency is still very competitive and attractive to foreign investors.

A big Indian conglomerate, Reliance, has purchased rights to explore for oil off the country's west coast. War-zone insurance rates that had made it too expensive to dock in Sri Lanka have disappeared, leading to a large increase in cargo traffic at the main port in Colombo. Meanwhile the government is pouring money into new terminals there, as well as new ports and harbors in formerly rebel-held regions. The reintegration of the marginalized Tamils—with their high levels of educational achievement and English fluency—should provide a huge boost to a nation that multiple consulting firms already rank highly as a potential destination for multinationals looking to outsource customer service, IT, and other back-office operations.

It would be a mistake to sugarcoat the postwar mood. There is evidence that Tamils, embittered by the bloody endgame of the war and suspicious of Rajapaksa, continue to leave the country. But many of those who remain seem determined to put the war memories behind them. I was surprised to see Tamils in Trincomalee working to attract Indian tourists to the "Ravana trail," named after a mythical king with a disputed legacy. In Tamil legend Ravana was one of the most powerful and inspired of ancient kings, while to Indians he was a devil incarnate, vanquished by an even greater Indian god. This difference of interpretation is of no small magnitude in Sri Lanka, which has long feared domination by its much larger neighbor. But in Trincomalee locals say that as long as the "Ravana trail" is drawing tourists, subjective spins on the myth don't matter.

It's only natural for nations to trade most heavily with their neighbors, and for most of East Asia, trade within the region has been growing faster than trade with the rest of the world. Indeed the success of East

Asia has been driven in no small measure by the willingness of China, Japan, Taiwan, and South Korea to leave old wars in the past, at least when they are cutting business deals. In contrast there is no region in the world with weaker trade among immediate neighbors than South Asia—including India, Pakistan, Bangladesh, and Sri Lanka—where isolation, lawlessness, and old grudges have made it difficult to move across borders, and trade within the region has stagnated at 5 percent of total trade with the world.

Sri Lanka could be the country to move the region toward a new trade regime. Ignoring the lingering fears of Indian domination, the government is proposing a grand deal that could unlock trade with India and provide a huge boost to the economy. The opposition comes from Sri Lankan businessmen fearful of Indian competition. But India welcomes the deal, in part as an opportunity to balance China's growing interest in Sri Lanka as a linchpin on its supply routes through the Indian Ocean. Many small nations in Europe and Asia have benefited from geographic good fortune, and Sri Lanka is only too happy to exploit its felicitous location in return for even a small share of China's gargantuan outbound investment. As part of its vision of a "string of pearls"—a series of ports along its preferred sea routes—China is investing heavily in the Sri Lankan port at Hamban-tota, the home base of the Rajapaksa family.

At peace, Sri Lanka finds itself in a very strong position, courted by both of Asia's emerging giants. There is some risk that the peace dividend could prove fleeting: the USAID study found that 40 percent of nations that end a civil war will revert to violence within a decade. There is a strong case to be made, however, that Sri Lanka's peace will hold. First there is the decisive end to the war. It left no rebel army to disarm, much less to revive the threat five to ten years down the road. Even if some rebels had managed to melt back into the woods, it's not likely they would command much support, for by the end their brutality had alienated even many fellow Tamils. In the Tamil provinces no more than a third of the adult population has bothered to vote in recent elections, and no more than a third of those voters have cast ballots for proxy parties representing the Tigers.

There is also a fundamental national consensus that the future should be decided based on what works, not on the ideological debates that retarded Sri Lanka's development for so long. Indian socialist ideals heavily influenced the founders of independent Sri Lanka, and state spending came to be seen as a tool to deliver economic justice to Sinhalese. At its peak in the 1970s, state spending accounted for 59 percent of GDP, and four in ten Sri Lankans worked for the government, an extraordinarily high number. But by the late 1990s even the main left-leaning party, the SLFP, was moving toward a more modern development model built on an open economy and trade liberalization. State spending has fallen to about 30 percent of GDP today, and most parties agree this is movement in the right direction.

Ultimately, the economic impact of Sri Lanka's civil war was relatively mild despite the personal suffering of the people it swept up. According to USAID research, a typical civil war of fifteen-year duration reduces national GDP by around 30 percent, and it typically takes a decade just to recover the prewar levels of income. Over the course of its war Sri Lanka grew its economy slowly but positively, by a total of 206 percent. The country has economic and administrative momentum. In the comparable cases of Mozambique and Uganda, the fundamental task was much more complex because the rebels won the decisive victory and had to learn how to govern. In Sri Lanka the government won and it can now build prosperity without interruption by suicide bombers.

Vietnam's Ports to Nowhere

Vietnam offers a classic case of a small country that had greatness thrust upon it. By the middle of the last decade, legions of investors were not only hyping Vietnam as the next China but also, relatively speaking, throwing more money at it than they had ever thrown at China. At its peak in 2007 this investment produced a net inflow of $17 billion in an $80 billion economy—a ratio four times higher than China ever achieved. As the hype meter rose, and the price of office space in Hanoi rose higher than that in Shanghai or Beijing, there was intense pressure to set up Vietnam-dedicated investment funds (which I resisted because I thought Vietnam was too small to handle the hype). At the time the total value of the local stock market was only $25 billion, roughly equivalent to the value of one decent-sized American company. By late 2007 more money was pouring into Vietnam than the nation could absorb. The leadership simply lost control of the economy, and in 2008 the bubble went bust.

Vietnam never was or will be the next China. That particular illusion was built by investors and the media on what looked like shared social and political cornerstones. Part of the Middle Kingdom until the ninth century, the people of Vietnam once wrote in Chinese characters and to this day practice a mix of Buddhism, Taoism, and Confucianism that is borrowed from China. Chairman Mao Zedong was invoking this shared past when he said the Communist bedfellows were as close "as lips and teeth."

In the early 1990s, when Vietnam began to experiment with pragmatic reforms very similar to those Deng Xiaoping had undertaken in China the decade before, the two countries began to look more and more alike. Even a small dose of market logic can produce dramatic results in a backward Communist state, and within a few years Vietnam was posting growth of 7.5 percent per year, second in the world after China. The notion of Vietnam as the next centrally planned success story was born: here was another disciplined Asian nation taking off under the stable guidance of an authoritarian party, as it unchained itself from a failed Communist economic ideology.

Subsequent events showed that authoritarian capitalism is not that easy. For one thing Vietnam's population of ninety million was less than one-tenth of China's, so the advantage of sheer market scale was diminished. Much was made of the country's untapped labor force and lower wages, but low labor costs don't do factory owners much good if there are no passable roads or ports to get products to market. And while China proved that an authoritarian government could succeed at running a command economy, Vietnam would show that success depends on who is issuing the commands, and to what ends. Vietnam is in fact strong proof of the 50/50 rule: political systems don't impact growth for better or worse; political leaders do.

Vietnam is a glaring example of a stable command capitalist system led by men who just don't get the basics of economic reform. Its rulers were neither prepared nor competent to handle the huge inrush of foreign capital in the last decade. Like Japan, Vietnam is a consensus-driven society, which can slow decision-making and drive up costs. When China wants to build a new road it simply seizes the land from farmers, often without adequate compensation. For all its strength the Vietnamese regime has no effective power of eminent domain. Instead of grabbing the land it needs, it ends up buying it at inflated prices, often from corrupt local figures. Some of the best current examples of this phenomenon are the planned highway and high-speed rail connections from Hanoi to Ho Chi Minh City, both priced at $50 billion, an extraordinary sum in a $100 billion economy.

Moreover what does get built is often so badly conceived that operating costs are much higher in Vietnam than in China. It's difficult to connect to international shipping routes from Vietnam because most of its fifty-four ports were built for river routes. The water is too shallow, the berths are too short, and dockside storage is inadequate to handle large ships. In the north and south the roads to the coast are generally in such poor shape that many of the ports were built far upriver, an hour or two inland. Even a planned road from the capital city of Hanoi to the coast has yet to be built.

The aging river ports mean that the average ship docking in Vietnam carries 169 shipping containers—a tiny amount. Standard international cargo vessels range from "feeder" ships that carry up to one thousand containers to "ultralarge container vessels" that carry up to fifteen thousand. These new behemoths are too large to fit through the Panama or Suez Canal, and the newest ports in Vietnam cannot handle them either. Even worse, half of the Vietnamese ports are in the central coastal region, where only 20 percent of the economic activity takes place. This is due in part to the fact that most of them are owned by a state company, which opens up development decisions to the influence of local politicians.

This blunder wouldn't happen in China, where the influence of politicians does not lead to consistently irrational economic decisions. We've already seen how, early on in the reform process, Deng Xiaoping chose to open up the southern coastal regions that would most quickly tie China into global trade even if the decision led to increased regional income inequality—and political risks—in the short term. The contrast between Vietnam and the hyper-rapid port development in China is night and day: even ten years ago China had no ports in the world's top ten in terms of traffic, and now it has four.

Vietnam is following the more typical route of authoritarian economies and distributing investment dollars for political reasons. The constant meddling of politicians is the basic reason why the new Dun Qat refinery was originally conceived in 1988 but work on it did not even begin until seventeen years later. Along the way three major international partners abandoned the project in frustration. The project is located in central Qang Ngai Province, more than six hundred miles from the oil fields in the south. There is no pipeline or new road to connect the refinery to the fields, and the project is designed to handle a high grade of petroleum, though the Vietnamese fields pump only a low grade. The early years of operation have seen so many malfunctions that the plant is depreciating in value at an unusually rapid pace, which will raise the price of its gas in the future.

Since 2008 foreign money has fled Vietnam, which is now starved of the capital it needs to get its roads and other basic infrastructure in shape. When foreign investors do come, they pour money into projects Vietnam does not clearly need, including real estate ventures, such as a new $4 billion casino three hours from Ho Chi Minh City, which will not be open to locals and will be hard-pressed to compete for international tourists with the more easily accessible casinos of Macao and Singapore.

Politics steers money in the wrong directions because the authorities still operate by a leveling instinct that makes them reluctant to allow the market to determine prices. That is particularly true if the profits are going to foreigners. To take just one example, the government sets utility rates artificially low, making the price of electricity in Vietnam the lowest in the region. Expected returns on new power projects are just 4 percent, compared to an average in Southeast Asia of 12 percent, when the local interest rates in Vietnam are about 24 percent. Not surprisingly, there aren't many takers.

Vietnamese leaders are so fixated on maintaining growth rates comparable to China's that they keep pouring money into an economy that cannot handle it. Vietnam will not be the next China unless it builds roads, ports, and solid companies that can make use of heavy investment. That was the basic problem in 2008, and it remains today. While foreign creditors now avoid Vietnam, the authorities still fueled the emerging world's fastest rate of increase in bank lending before the 2008 crisis and, incredibly, after it as well. Without solid companies to put that credit to good use, this version of printing money can produce only one thing: inflation. A general rule for spotting credit bubbles is that if bank lending expands by more than 20 percent a year for five straight years, problems usually follow. Namely, way too much credit goes to unworthy businesses, resulting in a mounting pile of bad loans. Countries all over East Asia violated this rule before the crisis of 1997–1998 and Vietnam has been violating it for more than a decade.

In late 2011, inflation in Vietnam, at close to 20 percent, was running out of control, and there is little confidence that the central bank can manage it because, like most agencies in the country, it is not independent. The State Bank of Vietnam has tried many times to sever ties to the political power structure, but to no avail. The demands of consensus-based rule still trump the basic requirements for a modern financial system, including eliminating political interference from the vital job of setting interest rates.

The government appears to be headed in the opposite direction, toward more meddling and bailing out state companies. Letting them fail would take down many of the state banks with them—roughly 50 percent of the loans from state banks are to big state companies. The central bank has tried to ease loan terms for the state companies, but that inspired many Vietnamese to move money out of deposits and into gold or the local stock market. That is putting so much pressure on the dong that as of late 2011, the central bank was spending $1 billion every six weeks to keep the currency from collapsing.

China's superior results stem in part from its leaders, who are more worldly than their Vietnamese counterparts. The Chinese elite started sending their kids to school in Europe and the United States in the 1970s, so many of today's leaders have been exposed to Western thought. In contrast, until the early 1990s, the Vietnamese elite were still sending their kids to universities in the Soviet Union and Eastern Europe, where they were exposed mainly to the best ideas of a defunct Communist system. While some analysts attribute China's prowess in the construction arts to the fact that eight of the nine top leaders are engineers, there are no engineers in the top Vietnamese leadership, which is populated largely by lawyers, with an economist and a philosopher among the top six. The emphasis on people skills is in keeping with the dictates of a consensus-driven society, but the current consensus excludes many of the best and brightest.

Chinese Communism is now much more meritocratic than its Vietnamese cousin, in part because its defining political event is farther in the past, argues Ben Wilkinson, associate director of the Vietnam Program at Harvard University. The first leaders of Communist China earned their stripes in the civil war of the 1930s and are long gone. While it still helps politicians to have ties to that generation, it's not critical. The formative event for Vietnam was the northern victory over the United States in the 1970s, and many Vietnamese leaders are veterans of the war, or children of veterans. If one's father fought for South Vietnam, chances of getting an important government job are slim. The highest national rank an official from Ho Chi Minh City—formerly known as Saigon, capital of South Vietnam during the war—has ever achieved in the ruling Communist Party politburo is number six, the position now held by economist Le Thanh Hai. His success is seen as a sign of diminishing bias against the south, but it will take a while for it to disappear completely.

In recent years Vietnam has actually been investing more heavily in education than has China, but most of the money has gone into the elementary and high school levels. While China has begun to produce some world-class universities, colleges in Vietnam are still in the educational dark ages. Foreign firms are increasingly disappointed with the lack of skilled labor and are turning back to alternative locations in Thailand and Indonesia. In 2010 Intel opened a $1 billion computer chip manufacturing plant in Ho Chi Minh City after a yearlong delay due in part to shoddy work by local contractors that led to a section of the roof collapsing. The plant was designed to employ four thousand people, but the failure rate on the test of basic English and technical skills was so high that only four out of the first twelve hundred applicants got hired. The company had to start training new workers on-site, but the plant is still undermanned, and it may be 2016 before the facility is operating at full steam.

In truth, there may be no country in the world with a per capita income of $1,300 that has a labor force ready to make computer chips when it has been making nothing more sophisticated than shoes and clothes until now. The point is that Vietnam has been trying (with much outside encouragement) to jump too high too fast. For now, a nation that aspires to grow its economy at least 1 percentage point faster than China is growing 3 to 4 percentage points slower, at about 5 percent. Foreign capital flows have slowed down dramatically and are unlikely to return until Vietnam's authoritarian leaders figure out how to run a command economy.

The Fastest Billion?

When there is reason for optimism about the Fourth World, it is often found in the nations of Africa. In fact the continent is such a hot fad right now that economists in Johannesburg are complaining about all the foreign investors who talk in broad-brush terms about the "Africa opportunity" presented by the "billion-strong population" and the "$1.7 trillion market." That is the economic size of the entire African continent. Foreign investors also like pointing out that $1.7 trillion is roughly the size of the economy of India or Russia today—as if the fifty-four nations of Africa comprised one economy.

In Africa perhaps even more than in the big emerging markets, nations have to be viewed as distinct entities or at best as clusters, when neighbors start working together in trade unions. For starters the four largest economies (South Africa, Nigeria, Egypt, and Algeria) account for more than $1 trillion of the $1.7 trillion market. Most of the rest are so small (thirty-eight have economies smaller than $20 billion) and so disconnected they really have only one thing in common: they rely on commodity exports, which makes them vulnerable to the coming slowdown in China.

But the continent has its share of surprises. In 2010 Indian telecommunications tycoon Sunil Bharti Mittal paid $9 billion for a mobile network spanning sixteen African nations. When Mittal thought about venturing into Africa, the first thing everyone warned him about was corruption. But in two years he says he has not been hit up for one bribe, only donations for local schools, health clinics, and football teams. "Nobody has asked for any money, not once," says Mittal. "That's huge."

He recalls driving past the swarming crowds and impoverished shops of Kinshasa to reach a meeting with President Laurent Kabila of the Democratic Republic of Congo, which took many hours of winding through the city because Kabila is always on the move, for security reasons. Once he reached Kabila, however, Mittal found him straightforward, sincere, and focused on one thing: bringing more Indian businessmen to his dirt-poor nation of eighty million, one of the most populous but also most remote in Africa. For all its riches—from diamonds to gold to "land so fertile all you have to do is throw seeds over your shoulder and they will grow"—very few outsiders come here. "Bring back Indian businessmen," said Kabila. "You can take all the land you want." Mittal left deeply moved by how much potential lies hidden in the Congo if only Kabila could solve his riddle: no one will come if he doesn't build roads, but he can't build roads if no one comes.

Back in the 1980s and 1990s, the story line about Africa was so dark no one could see through it to the good news. Between 1960 and 1990, elections were infrequent and rarely brought in new faces: in that thirty-year period only one African leader was defeated at the polls. In 1990 all but five African nations were run by dictators; but a wave of change began the next year with the victory of the opposition presidential candidate in Benin's first election since 1970. By 2009 Freedom House, a think tank based in Washington, D.C., was ranking thirty African nations as free or partly free, up from nineteen in the previous decade, as the rule of law started to trump the rule of dictators. Classic African "strongman" rulers like Daniel arap Moi in Kenya and Olusegun Obasanjo in Nigeria were actually being forced out of power by new rules imposing term limits. Though the 50/50 rule tells us that there is no clear connection between democratic elections and growth, elections were probably necessary in Africa to break a seemingly endless cycle of corruption and coups.

Further, as we've seen throughout this book, sometimes just modest reform or the arrival of a dynamic new leader can unleash growth, particularly in frontier markets. Leaders such as Mbeki in South Africa, Paul Kagame in Rwanda, and Joaquim Chissano in Mozambique started to get the basics right, though in some cases the improvements had begun before the new leaders arrived. Primary-school enrollment was rising fast, from a rate of 61 percent across Africa in 1975 to 96 percent by 2005. Secondary-school enrollment rose from a rate of 3 percent in 1960 to 39 percent by 2005. That is all movement in the right direction, though still very low by developed-nation standards.

Mittal says there is now a surprisingly "Eurocentric" quality to the business culture in sub-Saharan Africa. It has an "incredibly evolved" legal and regulatory environment: "In my industry the regulations are more like Europe. They get it, they want to keep prices low, they don't milk this industry and want to help the industry so it rolls out network and creates jobs. I am stunned at the quality of the human capital: educated, erudite, they have studied the U.S. and British systems." In the executive job market, where there is shortage of talent, those who have been educated in the United States or the United Kingdom come back knowing they can demand the standard Western package, including performance-linked incentives. The cost of hiring a country CFO in a place like Uganda runs to $250,000 a year, more than twice the salary for a comparable post in India, and about the same as in London.

The new African leaders also looked to success stories in Asia and started to realize that getting the economy right would give them more political leverage too. While some of the new leaders have started to act like strongmen, hanging on to office too long, most are still pushing economic progress. In this new decade the economic problems of Africa are starting to look like opportunities. The estimated $420 billion that African tycoons have squirreled away in foreign banks used to be seen as a symptom of corruption; now investment advisers cite this vast pool of money as potential investment capital that could come back home and drive African growth. The fact that African nations barely trade with one another—intraregional exports account for only 4 percent of GDP growth in sub-Saharan Africa—was once seen as a symptom of the bad roads, poor phone connections, and spotty power supplies that block

African commerce. Now it is seen as a big opportunity for construction companies.

Africa is a great case study in the contrarian value of cover stories. Front covers of popular publications often provide valuable insights—though many times not what they mean to. By the time a market trend becomes a screaming headline, it has likely matured and is fully factored into prices, setting the stage for a reversal. *The Economist* put Africa on its cover as the "Hopeless Continent" in 1999, the year when the income gap between the developed world and Africa was the widest in modern history. At the time the African continent's per capita incomes were less than a tenth those of its developed-country peers. As the most successful weekly news magazine on the planet, *The Economist* has become a voice of the consensus, its cover a reflection of current popular opinion. In November 2009, *The Economist* put Brazil on the cover, with an illustration of Christ the Redeemer, the giant statue of Jesus that overlooks Rio, taking off like a rocket. Over the next two years, the Brazilian market fell by around 30 percent in dollar terms, 15 percentage points worse than the emerging-market average. Lately *The Economist* has been rather hot on "Africa Rising" as "the hopeful continent." Let's hope that will work out this time.

Many nations in Africa are rapidly joining the global mainstream; their trade numbers are growing faster than the underlying economy. In particular, growth in information and telecommunications services is spectacular. Since 2007 the number of fiber-optic cables connecting sub-Saharan Africa to the world has increased by a factor of 12, Internet capacity has increased by a factor of 100, and prices for a connection have fallen more than 95 percent.

The later a nation develops, the more opportunity it has to learn from nations that came before, and to leapfrog entire development steps in the process. It's well known that rural China has gone from no phones to wireless phones, skipping the expensive, backbreaking, and time-consuming steps of digging trenches or erecting poles to run landlines. Two decades behind China along comes Africa, leaping from no telecommunications straight into the age of advanced digital services, delivered on mobile devices.

To cite just one example, consider the success of mobile banking, which offers a way for people on the low end of the economic scale to leap into the world of modern finance without having to build a single bank. With an M-Pesa "electronic wallet" a Kenyan can use his cell phone to pay for a ride in a taxicab, a service that is not available in the West. Since 2007 the number of Kenyans who keep money in a bank has risen from one in five to one in two, thanks in large part to M-Pesa. The increase in bank savings could serve as a new pool of money to finance the building of roads and other critical infrastructure, and its potential to grow is huge. Even in better-developed South Africa, the opportunity is substantial because while there are only twenty million South Africans with bank accounts, there are forty million with mobile phones.

Unfortunately a continent increasingly well connected by fiber-optic cable is let down by its shoddy networks for just about everything other than data. As South African executives point out, signs of opportunity in Africa can at times be misleading because many nations are so poorly served by basic transportation and utilities that the "route to market" is often prohibitively expensive, particularly in nations where the GDP is under $10 billion and the potential profits are limited. To move freight via road from the capital city of Abidjan in the Ivory Coast to Bamako in Mali, a trip of just 690 miles, can take up to five hundred hours, according to an IMF estimate. That averages out to less than walking speed, attributable to both the condition of the roads and the folkways of a trucking industry that is dominated by cartels, jammed with paperwork, and dogged by delays in loading and unloading that drive up the trucking cost to a very pricey $250 per ton. Yet even here, there is an opportunity for Africa to leapfrog into the future by learning from past successes.

One of the striking characteristics of the rare high-growth success stories is that they tend to appear in geographic clusters: the oil nations of the Gulf, the nations on the southern periphery of Europe after World War II, the nations of East Asia in the same period. Africa, moving past its warring-states period, is starting to look to the formation of the European Community in the 1950s, and the Association of Southeast Asian Nations, or ASEAN, in the 1960s, for ideas to overcome the hurdles facing nations that are too small and off the beaten trade paths to excite much interest on their own. The result is at least five separate efforts to create a common market in Africa, the most promising of which is the East African Community (EAC).

Bringing together Kenya, Rwanda, Burundi, Tanzania, and Uganda, this community aims to gain leverage in global trade negotiations through numbers and to begin laying the regional network of infrastructure—roads, rails, ports—required to accelerate commerce beyond walking speed. Modeled on the original European Community, the EAC set out to create a full-fledged common market with free movement of people and goods leading, perhaps, to a common currency by 2012 and political integration by 2015. The EAC has already eliminated all internal tariff barriers, but given the crisis in the Eurozone, it would not be surprising to see the EAC slow or drop its plan for an East African currency.

Talk of an African renaissance tends to skip over the practical hurdles, the political hurdles, and the source of the trade revenues: 80 percent of African exports are commodities, leaving the continent vulnerable to any slowdown in Chinese and global demand for raw materials like oil and precious metals. Mittal says he was amazed by the astronomical cost differences across the sixteen nations where his company operates: building cell towers in a landlocked nation of the African interior like the Democratic Republic of Congo is up to twice as expensive as it is in coastal states like Kenya, owing to the state of the roads and the power grid.

Too many people are now saying that because eleven African nations grew at 7 percent in the last decade, the entire continent can build on that momentum to grow at breakneck speed over the next one. Maybe, if they get all the basics right. Some are heading in the right direction, including major African economies such as those of Nigeria and the countries that are part of the EAC. They have a good chance to be breakout nations, but it's not likely that all their neighbors will break out with them.

Africa's Accidental Leader

Nigeria has been infamous for some of the most corrupt regimes in Africa, but today it is in the hands of an accidental but effective leader with an apropos name: Goodluck Jonathan.

Jonathan is not one of the charismatic champions of change like Erdoğan in Turkey or Lula in Brazil. He was a deputy governor of a state in the war-torn Niger Delta when the actual governor was pushed out of office on corruption charges in 2005. Then President Umaru Yar'Adua selected Jonathan as his vice president, largely because he wanted representation from the delta region. When Yar'Adua died suddenly in 2009, Jonathan became president. Although he was promoted largely because of chance and circumstance, Jonathan nonetheless provides the modicum of sound leadership Nigeria needs: There is no record of his ever saying anything outrageous, which is a badge of merit among leaders on the frontier. His reputation so far is down-to-earth, uncorrupt, a sharp departure from the history of presidential graft in Nigeria: Swiss authorities declared the family of President Sani Abacha (1993–1998) a criminal enterprise, with an embezzled fortune estimated at $2 to $5 billion. Though Abacha was once ranked the fourth-most-corrupt leader in modern history, close behind the likes of Suharto and Marcos, Nigerians have argued that both Olusegun Obasanjo (1999–2007) and Ibrahim Babangida (1985–1993) were worse. Together those three leaders ran the country for most of the two decades before Jonathan became president.

And yet, such was the power of rising oil prices and the economy's low base (per capita income is below $1,500) that Nigeria, along with its African neighbors in Equatorial Guinea, Angola, and Sierra Leone, was among the fastest-growing economies of the past decade. With GDP growth running at 6 to 7 percent, twice as fast as South Africa's, the West African country is well on track to be the largest economy on the continent by 2013.

Its greatest recent accomplishment, one that is likely to prove to be more valuable than oil, is the widely overlooked series of bloodless leadership successions that brought Jonathan to power after many years of coups, assassinations, and dictatorships. Jonathan's passage through high offices has also coincided with the rapid maturation of Nigerian democracy. Yar'Adua's victory in 2007 was rife with fraud, yet it marked the first democratic transition (that is, not a coup) in Nigeria's recent history. Every step since has grown cleaner and cleaner. The 2009 transition to Jonathan was conducted in accord with the letter and spirit of the constitution, and one of Jonathan's first acts was to bring in a trustworthy figure as head of a new election commission. Under its guidance, the presidential election of April 2011, which Jonathan won easily, was praised by international observers as strikingly clean and fair.

The significance of this turn to stability in Africa's most populous nation (155 million people) should not be underestimated, nor should Jonathan. The rebellion in the southern Niger delta region is in some ways a distant offspring of the 1967–1970 civil war, which pitted separatists in the Christian South against the rulers, then from the Muslim North. This divide still animates Nigerian politics, as Jonathan, a southerner, won all the southern states and none of the northern states. But as vice president he was central to the negotiation of a peace deal under which the southern rebels disarmed, in return for safe passage into civilian life. Oil production in Nigeria had been plummeting until the peace deal was reached in mid-2009, and it has since rebounded by more than 20 percent to 2.2 million barrels per day. If the newfound political stability holds, it could set the stage for higher output growth in the coming years.

There is more to the Nigerian economy than just oil. The $300 million-a-year movie industry, known predictably as Nollywood, is the second-largest producer of films in the world, just ahead of the United States and behind only India. Its rise from virtually nothing two decades ago to become the nation's second-biggest employer, after the government, is a remarkable example of how new cheaper technologies like digital cameras and some entrepreneurial zeal can create a mini tech-led boom even in the heart of Africa. Most of the movies are shot on a shoestring budget, completed in a matter of days, and go straight to video, for lack of public venues. The movie theaters in Lagos and other Nigerian cities were shut in the 1980s and 1990s during a crime epidemic, and have recently opened. Nigeria's most lucrative market for video sales is in the southwest, in and around Lagos, where a growing middle class is creating higher demand for consumer goods.

Jonathan's government looks to be targeting all the right steps to unleash growth from a low base. The first rule for a successful oil-rich state is "Thou shalt not steal." Over the past decade an estimated $400 billion in profits from Nigerian oil has simply disappeared into the pockets of politicians and businessmen, a huge loss in a nation with an annual GDP of $250 billion. To stem the flow Jonathan has created a sovereign-wealth fund that operates according to the Santiago Principles, an international standard designed to ensure that these increasingly popular investment vehicles are professionally managed and do not become political and personal slush funds for those in power. That may not guarantee that oil money does not end up in the wrong pockets, but it reflects honest intentions.

A nation at Nigeria's income level should be spending well more than 20 percent of GDP on the staples of a modern economy: better roads, telecommunications, and power. Nigeria invests only around 10 percent, which leaves gaping holes, especially in the power grid. With total output of just four thousand megawatts a year, the country generates as much electricity as Bradford, a postindustrial town in the north of England. In fact Nigeria generates just 162 kilowatt hours per year per person, ranking 175th in the world; by comparison Mexico generates fourteen times more power per person, and Kazakhstan generates thirty times more.

Economists who look at these factors call Nigeria "underinvested," but visitors encounter it as just plain chaos; Lagos, one of the fastest-growing megacities in the world, has ten million people and counting. Visitors are jostled everywhere and constantly have to work around the power failures, which are likely to shut out the lights in the middle of meetings or trap the unprepared in elevators. Those in the know always take the stairs. The luxurious Federal Palace Hotel in Lagos has multiple backup generators, but the lights still go out for five to ten minutes a couple of times a day while the generators crank into operation.

For the moment Nigerian companies get power any way they can, and frequently generate their own. MTN, the South African mobile-phone company, has to equip each of its towers in Nigeria with a generator, a backup generator, and a fuel tank. It needs a truck to resupply those tanks and guards to protect the entire operation. It's little surprise that MTN's operating costs here are three times higher than those in its native South Africa. If there is a business upside to the power shortfall, it is that Nigeria is the world's biggest market for private generators; many middle-class homes have one. But as we've seen with Brazil's roof-hopping CEOs, a private solution to a public problem is a symptom of wider dysfunction. The costs can be extraordinary: Lafarge, a global supplier of construction materials, charges $180 a ton for cement in Nigeria, compared with $120 elsewhere in sub-Saharan Africa and $65 in emerging markets such as Turkey. The reason, it says, is the high cost of doing business in Nigeria, including the fact that only one-third of the roadways are paved.

Perhaps the most dramatic result of the lack of investment is the absence of formal stores and malls, leaving the street as the main distribution channel for goods. Sidewalk vendors in Lagos sell an array of merchandise unsurpassed anywhere in the world: watches, wallets, bed linens, biscuits, healing remedies, newspapers, chessboards, toys, pots and pans, shoes and clothing, appliances. Hawkers carry night tables on their heads at the busiest junctions of downtown Abuja, the national capital. This overflowing street life is part of Nigerian culture, but it's also evidence of too little retail space and the resulting high prices per square foot in the major cities of Abuja, Kano, and Lagos and along all the major roads throughout the country.

The more obvious the problem in a frontier market, the bigger the opportunity, particularly when the national leadership is making moves to get some basic things right. Based on plans laid down during Yar'Adua's administration, the Nigerian government is working hard to turn the power up. It hopes to raise $35 billion in new energy-sector investment for new plants that will increase overall output by a factor of 10 by 2020, for a total of forty thousand megawatts. Jonathan is also taking steps to lower "domestic content" rules that limit foreign investment in the oil sector, and to lift the subsidies that make the price of domestic fuel too cheap.

Nigeria's government has more low-hanging fruit than it can possibly pick in the next five years. It could establish a Nigerian identification card; currently there is no official form of ID in the country, making it virtually impossible for businesses to know their customers and creating enormous opportunities for scams. At another level it could clean up the fast-track channel at Lagos airport, run by touts who charge ten dollars to ferry travelers through immigration checks, in league with border guards who work extra slowly on the regular lines to make the fast channel appealing. Or it just could clean up the system in some Nigerian states where governors must personally sign off on property sales, for a fee. This arrangement is one of the reasons why the International Finance Corporation ranks Nigeria one of the worst property markets in the world. Any advance on even one or two important fronts could unleash new sources of growth—and Nigeria may now have a government stable enough to move on several fronts at once.

A World unto Itself

At the 2007 peak of the emerging-market boom, the Wall Street chorus was singing, "It is all about Shanghai, Mumbai, and Dubai." Dubai has fallen off the refrain since 2009, following the burst of a credit bubble that exposed problems common throughout the Gulf. Many companies are privately held, either by wealthy merchant families or by the ruling monarchies, so it is difficult to see trouble coming. Numbers arrive late and are unreliable. The huge debts exposed in 2009 at Dubai World, a state holding company, reminded outsiders that in the Gulf what you see is still not what you get. Even though Dubai has staged a comeback of sorts, most foreign investors have stayed away.

Historically, stock exchanges in the Gulf have listed so few quality companies that they have never captured the region's economic growth, but today the disconnect is growing. Between 2005 and 2010, the GDP of the Gulf region expanded at an annual pace of 6 percent, a rate in line with the average for all developing economies. Yet the value of Gulf stock markets (including in Bahrain, Kuwait, Oman, Qatar, and the United Arab Emirates) fell 30 percent, while mainstream emerging markets gained 50 percent. Why Gulf markets are out of sync with economic growth is just one more puzzle in a region I've increasingly come to see as a world unto itself.

It is a world built entirely on revenues from oil and gas. The old Benjamin Franklin line about how the only certain things in life are death and taxes does not apply in the Gulf, where there are basically no taxes. Government, too, survives off oil wealth. Saudi Arabia abolished the income tax for locals and foreigners alike back in 1975. At just over 2 percent, the United Arab Emirates has the lowest effective corporate tax rate in the world after Venezuela (where the Chávez government gives so much money back to favored businesses that the total corporate tax rate is negative). By many metrics—total amount of money in foreign reserves, population growth, energy consumption—the Gulf is at the top of global charts, or off the chart.

Black gold has flowed so easily for so long that the typical Gulf state has become an oil-fueled jobs machine with subsidies on offer for every essential item, ranging from food and power to schooling. This raft of freebies means that there are no effective price signals. Normally people cut back on driving when their incomes fall but not in the Gulf, where the price of gas is inconsequential; a gallon of gas goes for forty-five cents in Riyadh. The cost of diesel is just 3 percent the cost in the United Kingdom. While the rest of the world is raising (or at least debating) higher taxes on gas to restrain consumption, the subsidies in the Gulf are spurring a consumption boom. Saudi Arabia spends nearly 10 percent of GDP on subsidies, including support for electricity, transport fuel, and gas prices. Add in the rapidly growing population, and it's easy to see why energy consumption is growing at 5 percent a year, one of the fastest rates in the world. Today Saudi oil consumption—more than thirty-three barrels per person each year—is by far the highest among the Group of Twenty (G20) major economies, and 50 percent higher than the next-most-gluttonous nations, Canada and the United States.

When asked why they keep the costly subsidies in place, officials have said that the gas subsidies are cheaper than building public transport, despite the fact that the subsidies eventually end up in the pockets of foreign companies. Saudi Arabia, the largest crude oil producer in the world, has never gotten around to building enough refineries, so it must import finished fuel, a situation typical for the region. The Middle East holds nearly half the world's oil and natural gas reserves but runs one of the world's largest gasoline deficits. This paradox of scarcity amid plenty is not unique to the Gulf—there are other oil exporters that have to import refined gasoline—but except for Qatar, the world's largest exporter of gas, the discrepancy in the Gulf region is the most extreme in the world.

The "Arab Spring" revolts that swept the region in 2011 could drastically alter the economic picture. The Gulf monarchies have been startled by uprisings that toppled authoritarian regimes in Tunisia, Egypt, and Libya—and as of this writing still threaten those in Yemen and Syria. Fomented in no small part by economic stagnation under unyielding rulers, the revolts have put a scare into Gulf regimes. Despite rising oil wealth, the population in Saudi Arabia is increasing so fast that per capita income ($20,000) is at about the same level as in the early 1980s.

To ease discontent at home the Gulf States have been spreading around oil profits with even greater generosity than normal. In 2011 Bahrain gave $1,000 to every family in the country, only to be trumped by Kuwait's payout of $2,600. There are also targeted benefits for key political constituencies, like Qatar's decision to raise pension payments to retired military personnel by 70 percent. In many cases the spending plans—on new housing, new jobs, wage hikes—are major long-term commitments that will weigh on the region for years.

The impact varies widely across the Gulf, but looking just at the largest and most restive nations reveals that spending has risen so fast of late that the oil price these nations need in order to cover their surging budgets has roughly tripled to around $80 in Saudi Arabia and Oman and to more than $110 in Bahrain, one of the monarchies hardest hit by street protests. Oman and Saudi Arabia also have much larger cash reserves than Bahrain, which means they can continue to spend for another ten years as heavily as they did during the turmoil of 2009, even in the event of another financial crisis. Bahrain by contrast is already getting billions in aid from its neighbors. Whether it can continue to pay off its restive population remains an open question.

More broadly, a region oriented entirely around the discovery of oil is now ever more dependent on that original resource. If emerging markets are entering a phase of slow growth, the high oil prices that keep the whole region afloat are under threat. The Gulf States don't have a great plan B to fund their recent largesse if oil prices do fall. Though the Saudi government's effort to forestall unrest will hike spending by 40 percent in 2011, there is no discussion of taxes to cover the cost. In a society where the population is accustomed to receiving checks from the government, raising taxes isn't a live political option.

What top foreign advisers such as the IMF tell Saudi Arabia, Bahrain, and Oman is that they can afford their spending habits only in the short term, so long as the price of oil stays high, but this gets riskier as the region's oil reserves start to run down. Oil and gas production is believed to have peaked everywhere in the Gulf outside Qatar, which has hit the resource-wealth lottery. Qatar still has a century or two of natural gas left at current production rates—and so restraint is not in its lexicon. Massive spending has been driving extraordinary growth—an average pace of 17.5 percent for the five years through 2010—that looks likely to continue for a while. With a per capita income of $100,000, twice that of the United States, Qatar is unique, a world unto itself, hidden within a world unto itself.

While the Gulf monarchies are ramping up spending to unsustainable levels in an effort to forestall popular revolt, the threat to their hold on power should not be overstated. As Jack Goldstone of George Mason University has pointed out, the Gulf monarchies are not "sultanistic regimes" like those in Tunisia or Egypt, which existed mainly to enrich the reigning leader and his inner circle, with no plan either to develop the nation or to pass on power in an orderly succession. The monarchies of the Gulf are widely viewed as legitimate, rooted in the local culture, and working hard if not always effectively to carve viable economies out of the desert.

There are some reasons to be optimistic about the Gulf, largely due to the reforms in Saudi Arabia, which accounts for about half the region's population and GDP. Back in the 1970s as much as 80 percent of the overall oil windfall went into regional conflicts, higher defense spending, and the related kickbacks. Budgets were deep in the red. When oil prices collapsed in the 1980s, the ensuing financial crises forced many Gulf nations to get a grip on spending. By the middle of the last decade, 70 percent of the oil revenue was going into savings, or to pay down debt, and today financial management remains top notch. Virtually every state in the Gulf has adopted the model established by Norway, which has a hugely successful sovereign-wealth fund to reinvest its oil profits. While some researchers have suggested these funds were a kind of fad in the Gulf, an attempt to look at least as modern as the neighbors, they continue to achieve their basic purpose: to manage money strategically and honestly in the long-term interest of the state.

Even in Egypt, which was characterized by some as a sultanistic regime, there was real momentum for economic (if not political) reform in the last few years under the Mubaraks. In March 2009, when the collapsing world economy was inspiring global headlines about the death of capitalism, I spent some time with Gamal Mubarak at an annual conference I regularly attend in the seaside town of Sharm el Sheikh. Mubarak was then widely seen as the likely successor to his father as Egyptian president. I asked him about the crisis, whether it would take the momentum out of economic reform in places such as Egypt, and he said, "Absolutely not. There's still a lot of support for reform because memories of socialism and its downsides—low growth and high inflation—have not faded. We need better regulation, not more regulation." At a time when headlines in the West were heralding "the end of capitalism," it was reassuring to hear such words in a country that had been on the margins of globalization.

Saudi leaders seem most aware of the key challenge they face: building a better-educated, more motivated native workforce capable of creating an economy beyond oil. They are spending heavily and wisely on improving schools, from kindergarten to PhD programs, on modernizing transport networks, and on building new power plants. Even without new non-oil industries, it still looks like smart spending, and oil profits alone could keep growth chugging along at a 4 to 5 percent rate, which is not bad for a region with already high incomes. This outlook, however, is far from assured.

For the last decade the discussion throughout the Gulf has focused on life after oil, on developing new industries, starting with those that use oil as a raw material, the region's clear competitive advantage. There are new plants producing petrochemicals and fertilizer throughout the region, but so far the actual economic impact of the new industries does not match the urgency of the discussion: between 2001 and 2010 the oil share of GDP dropped a few percentage points in Bahrain, Kuwait, and Oman, but several Gulf States have actually become more dependent on oil, with petroleum's share of GDP rising 10 percentage points in Saudi Arabia to 45 percent, and 2 percentage points in the United Arab Emirates to 31 percent.

It's particularly surprising to see the United Arab Emirates becoming more oil dependent, because one of the emirates is Dubai, which became internationally renowned during the same ten-year period for its over-the-top campaign to build a finance and tourism mecca in the desert. Part Vegas, part Singapore, the idea was to house serious businesses in attention-grabbing architecture like the sail-shaped Burj Al Arab, which became the inspiration for similar visions in the emirate of Abu Dhabi, Qatar, Oman, and elsewhere in the region. But there is a limit to the economic potential of finance and tourism industries in the desert. Those following Dubai's lead all claim slightly different spins on the model—Qatar is focused on sports tourism and will host the 2022 World Cup soccer tournament; Oman has embraced non-sports tourism. But Qatar also has its impressive new Islamic Museum, and Abu Dhabi is both hosting major sports events like Formula 1 races and building a spectacular $25 billion island to house extensions of the Louvre and the Guggenheim, as well as top international universities. These are grand but competing visions, and they can't all work in one small region.

The Gulf has also made very limited progress in putting its own citizens to work. It's pretty well known that the Gulf States are home to a vast army of expat workers that accounts for about a third of the region's population, and as much as 75 percent in Qatar, 66 percent in Kuwait, and more than 80 percent in the United Arab Emirates. What's less well known is that most of these countries are essentially run by consultants: in the typical oil company the board of directors and the CEO will be drawn from the royal family, but the president and everyone below him will be British, Indian, or Lebanese. Essentially the system is employing foreign talent to generate a trust fund for the locals as oil and petrochemical companies in the region churn out profits—which have contributed to an estimated $2 trillion in reserves—much of it now held in sovereign-wealth funds. These funds, in turn, invest outside the Gulf for the same reasons foreign investors avoid the Gulf: murky rules, opaque books, too few world-class companies.

Local individual investors, however, are another story. This population holds enough wealth to create major bubbles in the Gulf stock markets. They live in liquidity hothouses, built on trade surpluses rising at the rate of more than $200 billion a year, or more than 20 percent of GDP.

Estimates put the total financial wealth in the region at over $3 trillion, compounding at 20 percent a year as oil revenues continue to spill over. This kind of wealth is beyond imaginations anywhere else in the Fourth World, and it has to go somewhere.

In 2005 and early 2006 the oil wealth sloshing around the Gulf created a bubble of epic proportions. With oil prices rising and some nations starting to follow the Saudi reform lead by privatizing arms of their oil industries, investing got hot. Private lending started to grow, and investors started to borrow to buy stock, leading to a spiraling cycle of rising credit feeding rising stock prices. Small investors started to rush in, gambling family savings, falling deep into debt, even selling cars and houses to buy stock. Most of the newcomers were women who had never traded before, and some exchanges in the region set up special trading floors for them, in keeping with Muslim strictures on separation of the sexes.

Trading became a nationwide mania in Saudi Arabia. Teachers were publicly admonished for day-trading during school hours. In December 2005 fully half the population of seventeen million purchased shares in the IPO of a petrochemical company. At the fever's peak one in five Saudis was day-trading—compared to one in one hundred Americans at the height of the tech bubble in 2000. When the pop finally came in early 2006, it was devastating to Saudis. The luxury shops of Riyadh emptied out, and Saudis rushed to car dealerships to sell their cars, this time to pay off stock market losses. As the dust settled, the market supervisors shut down dozens of Web sites that had sprung up to spread stock rumors, and today the market is still down about 50 percent from its peak, to a total value of around $300 billion, roughly in line with where it should be for an economy of Saudi Arabia's size ($560 billion).

While the oil bounty encourages such speculative outbreaks, the Gulf appears immune to the Dutch disease that afflicts many commodity-rich countries, including Brazil, Russia, and South Africa. Rising commodity prices are driving up the value of the currency in these countries, which makes all their non-commodity exports more expensive, and less competitive on world markets. The Gulf States are largely immune to Dutch disease because they have never had significant exports outside of oil. There is no manufacturing or service sector to hollow out. Besides oil the Gulf has no competitive advantages, and has to import just about everything. Even local glass companies—surrounded as they are by millions of acres of sand—have to import their main ingredient. None of the local sand is of high enough quality to use in glass. This is no fault of the Gulf nations; it is simply a sign of how difficult it is to build a modern society with a diverse economic base in an inhospitable desert.

The Gulf States are thus an extreme example of why no two emerging or frontier nations can be treated alike, and no nation's economic path can be understood through a simple set of rules. The Gulf States have broken dozens of basic rules of economic development—the lack of a manufacturing base, a much-too-small skilled native workforce, the most generous subsidy culture on earth, with no taxes demanded to pay for it—and yet it is possible that they can grow reasonably well for the foreseeable future, thanks to oil's bounty. And within this world unto itself, there is an even smaller state, the world's richest, that looks like it can prosper on oil for decades. The Gulf is proof positive that every emerging nation—and every emerging region, particularly in the Fourth Worl—is unique.

"Those who leave early may be saved, but the music and wines are so seductive that we do not want to leave, but we do ask, 'What time is it? What time is it?' Only none of the clocks have any hands."

13

After the Ecstasy, the Laundry

As PLAYWRIGHT ARTHUR MILLER once observed, "An era can be said to end when its basic illusions are exhausted." Most of the illusions that defined the last decade—the notion that global growth had moved to a permanently higher plane, the hope that the Fed (or any central bank) could iron out the highs and lows of the business cycle—are indeed spent. Yet one idea still has the power to capture the imagination of the markets: that the inexorable rise of China and other big developing economies will continue to drive a "commodity supercycle," a prolonged upward rise in the prices of commodities ranging from oil to copper and silver, to textiles, to corn and soybeans. This conviction is the main reason for the optimism about the prospects of the many countries that live off commodity exports, from Brazil to Argentina, and Australia to Canada.

I call this illusion commodity.com, for it is strikingly similar in some ways to the mania for technology stocks that gripped the world in the late 1990s. At the height of the dotcom era, tech stocks comprised 30 percent of all the money invested in global markets. When the bubble finally burst, commodity stocks—energy and materials—rose to replace tech stocks as the investment of choice, and by early 2011 they accounted for 30 percent of the global stock markets. No bubble is a good bubble, and all leave some level of misery in their wakes. But the commodity.com era has had a larger and more negative impact on the global economy than the tech boom did.

The hype has created a new industry that turns commodities into financial products that can be traded like stocks. Oil, wheat, and platinum used to be sold primarily as raw materials, and now they are sold largely as speculative investments. Copper is piling up in bonded warehouses not because the owners plan to use it to make wire, but because speculators are sitting on it, like gold, figuring that they can sell it one day for a huge profit. Daily trading in oil now dwarfs daily consumption of oil, running up prices. While rising prices for stocks—tech ones included—generally boost the economy, high prices for staples like oil impose unavoidable costs on businesses and consumers and act as a profound drag on the economy.

That is how average citizens experience commodity.com, as an anchor weighing down their every move, not the exciting froth of the hot new thing. The dotcom sensation broke the bounds of the financial world and seized the popular imagination, attracting thrilled media hype around the world and enticing cubicle jockeys to become day traders. There was the dream of great riches, yes, but also a boundless optimism and faith in human progress, a sense that the innovations flowing out of Silicon Valley would soon reshape the world for the better.

Tech CEOs became rock stars because they promised a life of rising productivity, falling prices, and high salaries for generating ideas in the hip office pods of the knowledge economy, or for trading tech stocks from a laptop in the living room. It was impossible in those days to get investors interested in anything that did not involve technology and the United States, so some of us started talking up emerging markets as "e-merging markets," while analysts spent a lot of time searching for the new Silicon Valley, which they dutifully but often implausibly discovered hiding in loft offices everywhere from Prague to Kuala Lumpur.

A decade later the chatter was all about the big emerging markets and oil, but with a darker mood. Commodity.com is driven by fear and a total lack of faith in human progress: fear of a rising phalanx of emerging nations with an insatiable demand led by China, of predictions that the world is running out of oil and farmland, coupled with a lack of faith in the human capacity to devise answers, to find alternatives to oil or ways to make agricultural land more productive. It's a Malthusian vision of struggle and scarcity: of prices driven up by failing supplies and wages pushed down by foreign competition.

Excitement about rising commodity prices exists only among the investors, financiers, and speculators who can gain from it. Commodity.com has inspired many an Indian and Chinese entrepreneur to go trekking across Africa in search of coal mines, yet it has no positive manifestation in the public mind at all. At the height of the tech bubble millions of American high school students aspired to become Stanford MBAs bound for Silicon Valley; today the growing number of oil, gas, and energy-management programs represents a small niche inside the MBA world. The only popular manifestations of commodity.com are complaints about rising gasoline prices and outbreaks of unrest over rising food prices in emerging markets.

It is well-justified unrest. If anything, the negative impact of sky-high commodity prices on the larger economy is underestimated. The price of oil rose sharply before ten of the eleven postwar recessions in the United States, including a spike of nearly 60 percent in the twelve months before the Great Recession of 2008 and more than 60 percent before the economy lost momentum in mid-2011. When the price of oil trips up the United States, it takes emerging markets down with it. In 2008 and 2009 the average economic growth rate dropped by 8 percentage points in both the developed and the emerging world, from its peak pace to the recession trough.

The strongest common thread connecting the dotcom and commodity.com eras is the fundamental driver of all manias: the invention of "new paradigms" to justify irrationally high prices. We heard all sorts of exotic rationales at the height of the dotcom boom, when analysts offered gushy explanations for why a company with no profits, a sketchy business plan, and a cute name should trade at astronomical prices. It was all about the future, about understanding why prices in a digitally networked economy "want to be free," while the "monetization" problem (how to make money on the Internet) would solve itself down the line. The dotcom mania, while it lasted, was powerful enough to make Bill Clinton—who campaigned as the first U.S. president to fully embrace the "new economy"—a living emblem of American revival, just as the commodity price boom played a role in making Vladimir Putin a symbol of Russian resurgence and Inácio Lula da Silva the face of a Brazilian recovery. When the rapture is over, the nations and companies that have been living high off commodities will also share the sinking feeling that followed the dotcom boom.

Two Hundred Years of Decline

The hype for nations like Brazil has been stoked by outlandish rationales for why the spike in commodity prices of the past few years suggests a permanent upward shift—a high-speed edition of the "new normal." Much of the case for rising commodity prices builds on the assumption that demand from emerging markets will continue to roll forward in one great wave as it did in the last decade, but that wave has already broken up. Given the burdens of high commodity prices, the coming bust will encourage the revival of confidence in the West, where most nations are major commodity consumers.

Over the last two hundred years, the prices of commodities as a group not only have declined steadily but also have traveled along predictable lines. Prices for a given resource rise continuously for a decade, which inspires inventors to come up with ways to conserve existing stocks, to extract the commodity more efficiently, or to invent cheaper substitutes. Then prices fall for two decades. This pattern of one decade forward, two decades back has pushed prices of major industrial commodities down 70 percent below where they were in the year 1800, after adjusting for inflation, according to data from the Montreal-based research firm Bank Credit Analyst. There are exceptions to the rule, such as gold, and to some extent oil and copper, which have at least retained value over time, but they have not seen extended "supercycles" of rising prices.

Today we are nearing the end of a decade of sharp increases in the price of oil, and the historical pattern is indeed repeating itself. We are already seeing huge gains in energy efficiency, and high oil prices have inspired heavy new investment in alternative energy sources and alternative-fuel vehicles, most of which have yet to deliver big, but hopefully that is only a matter of time.

No nation has more incentive to economize on oil or innovate than China, which is pushing to create green cities, electric cars, energy-efficient homes, and factories that are less energy-intensive. China is also delivering on these goals as perhaps only an aggressive command economy can. Take a summer business trip to Beijing, where government offices have been ordered to turn thermostats no lower than 25 degrees Celsius (77 degrees Fahrenheit), and you will feel what I mean.

The Oil Billionaires

The longer the illusions of commodity.com grip Wall Street, the more trouble they will cause, guiding vast personal and national fortunes to the wrong targets and into increasingly undeserving hands. At least back in 2000 the newly minted billionaires were truly creative people, many of whom endured the crash and are still advancing the tech revolution, delivering new generations of smart phones, e-readers, and many other innovations. Unfortunately today's newly minted billionaires are mainly in oil and other commodities: energy and materials stocks appreciated 300 percent in the last decade, and the big players are still making money by essentially digging stuff out of the ground. In 2001 the world had twenty-nine billionaires in the energy industry, seventy-five in tech; by 2011 the numbers had reversed, with thirty-six in tech and ninety-one in energy, mostly in oil. These new tycoons will make a lasting contribution only to the extent that they inspire competitors to come up with alternatives to oil that will help break the cycle.

Bullish attitudes about commodity prices have spawned an entire industry offering investment products including exchange-traded funds that essentially allow even lay people to trade commodities like stocks. The growth of this trend, labeled the "financialization of commodities," has been dizzying. The total sum of money invested in commodity funds has more than doubled over the last five years to more than $400 billion in 2011. According to the U.S.-based energy research firm Cornerstone Analytics, the total volume of trades in energy futures in 2011 was the equivalent of nearly two billion barrels a day, a staggering twenty-two times higher than the daily total global demand for energy, up from three times higher just a decade ago. Speculators rule the commodity markets, and prices of goods including silver, corn, and cotton have surged well past the cost of producing these goods at even the least-efficient farms and mines (which, in a normal market, will lose money). Commodity prices always rise after a downturn, but this boom was different. In the twenty-three economic recoveries since 1900, commodity prices have risen faster in only one case—after the recession of 1914—and have never risen faster relative to economic growth. From the end of 2008 through mid-2011, commodity prices led by oil and gold more than doubled. That makes this the sharpest commodity price boom ever recorded in a period of slow growth.

The Most Dangerous Herd Behavior

Inflated prices for commodities like oil carry the seeds of their own destruction, because the higher they rise, the more likely they are to stall the entire economy. In a way oil prices have become the new interest rate—effectively capping growth when central banks insist on flooding the system with liquidity. This is exactly the point we reached in mid-2011: with oil prices well over a hundred dollars a barrel, global spending on oil was 8 percent of GDP, the point at which the price traditionally starts to destroy demand.

The impact of sharply rising oil prices has always been destructive, but it has been magnified by the strange herd behavior of global markets in recent years. Like never before, the price of oil and the price of stocks have been moving in complete lockstep. And it's not just oil: in recent years investors have been treating all risk assets—meaning any investment that has a history of sharp up-and-down price movements, from copper to currencies and stocks in commodity-rich nations and even junk bonds—as the same animal. When investors are feeling confident, they pile into all these assets all at once, and when confidence ebbs, they pull out all at once.

It is popular to attribute the new herd behavior to the effects of globalization. Studies indeed show that as nations lower barriers to the movement of trade and money across borders, those money flows narrow the differences between markets across the world. Markets tend to move up and down together, as do the economies, because of the increased trade and capital linkages. However, in recent years, markets have become exceptionally synchronized, and that suggests a force other than globalization must be at work.

The Ariadne's thread that may solve this puzzle is easy money. Ebbs and flows in liquidity now dictate many trends across the world, and the abnormally low interest rates of recent years have led to a surge in easy money, as central banks tried to fuel an endless boom. When money is loose, investors borrow to buy hard assets, which is why the prices of oil, copper, and other commodities have become disconnected from actual demand, and are moving together. All the factors that used to have influence—weather on food, interest rates on gold, and industrial demand on base metals—came to be overridden by the growing demand from China and from speculators juiced up on easy money. As a result any efforts to stimulate the economy with more easy money just don't work; a big chunk of the money gets sucked into higher commodity prices, which undercuts the economy.

Central banks intend to promote real economic growth, not speculation and crippling oil price hikes. The diversion of all this money into commodity plays is disastrous, not only because it derails growth but also because it greatly increases inequality and the political tensions that go with it. Rising stock prices disproportionately benefit the richest 20 percent of the population, who in the United States own 75 percent of all stocks. Meanwhile rising oil prices disproportionately hurt the poorest 20 percent, who spend a four-times-larger share of their income on gas than the richest 20 percent.

Any social democrat who supports easy money as a way to promote jobs needs to rethink that position, as the current wave of liquidity is leading mainly to speculation, benefiting only the rich and effectively taxing savers (with interest rates below the rate of inflation, savers are getting a negative real return on their money). Cheap-money policies also tend to fuel what the research firm GaveKal Dragonomics has aptly called "the worst kind of bubbles," because zero interest rates encourage investors to pile into assets that are priced on scarcity (gold, fine wines, collectibles, trophy properties), not on productivity (tech, machine tools, ships). When the bubble pops, capital is simply destroyed and society is left with no more gold, diamonds, or fine wines than when it started. At least the tech bubble helped wire the world and left behind a whole new range of Internet tools and services, which have grown ever more valuable since.

The other force behind commodity.com is China's inexorable rise. China and commodities have become thoroughly entwined with the tide of easy money in the minds of investors. However, it makes no sense to believe that the price of commodities such as oil will rise indefinitely based on an expanding China, because the price of oil will eventually reach a height where it acts to slow China's factories. Further, the hype about China's manufacturing prowess and its exploding oil demand misses a basic point: the shift of global manufacturing to China is essentially a zero-sum game. Commodity prices should reflect overall manufacturing output and overall demand for oil, but neither is in fact rising sharply. Even though China's share of global manufacturing has risen dramatically in the last two decades, from 4 to 17 percent, the manufacturing share of the global economy has fallen in the same period, from 23 to 17 percent, largely at the expense of Europe, Japan, and the United States. Little wonder that demand for copper in the developed world has declined by an average 3 percent a year since 2005. Over the past decade American multinationals have shed two million jobs and moved an equal number overseas, but mainly in service industries; the manufacturing jobs are just gone. In the manufacturing sector China is a big, growing fish in a shrinking pond, which does not imply insatiable global demand for oil or any other commodity.

The rise in commodity prices has also magnified the problems associated with the "resource curse." The discovery of oil in poor nations tends to lead to tragedy, because the windfall profits breed corruption in government, attract excessive foreign lending, and trigger violent competition for oil profits while discouraging the pursuit of non-oil-related business ventures. An economy totally dependent on oil, and mired in foreign debt, results. Nations that have managed to save and invest commodity profits—such as Norway—were rich already, so the discovery of oil or copper did not land like a winning lottery ticket in the hand of a destitute and unprepared man. In the commodity.com era, however, the profits have been so high that even nations once on the right track have fallen off. As we've seen, the most striking example is probably Russia, which has blown through much of the rainy-day fund it had established with oil profits, and has failed to create even one non-commodity global brand.

It's my conviction that the China–commodity connection will fall apart soon. China has been devouring raw materials at a rate way out of line with the size of its economy, and the results of this investment are indeed stunning, from the maglev trains that flash from Shanghai to its airport, to sweeping highways that connect all of China's major cities. Since 1990, China's share of global demand for commodities ranging from aluminum to zinc has skyrocketed from the low single digits to 40, 50, 60 percent—even though China accounts for only 10 percent of total global output. In the case of oil China accounts for only 9 percent of total demand but is responsible for nearly half of the growth in demand, so it is the critical factor driving up prices. The extent to which the commodity boom is inflated by China becomes clear in a closer look at some possible slowdown scenarios. If, for example, growth in China's annual demand for copper slows by even 20 percent over the next five years, then demand growth in the rest of the emerging markets will need to double from 7 to 14 percent to make up the difference. That's not likely.

Malthus Is Back

Food offers a somewhat different story line, but with the same ending. It's possible that food prices will continue to increase in the near term, buffeted by a combination of underinvestment, erratic weather patterns, and other factors, but here, too, forecasts of a dismal new paradigm smack of Malthusian doom-mongering and a fundamental failure to understand the human capacity for transformation. The spike in food prices in the 1970s led to massive government investment in a "green revolution" that increased output to the point where farmers in the developed world were paid not to grow crops. Today governments have every bit as much incentive to mobilize, given the outbreak in recent years of protests against high food prices from Tunisia to Egypt, and there are signs that a new round of investment in food technology is already under way.

Those who see a long-term food crisis point to the growing world population but fail to note that the rate of population increase has been fall-ing steadily for a century. Further, 80 percent of the population increase between now and the year 2100 is expected to come in age groups of fifty years or older, and since caloric intake declines sharply with age, this would take a lot of the pressure off food supplies.

In the United States and Europe, there is some truth to the argument that nearly all of the most fertile farmland is already under cultivation, but the same is not true in developing nations. Africa has 60 percent of the world's arable land, and only a third has been cultivated. In other regions there is ample room to improve yields: In the last five years Rus-sia has improved its wheat output 20 percent, to 2.3 tons per hectare, but that yield still pales in comparison to a country like France, which gets 8 tons per hectare. In Brazil simply improving the roads would lower the cost of food, because it costs more to truck soy from the plantations of Mato Grosso to the coast than it does to ship the soy from those ports to China.

If It Feels Too Expensive, It Probably Is

Brazil, the top exporter of many agricultural commodities, is one of the leading examples of how the price boom has driven up the value of the currency in most nations that rely on the sale of oil, or iron ore, or sugar cane, or coffee. The rising value of the Brazilian real, the Russian ruble, and the South African rand ends up inflating the price of every other kind of good these commodity-driven nations try to sell, from cars to consult-ing services to hotel rooms in their leading cities. The chart below com-pares the price in dollars of a night's stay at a leading hotel in many of the major emerging-market capitals. I use the Four Seasons chain because it is frequented by elite business travelers, so it reflects a recurring cost for high-end businesses. A country's ranking on the index can tell a lot about its competitiveness in world markets.

A quick glance at this chart shows that commodity capitals like Mos-cow and São Paulo have been pricing themselves so far above other major cities, they are putting their future growth at risk. At the other end lies Jakarta, a commodity capital that is still strikingly reasonable—a big rea-son why Indonesia could be a breakout nation in coming years.

THE FOUR SEASONS INDEX

Country	City (Name of alternate property if applicable)[1]	Rates in USD ($)[2]	Differences vs. Emerging Average
Russia	Moscow (Ritz-Carlton)	924	109%
Brazil	Sao Paulo (Fasano)	720	63%
	DEVELOPED MARKETS AVERAGE[4]	704	60%
Turkey	Istanbul[3]	659	49%
United Arab Emirates	Dubai (Ritz-Carlton)	613	40%
Nigeria	Lagos (Federal Palace)	597	35%
Argentina	Buenos Aires	520	18%
Czech Republic	Prague	517	17%
Saudi Arabia	Riyadh	460	4%
	EMERGING MARKETS AVERAGE	441	–
Mexico	Mexico City	440	−0.3%
Hungary	Budapest	421	−5%
Egypt	Cairo[3]	380	−14%
India	Mumbai	378	−14%
South Africa	Johannesburg (The Westcliff)	365	−17%
China	Shanghai	359	−19%
Poland	Warsaw (Le Royal Meridien)	271	−39%
Thailand	Bangkok	234	−47%
Indonesia	Jakarta	230	−48%
Malaysia	Kuala Lumpur (Ritz-Carlton)	160	−64%
Sri Lanka	Colombo (Galle Face Hotel—Regency Wing)	156	−65%

1. If the city has no Four Seasons, the first alternate is Ritz-Carlton, followed by comparable hotels.
2. Rates are based on standard rooms from the hotel websites as of August 8, 2011.
3. In cities where two Four Seasons are located, the average price was used.
4. Developed markets average based on Four Seasons in the following cities: Chicago, Geneva, Hong Kong, London, Milan, New York, Paris, San Francisco, Singapore, Sydney, and Tokyo.

Adam Smith's Black Horsemen

A slowdown in China could shock the stars of the past decade, when the best-performing stocks in the world were materials and energy companies, and the best-performing stock markets were in resource-rich Brazil and Russia, which rose by around 300 percent in dollar terms, with large gains in their currencies boosting returns. In these countries high commodity prices underpin the stock market and the popularity of high-spending governments as well: Russia's 2011 budget will balance only if oil averages over one hundred dollars per barrel. Falling commodity prices could change all this in a snap, not only adding to the threat of instability in the Middle East but also shrinking the ambitions and the financial war chests of disruptive petro-states like Venezuela, and even of aspiring regional powers like Brazil.

In 2000 the major commodity producers were investing very little in extraction efforts following a twenty-year decline in prices, and hardly anyone could foresee the coming boom in demand from China. When it arrived unexpectedly, the hike in prices led to windfall profits, and the supply response was slow in coming. In recent years producers of commodities from iron ore to oil and copper have been spending tens of billions of dollars expanding operations based largely on projected demand from China that may not materialize. The global mining companies, for example, are expanding iron ore mines on the assumption that shipments will rise 60 percent by 2015—a level that requires Chinese demand to double over that period despite the clear message from Beijing that its investment surge is about to slow.

The commodity bulls tend to talk mainly about skyrocketing demand, but the rising price of oil over the last decade has inspired enough investment in new supply—new oil fields, new pipelines, new refineries, and alternative sources of energy such as shale gas—that a glut may emerge this decade. And what goes for oil goes for many commodities, from steel to soybeans. This overbuilding is typical of the late stages of a bubble, putting many investors, companies, and countries at high risk. The author George Goodman, best known by his pseudonym, Adam Smith, captured the closing moments of all manias perfectly in his book *The Money Game*, written at the height of a market boom in 1967: "We are at a wonderful party, and by the rules of the game we know that at some point in time the Black Horsemen will burst through the great terrace doors to cut down the revelers; those who leave early may be saved, but the music and wines are so seductive that we do not want to leave, but we do ask, 'What time is it? What time is it?' Only none of the clocks have any hands."

The Black Horsemen will crash the commodity party, too, and some will be saved. As the China–commodity connection breaks, one obvious group of beneficiaries would be commodity importers, including India, Turkey, and Egypt. A decline in commodity prices will ease inflationary pressures that can be a major obstacle to growth in these nations. Such an outcome would be consistent with the postwar record, which shows that the overwhelming majority of miracle economies were manufacturing powers—commodity importers, not exporters. In 2008 a report from the World Bank Commission on Growth and Development showed that since 1945, thirteen countries have been able to sustain growth of 7 percent or more for twenty-five years at a stretch, and only two of those were commodity economies, Brazil and Indonesia. The other major success stories were manufacturers, makers of useful things at affordable prices. First came Japan, starting in the 1950s, followed by Korea, Taiwan, and then China and Thailand. Hong Kong and Singapore joined this crowd by becoming the conduits through which Asian manufacturers reached the world.

Nothing Is Lost, Everything Is Transformed

A common mistake of bearish forecasters is to believe that as a current fad ends, the world will come to a shuddering halt rather than move on to a new chapter. In the late 1980s, when the Tokyo exchange represented nearly half of the total value of global stock markets, the bears forecast that problems in the Japanese economy would produce a global crash, but Japan's stock market collapsed in the early 1990s and it caused hardly a ripple. The United States came on strong, creating a sensation with new technology out of Silicon Valley and replacing Japan as the big growth engine. Similarly, midsize manufacturing economies like Thailand and Malaysia represented 30 percent of global emerging-market stock indexes before the Asian financial crisis of 1997–1998 provoked new warnings of planetary collapse, which never came. The economies of Thailand and Malaysia shrank back to represent 5 percent of global markets and were replaced by the economies of two giants, China and Brazil, which now represent about a third of emerging-market stock indexes.

Antoine Lavoisier, the father of modern chemistry, best captured the reality of such evolutionary changes in his observation "Nothing is lost, nothing is created, everything is transformed." This is what the coming slowdown in China and the end of commodity.com will bring: transformation, not disaster. China will not collapse, it will transform. The coming decline in investment will slow overall growth, but it will not derail the continuing strong growth of the consumer sector in emerging markets, which will make up a larger and larger share of the Chinese and the global economy.

The big shift in opportunity for emerging markets will be from the mining of raw materials that feed factories, to the production of goods that satisfy the new consumers. Asia's share of the global middle class rose from 20 percent in 1980 to 60 percent today, and in 2010 the number of millionaires reached three million, the same as in Europe. At one level this suggests investigating markets in China that may expand even if the investment side of the economy slows. One example could be tech products ranging from smart phones to LCD TVs, for which there is still wide, unmet demand.

This swelling consumer class will also boost demand for staples, from soap to packaged food, but the really striking growth possibilities lie at the high end. Asian aspiration for the good life is producing an upswing in sales of luxury goods with no end in sight. Luxury sales currently are rising two and a half times faster than growth in the global economy. China now accounts for 10 percent of global GDP but 20 percent of luxury goods sales, and with just over 1 percent of the world's millionaires, it's already responsible for 32 percent of Swiss watch sales.

The New Old Thing

A sharp decline in commodity prices is likely to be a major plus for the beleaguered Western economies, which spend heavily on importing oil and other raw materials. More capital could also then flow to the productive parts of the global economy, and I would not be surprised if U.S. technology again becomes the mania of the coming decade—mirroring the nineteenth century, when the United States saw two railroad booms in the space of three decades. In the 1980s and 1990s, the United States cut way back on investment in roads and buildings—exactly the investments that were taking off in China—and moved to embrace its new role as the premier knowledge economy. The state of American roads is now seen as a national scandal, but much less attention is paid to the upside: spending on software and equipment more than doubled in the period between 1980 and 2000, unleashing a productivity boom that drove the strong U.S. recovery through the 1990s.

U.S. strength in technology looks overwhelming in comparison with even the fastest-rising emerging markets, and in comparison with Japan and Taiwan, nations that also spend heavily on tech research and development but generate a lot less growth out of it. Business strategist Anil K. Gupta and research consultant Haiyan Wang, in a recent article for the *Wall Street Journal*, pointed out that for all the hype around rising Chinese prowess in innovation, with burgeoning billions devoted to R&D, the world's largest research workforce, and a rising number of patent applications, there is a lot less there than meets the eye. Much of the workforce remains hamstrung by a tradition of rote learning, and most of the patents, filed only in China's patent office, represent trivial changes to existing designs or attempts to claim credit for foreign ideas in a system that does not recognize overseas patents. Gupta and Wang argue that the relevant metric is the number of ideas recognized in the three premier patent offices: the United States, Europe, and Japan. China gets roughly one idea through this triple screen for every thirty that get through from the United States, Europe, and Japan.

Even Japan gains a lot less from its heavy commitment to R&D than the United States. For one thing sheer size favors the United States, which accounts for more than a third of global R&D spending. But just as important, Japan looks inward, and though it is frequently first to the market with new ideas, they often work only in the Japanese market. Examples abound: Japan introduced mobile payment systems to replace credit cards as early as 2004, but has yet to generate any global brands out of the concept. Dozens of different mobile devices, including piston-shaped cameras that double as smart phones, have made it big in Japan but are found nowhere else.

Japan's insular technology culture contrasts with the wide-open style of the tech industry elsewhere, from California to Finland. Silicon Valley is so rich in immigrant Indian and Chinese talent that it's little surprise

Google has traveled so well. The broader ecosystem that nurtures tech start-ups, including the venture capital industry, the top-notch university system, and the strong legal protection for intellectual property, is also arguably far stronger in the United States than anywhere else in the world, certainly more so than in China or in Japan. While venture capital still barely exists in big emerging markets, according to a 2011 research report by the brokerage firm CLSA, in the United States venture capital–backed companies accounted for 11 percent of U.S. private-sector jobs in 2010, up from less than 8 percent before the crisis of 2008.

The larger point here is that technological innovation follows its own muse, at least partly impervious to recession. The ebb and flow of funding matters, but the busts of 2001 and 2008 have not stopped U.S. firms from continuing to push the innovation frontier in fields ranging from 3D printing to genomics. To a degree that is unmatched outside small nations such as Finland, the U.S. economy is built to innovate: there are whole industries dedicated to refining the next wrinkle in innovation—the latest are open innovation (basically using open-source software systems on the Linux model) and light innovation (optimizing the use of cheap new software sources like the Amazon cloud for business). So American innovation is no accident. As Albert Einstein said, "Innovation is not the product of logical thought, although the result is tied to logical structure."

The United States is strong across the board in technology, but it's really in the field of software—the ideas that drive the emerging knowledge economy—that the system produces its greatest advantages and generates the most wealth. While Apple employs fifty thousand people and has a market capitalization that has risen fivefold over the last five years, the Taiwan companies that make gadgets for Apple employ millions but have seen their stock prices stagnate for lack of pricing power. The hardware is easy to replicate, which in turn cuts profit margins, while the software is highly profitable so long as it continues to evolve.

Netscape founder Marc Andreessen has argued, in a *Wall Street Journal* essay called "Why Software Is Eating the World," that two decades after the invention of the modern Internet, and a decade after the collapse of the Internet bubble, the software industry is at last reaching critical mass. The technology required to transform industries through software finally works and is accessible. Two billion people have access to broadband, and by the end of the decade, Andreessen predicts, five billion will have access to the Internet through smart phones. The fully wired and mobile global economy, the dream of the early 1990s, is becoming a reality, and American companies are at the forefront of making it work. This is why Amazon is now the world's biggest bookseller; why Netflix is now the world's largest video service; why the surviving telecom and music companies are the ones that transformed themselves into software companies; and why the fastest-growing video game company is one that delivers games online, Zynga. Andreessen makes a powerful case that this same transformation—the spread of useful software to new industries— is now about to hit new fields such as defense, agriculture, education, and schools, in ways that go beyond the dabbling we have seen so far.

All the hottest new things, from tablet PCs to cloud computing to social networking, are emerging largely from the United States. China is one of the few other countries that has its own social networking sites, largely because of language barriers and other imposed media restrictions. America is the leader in Internet search, in business networking, in online commerce. All of these services are attracting millions of users, revolutionizing the way we interact with the Web—and one another— and threatening established businesses. These Web services find commonality in their U.S. origins, even if final demand for these products is increasingly from emerging markets. This is likely to keep the United States well up to speed in the global growth game. Meanwhile the nations that have reveled in the commodity boom are likely to face a disheartening return to the mundane ordeals of a normal life. Buddhist monks have a phrase for it: "After the ecstasy, the laundry."

If there is no wind, row.

14

The Third Coming

IN ECONOMIC LIFE, happiness is relative, not absolute. What matters is not what you have but what you have relative to those around you. Studies have shown that most people would prefer to live in a world in which they make more than their neighbors, rather than one in which they just make more. They would choose a salary of $50,000 in a neighborhood of people making $25,000 over a salary of $100,000 in a community of people making $200,000, according to a Harvard School of Public Health survey.

This psychology is behind the hand-wringing in the United States and Europe over the decline of the West, because the rise of China and India threaten to reduce the relative prosperity and power of the West, not its absolute prosperity. While the West's status and leverage relative to the rest of the world are very much at risk, its prosperity can only increase in absolute terms because richer neighbors make better customers. Yet the prospect of living among rapidly prospering neighbors proves so unsettling that Westerners fear the turning point is coming much faster than it really is. In an early 2011 Gallup poll that asked Americans to identify the world's leading economy, 52 percent said China and only 32 percent cited the United States—an astonishing misperception. China's economy is still a third the size of the U.S. economy, and the average Chinese income is just a tenth of the American average.

The awe of China is not entirely unreasonable, given recent events.

After all, China's growth has averaged 10 percent since 1998, never dipping below 8 percent despite a series of global crises. Investors now view a growth rate of less than 7 percent in China as a "hard landing," and today polls show that more than 80 percent of global fund managers believe China will have no hard landing in 2012 or in the foreseeable future.

As George Orwell once observed, "Whoever is winning at the moment will always seem to be invincible." China's economy has been rising for so long, it's not surprising that its aura of invincibility has grown to outsize proportions in the Western imagination. In the fourteenth century, Chinese maps showed China occupying most of the planet, and the page, with the other continents rendered as tiny places and squeezed into the margins. In the first decade of the twenty-first century the Western view of the world was starting to look like that old Chinese map. Most Westerners would say that China's landmass is considerably larger than that of the United States, when in fact it's so similar that geographers dispute which is bigger.

China's looming shadow is about to retreat to realistic dimensions. Over the next decade, growth in the United States, Europe, and Japan is likely to slow by a full percentage point compared to the post–World War II average, owing to the large debt overhang, but that slowdown will pale in comparison to a 3 to 4 percentage point slowdown in China.

The big story will be that China is too big and too middle-aged to grow so fast. And as it starts buying less from other emerging nations, the average pace of growth in emerging markets is likely to slow from nearly 7 percent over the past decade to the 1950s and 1960s pace of around 5 percent. To people living in rich nations, the dispiriting sense that everyone in the neighborhood but you can afford a new pool will diminish greatly. The sense many Americans have of being rapidly overtaken by Asian juggernauts will be remembered as one of the country's periodic bouts of paranoia, something like the hype that accompanied Japan's ascent in the late 1980s.

The Miracle Is Younger Than It Looks

Emerging markets have become such a celebrated pillar of the global economy that it's easy to forget how new this concept is, at least from an

investment standpoint. The First Coming of the emerging markets dates
to the mid-1980s, when Wall Street started to track them as a distinct
asset class. First labeled "exotic"—a name that scared off investors—many
of these nations were opening their stock markets to the outside world for
the first time: Taiwan opened in 1991, India in 1992, South Korea (to
small minority shareholders) in 1993, followed by Russia in 1995. It was a
chaotic period of discovery and excitement for foreign investors, unleashing a helter-skelter 600 percent boom in prices (as measured in dollar
terms) between 1987 and 1994. Over this seven-year stretch the amount
of money invested in emerging nations rose from less than 1 percent to
nearly 8 percent of the global stock market total.

The First Coming skidded to a close with the series of economic crises
that struck from Mexico to Turkey between 1994 and 2002, when emerging stock markets lost almost half their value and slid back to represent 4
percent of the global total. Even more strikingly, over the duration of the
period from 1987 and 2002, the emerging-market share of global GDP
actually fell from 23 to 20 percent, and the one big exception was China,
which saw its share of global GDP double to 4.5 percent. The story of the
hot emerging markets was really about one market. As recently as 2002
many big investors often wondered why they should bother investing in
such a marginal class of countries at all.

The Second Coming began with the global boom in 2003, when
emerging markets really started to take off as a group, and their share of
global GDP began a dramatic climb from 20 percent to 34 percent today
(attributable in part to the rising value of their currencies), while their
share of the global stock market total rose from under 4 percent to more
than 10 percent. The huge losses of 2008 were mostly recovered in 2009,
but since then it has been slow going.

We are now entering the Third Coming, a new era that will be defined
by moderate growth, the return of the boom-bust business cycle, and the
break-up of herd behavior. Lacking the easy money and the blue-sky
optimism that has fueled investment, the stock markets of developing
countries are set to deliver more measured and uneven returns. Gains
averaged 37 percent a year between 2003 and 2007 and that is likely
to slow to an average annual pace of 10 percent in the coming decade,

especially because many emerging-market stocks and currencies are no longer outright cheap.

The Breakout Nations

The growth game is all about expectations. People are always asking me, "So what if India slows from 9 percent to 6 to 7 percent—that is still three times faster than growth in the West, right?" Well, for India that slip would initially feel like a recession, because it is one of the poorer nations in the low-income group—the economies with per capita income under $5,000—and every Indian has come to enjoy the levitating sensation of rising fast from a low base, the bounty of higher incomes and new jobs. New Delhi has built its budget based on the revenue it could expect at 9 percent growth, and the prices in the Mumbai stock market are based on what Indian companies would be worth down the road if the economy continued to grow at a pace of at least 8 percent. In 2011, therefore, a growth rate of 7 percent was enough to trigger a bear market in Indian stocks.

Since the last decade was so unusual in terms of the wide scope and rapid pace of growth in emerging markets, much of the world suffers from unreasonable expectations. Nations with an average per capita income ranging from $5,000 and $10,000 have come to expect at least 5 percent growth, and those at risk of falling short include South Africa and Malaysia. Nations with an average per capita income from $10,000 to $15,000 expect 4 percent growth, and those at risk include Russia, Brazil, Mexico, and Hungary. In countries with an average per capita income from $20,000 to $25,000, growth needs to remain in the 3 to 4 percent range, and Taiwan may not sustain that pace. The exceptions in this category are in the Gulf, where the populations are growing so fast—at an average annual pace of 2.6 percent in recent years, much faster than other emerging regions—that the Gulf economies need to grow much more rapidly than 4 percent to keep per capita income rising. The happiness and satisfaction that nations derive from growth are relative not only to expectations but also to population, and to how rich they are in the first place.

So which are the breakout nations of the coming decade? The answer depends on which wealth category one is looking at. In the $20,000 to $25,000 income range, the nations with the best chance to match or exceed the expected pace of 3 percent are the Czech Republic—the safe haven from the chaos in Europe—and South Korea—the manufacturing barrier-buster. In the very large $10,000 to $15,000 category, possibly one nation has a chance to match or exceed the 4 to 5 percent pace of the last decade: Turkey, as Prime Minister Erdoğan frees the Muslim heartland to resume a normal role in the economy. Poland also has a shot, in part because it needs to hit only the low end of the range to feel like a fast-growth nation (since its population is not increasing). It is difficult to spot a breakout nation in the $5,000 to $10,000 class; the one with the best shot is probably Thailand, where a new leader could heal the capital-versus-countryside divide.

The next group includes the big kahuna, China, and it is a very special case. The breakout speed for countries with an average per capita income of $5,000 or less is 5 percent or faster, but expectations are higher in China because almost every mainstream economist still projects the Chinese economy to grow at 8 to 9 percent in the foreseeable future. Even though its per capita income is about to pass $5,000 and enter the next category, growth expectations in China are as high as in poorer nations like India It's impossible to break out when expectations exceed the maximum possible growth rates of the relevant income group. There are, however, many legitimate breakout nations in the under-$5,000 income class: Indonesia, the commodity economy that works; the Philippines, with a new Aquino in charge; Sri Lanka, riding its huge peace dividend; Nigeria, where an honest leader has ended a string of spectacularly corrupt ones; and a number of nations in East Africa, where an economic union is taking shape.

It is far from certain that all the nations on my list will actually break out, because it is so difficult to grow rapidly over an extended period. A recent paper from the Harvard political economist Dani Rodrik catches the reality well. It shows that before 2000 the emerging markets as a whole did not "converge" or catch up to the developed world at all. In fact the per capita income gap between advanced and developing economies steadily widened from 1950 until 2000. There were a few pockets of nations that did catch up to the West, but they were limited to oil states in the Gulf, the nations of southern Europe after World War II, and the economic tigers of East Asia. It was only after 2000 that emerging markets as a whole started to catch up, but as of 2011 the difference in per capita incomes between the rich and the developing nations is back to where it was in the 1950s.

The uneven rise of the emerging powers over the next decade will reshape the global balance of power in countless ways, reviving the self-confidence of the West, dimming the glow of recent stars like Brazil and Russia, and making the apparent threat from petro-dictators in Africa, the Middle East, and Latin America disappear like a passing meteor. The upside will be just as dramatic, with possible new giants emerging from relative obscurity. There are currently fifteen economies worth more than $1 trillion a year, and the next two nations in line to join that elite group, probably within the next five years, are Muslim democracies with increasingly market-oriented economies: Indonesia and Turkey. The implications of that development could be profound, both as inspiration to many Muslim nations that are struggling, and as an object lesson to Westerners who think that Muslim modernity is an oxymoron.

The Rediscovery of the West

Though post-crisis America is starting to look like post-crisis Japan in the 1990s, when massive debt led to the long stagnation that persists to this day, differences will come to the fore as several of the big emerging markets slow. Far more than Japan, the United States remains flexible and innovative—the center of creativity in technology, still wide open to people and ideas, with the youngest population in the developed world and a very competitive (cheap) currency. Restoring balance to American self-perceptions, based on a reasonable calculation of weakness and strength, will have healthy political ramifications, reducing the pressure on Washington to raise new barriers to global trade, and to cast China as a growing geopolitical and military threat.

There are already signs that this is happening: in August 2011, Boston Consulting Group published *Made in America, Again*, a persuasive argument for why U.S. manufacturing is poised for a comeback. China is suffering from a strengthening currency and rising wages, land prices, and transport costs, while the United States has a falling currency, stagnant wages, and rapidly rising productivity. Boston Consulting Group predicts that by 2015, these shifts will have wiped out China's competitive advantage, sparking a U.S. factory revival particularly in low-cost states like South Carolina, Alabama, and Tennessee, and especially for sales to North America. Already companies like Coleman, Sleek Audio, and Peerless have started to move manufacturing facilities back to the United States from China.

The same reversal is possible in some parts of Europe, where the spectacle of a more normal China should also produce a collective sigh of relief and a rediscovery of basic strengths. This is especially true in Germany, the only rich nation that has managed to defend its manufacturing base from foreign competition and to expand production in emerging markets as well. German reforms early in the last decade slowed the rise in labor costs to the lowest pace in Europe, while German companies also moved to open plants in low-wage countries of Eastern Europe. The result has been an astonishing jump in the export share of German GDP from 24 percent in 1995 to 45 percent in 2011, relatively low unemployment rates, and the world's second-largest trade surplus, which is spilling over into a rise in consumer spending.

No corresponding decline in the sense of triumphalism in China will occur because that feeling has never taken hold. Though the rising national pride of the Chinese and their strong support for the Communist government are well documented, the Chinese are also far more realistic about the likely future course of their economy than foreigners are. Polls show that the Chinese are much less likely than any other nationality to believe that China is destined to be the number one economy in the world anytime soon, and are more likely to understand the possibility of pitfalls ahead. As the rich world comes to view China and other big emerging markets more in the way they now see themselves—well behind the West in per capita GDP and with much still to do—the edge will come off the growing sense of East-West rivalry.

What the Misery Index Shows

The return of inflation has already taken some of the gloss off the big emerging markets over the past couple of years. Too many of these nations were trying to sustain the boom of the last decade and were reluctant to withdraw the monetary and fiscal stimulus (cheap interest rates and heavy public spending) they put in place following the 2008 financial crisis. Money alone does not foster growth, and much of that excess money flew straight into higher prices; average emerging-market inflation rates rose from 4 percent in 2009 to 6 percent in 2011, gradually feeding the cancer that has stopped many rising economies and taken down the politicians who run them. Between 2010 and 2011, Russia, Brazil, and China have all seen inflation accelerate by about 2 percentage points, and Vietnam—the dysfunctional Communist outlier—has seen it jump 9 percentage points, to 18 percent.

The misery index, popularized in the United States during the final, ugly years of the Jimmy Carter administration in the late 1970s, has started to edge up all over the emerging world. It is a simple index, the inflation rate plus the unemployment rate, and its rise into double digits under Carter was seen, accurately, as a harbinger of his political demise. To be sure, emerging markets have a much higher tolerance for pain than rich nations. The emerging-market misery index averaged over 100 as recently as the 1990s, before plummeting to 10 when the recession of 2008 began. Since then it has crept up to about 12, and in some countries considerably higher. One of the sharpest turns has come in China, where the misery index rose from 2 in 2009 to 9 in mid-2011, mainly because of higher inflation. Little wonder that controlling inflation became the Chinese government's top policy objective for 2011. The recent rise in the index is also contributing to a revival of hostility against incumbents in India, and making it very difficult for the successors to political rock stars like Lula in Brazil to retain that popularity.

The return of inflation will not be felt everywhere to the same degree, and there is a strong case that the threat is only short term. One piece of the prevailing optimism argues that inflation can be contained, at least much more effectively than it was in the past, and indeed there are new bulwarks against inflation. In the early 1970s global inflation surged above 10 percent and remained high throughout the decade as higher oil and food prices triggered a vicious price-wage spiral. In today's globally integrated world, production can move swiftly to the lowest-cost factory, trade flows freely, and it is difficult for workers to demand wage increases that are not supported by productivity growth.

Furthermore at least some key central banks are now officially committed to controlling inflation rather than just pumping up growth by printing money, and many are increasingly independent of the political process. Even where politicians do have a say, many societies have already learned how painful double-digit inflation can be, making the fight against inflation politically popular. Since 1990, when New Zealand's central bank became the first in the world to declare explicitly that fighting inflation would be its number one priority, twenty more have followed suit, and many nations, including Poland, the Czech Republic, the Philippines, Indonesia, and Turkey, have seen marked declines in inflation after adopting an inflation target. Since the 1980s the share of emerging markets running inflation in the double digits has fallen from 47 percent to 7 percent. In the long run that trend seems likely to continue.

In the coming years we can expect the least misery in breakout nations and the most in nations where slowing growth will drive up the unemployment measure in the misery index, rather than the inflation component. In these nations, which include Russia, South Africa, and Brazil, the fallout will land hard on incumbent politicians, who have ridden the boom of the last decade to high popularity and a series of election victories.

Volatility Strikes Back

When asked why evil exists in the world, the Indian saint Ramakrishna answered, "To thicken the plot." The same could be said of recessions. While most economies tend to expand steadily over time, recessions are the twists that add dramatic tension, not only by imposing pain but also by setting the stage for reform and resurrection. Now the global plot, which had thinned out in recent decades, is about to thicken.

Between 1861 (the first year for which records are available) and 1982, the United States was in recession about a third of the time, meaning that it was in a state of constant renewal. Since then it has been in recession only 11 percent of the time, taking much of the drama out of economic and political life too. The good times have been lasting longer, and the bad times hitting less hard, with happy ripple effects for economies and leaders across the globe.

The impact has been huge. From 1982 to 2007, the United States enjoyed unusually long expansions, and unusually short and shallow recessions, compared to the averages established over the preceding century. The three upturns in this recent period lasted six to ten years—nearly triple the historical average of three years. And the two recessions saw economic output fall barely 1 percent over two quarters, much less painful than the prior average of 2.5 percent stretched over five quarters. The data for the rest of the world are sketchier but similar. Since the early 1980s in the developing nations, the economic cycle of recovery and recession has typically run for around eight years, double the historical average of four years.

In the United States the flattening of the business cycle came to be known as "the Great Moderation," and at its peak, debate raged about whether this comfortable new environment was here to stay. The agony of 2008 ended that wishful discussion. Before the crisis, recessions had moderated in depth and length, due in large part to the almost limitless ability of the United States to fund growth by borrowing, mainly from the rest of the world. Globalization was forcing companies to become more productive, producing more for less and lowering the threat of inflation. Low inflation made it possible for the Federal Reserve to keep interest rates low and to cut rates even more at the first sign of a downturn. Expansions lasted longer, recessions hit less sharply. The United States became addicted to the sweet rhythm of a long, debt-induced business cycle, and to its booster effect on the stock market, where bull runs were extending from an average length of twenty-two months before 1982 to thirty-seven months in the subsequent years. But all the while credit was building up in the veins of the economy.

Now the U.S. government is running out of syringes. Its massive stimulus programs have driven government debt up from 40 percent of GDP in 1980 to more than 90 percent of GDP in 2011, a level that can weigh down on growth. With short-term interest rates close to zero, the Federal Reserve has run out of easy money to pass around, though it has still tried. Its inventive crisis policy of "quantitative easing" has done more damage than good because much of that easy money found its way into speculative investments—the bulk of it in commodities like oil and gold—rather than new lending by banks to new businesses at home. The end result is likely to be a return to shorter expansions and sharper recessions in the economy, as well as shorter bull runs in the stock market, and not only in the United States.

Emerging markets have much less debt than the United States, so they can still borrow to fight off a downturn. But the surge in global trade and capital flows has connected them to the United States more closely than ever. Today U.S. manufacturers buy 15 percent of their parts and materials from emerging markets, up from 9 percent just fifteen years ago, and these connections are still growing. Trade between nations is rising much faster than income within nations. Back in 1960 every percentage point increase in global income was accompanied by a 2 percent increase in trade flows; today every percentage point increase in income is matched by a 4 percent rise in trade. The increasing integration of global supply chains is a major reason why developed and developing economies began to expand and contract in sync over the last decade. It is also why emerging markets, too, can expect a shift to more frequent downturns. If the historical record cited above is any guide, the expansion phases are likely to shorten by a half or more to around three years across the global economy.

The Upside of Hard Landings

Volatility may be scary, but it is not necessarily bad for long-term growth. The Great Moderation of recent decades did nothing to increase the long-term growth rate of the United States, nor did the sharp booms and busts of the late nineteenth century do anything to slow the overall explosion of U.S. economic growth. What we have often seen is that nations with the wherewithal to pay for a soft landing out of recession frequently end up sinking in this expensive pillow.

This deep preference for soft landings is understandable, but it is equally clear that hard landings often force reforms that set the stage for rapid growth. This has happened repeatedly in recent years, from Sweden and Finland in the early 1990s to Asia after the 1997–1998 financial crisis. Economist Andy Xie, a well-known expert on Asia, has created an interesting taxonomy of winners and losers after the crisis, citing South Korea for pushing perhaps the most aggressive reforms. Xie argues that if South Korea had not suffered a hard landing in 1998 and moved decisively to tighten its belt afterward, it probably would not be a member in good standing of the club of leading industrial powers today. On the other hand Malaysia imposed capital controls to avoid the brunt of the hit in 1998, never reformed its system, and is falling behind its neighbors.

Xie is most critical of Japan, where, he says, "the greatest bubble in human history" burst in 1990 with no pain at all, like falling off Everest without breaking a bone. At its peak Japan accounted for 40 percent of all the property value on the planet, but instead of collapsing, the price of real estate slowly declined at a 7 percent annual rate for two decades, ultimately falling by a total of about 80 percent. There was never a major round of foreclosures or bankruptcies, as the government kept bailing out debtors, ruining its own finances.

China, intriguingly, is moving from the hard path to the Japanese path. In 1998 China was still largely isolated from the capital flows that carried the Asian contagion, but it pursued tough reform anyway, streamlining state-owned enterprises and privatizing the real estate market. That put China in a position to create factories to the world, but it faces tougher circumstances now. In China both the banks and their corporate customers are typically owned by the government, which controls most of the economy, and the government never forces its own debtor companies to liquidate. The debtors just hang on, hoping another round of easy credit will put them back in the black. Since 2008 total debt has risen from 115 to 170 percent of GDP, and the richer that China gets the less likely it is to be hard on itself.

The growing ties between nations over the last decade have made every one of them less inclined to allow their trade partners to go under. For all the current discussion about debt defaults, stemming from the crisis in Greece, the reality is that default has largely disappeared from the international economic scene. In their book, *This Time Is Different*, Carmen Reinhart and Kenneth Rogoff chart how surprisingly commonplace default used to be: In a typical year between the 1920s and 2003, nations representing at least 5 to 10 percent of global income were in default, and that proportion spiked up to 40 percent during the Depression and World War II, and close to 15 percent in the late 1980s. But since 2003, when the synchronized global boom began, the share of defaulting nations has dropped from 5 percent in any year to zero. No rich nation wants to suffer a default, which can lead to a hard landing, or to risk the spillover effect of a hard landing among its neighbors.

The worst-case scenario, however, is not countries that accept no pain when they reach bottom, but those that take no risks on the way up. I was always amused by the sense of accomplishment that exuded from Indians when they dodged the Asian crisis of 1998, having grown only tepidly in the preceding years. I still feel that same lack of urgency today in many emerging markets, from India to Brazil, which interpreted the boom of the last decade as a credit to their domestic policies, not as a function of global free-money flows. That complacency will be a huge handicap as the world economy enters a new era.

In this slower and more volatile world, the growth rates of countries and companies will start to diverge, so the Third Coming will be about understanding emerging markets as individual nations. This is as true in politics as economics. For example, the concern in the West over the rise of the major emerging markets as a political bloc, coming together in BRICS-type summits, is greatly exaggerated. The core of this group—Brazil, Russia, India, China, and South Africa—consists of nations with competing political interests. They are a group of commodity exporters versus importers, and trade links among them are surprisingly limited; although China has rapidly growing trade and financial links with the other four, those four don't do much business with one another. More-over, all will be hard-pressed to find a common program for growth in a slowing world economy.

The economic role models of recent decades are going to give way to new models, or perhaps no models, as growth trajectories splinter off in many different directions. In the 1990s global growth averaged 2.7 percent, powered mainly by the United States, before spiking to 3.7 percent from 2003 to 2007, driven mainly by the big emerging markets. In the next decade global growth is likely to return to the less than 3 percent pace of the 1990s, but few if any nations are going to look like heroes.

In the past, Asia tended to look to Japan for lessons on how to get growth right, nations from the Baltics to the Balkans tended to look to the European Union, and nearly all countries looked to some extent to the United States. But the debt crisis of 2008 has undermined the credibility of all these role models; economies that were once clamoring to get into the Eurozone, like Poland, the Czech Republic, and Turkey, wonder if they want to join a club so many of whose members are struggling to stay afloat. Japan's recent mistakes are much more visible than its past successes, so it's not clear why anyone would study Japan's economic model more closely than Korea's emergence as a manufacturing powerhouse.

The Mantra of the New Era

Creating the right conditions for rapid growth is more art than science, and while it can look easy when a nation gets a few key reforms right, or when foreign investors get excited about a country, it can all fall apart fast. Some of the biggest growth stars, such as China, South Korea, and Taiwan, started on the path to success with unconventional policies that defied the usual free-market prescriptions: subsidizing or granting tax breaks to favored industries, promoting free trade only in special zones, and providing investment guarantees. Even getting the basics right—stabilizing debts and inflation—is no guarantee that business will rise off this foundation. Since there is no blueprint for what will work, says Rodrik, "our baseline scenario has to be one in which high growth remains episodic."

My own rules of the road offer many possible scenarios that could derail breakout nations or move laggards into the breakout class. If the leadership in Indonesia slips and strives to create a family dynasty as in Argentina, the country could quickly lose its economic momentum. If China lets its currency appreciate too fast, it could remove one of its key cost advantages and precipitate an even deeper slowdown. On the positive side, if India once again starts generating new billionaires in productive industries like technology, rather than politically connected sectors like mining and real estate, it will be clear evidence that the country is correcting for its corruption and overconfidence problems. If Thailand's new leadership can succeed in bridging the yawning gap between Bangkok and the rest of the country, it could ascend into the breakout category. And if money begins to come home to Russia, it will be a sign that the state is no longer intimidating private enterprise into fleeing the country.

What is increasingly apparent is that not all emerging markets will be breakout nations, and their paths will vary significantly. Already, in a sign of increasing differentiation at the micro level, since 2010 there has been a greater flow of emerging-market investment to firms that sell consumer goods and get high ratings for solid management and away from state-run companies and firms with unstable revenues. These trends are bound to continue and to be a defining feature of the Third Coming: investors will become increasingly discerning, not only in their choice of companies but also in their choice of countries, and will treat emerging markets as individual stories, not a homogeneous class. No nation can hope to grow as a free rider on the tailwinds of fortuitous global circumstance, as so many have in the last decade. They will have to propel their own weight, and the breakout nations of the new era will take their mantra from a Latin proverb: "If there is no wind, row."

EPILOGUE

Where Are We Now?

Much like the Frenchman who said the Eiffel Tower reminded him of sex, because so did everything else, most Wall Street salespeople still can't help but think in acronyms when it comes to emerging markets. The popularity of "BRICS" continues to inspire mindless copies, like "MIST," which inexplicably combines Mexico, Indonesia, South Korea, and Turkey. My favorite is "CIVETS," a reference to an exotic cat.

Acronyms are so last decade. Bundling diverse nations into marketable catch phrases appeared to make sense during the market euphoria of the mid-2000s, but that boom is over. As the global economy has slowed, the Third Coming of emerging markets is playing out along the lines outlined in the previous chapter: it is an era defined by moderate and uneven growth in emerging economies, a breakup of herd behavior in the markets, and new stars rising to the top—including some in the West.

The Wall Street metrics used to gauge the dispersion of the herd suggest that change is under way. To take a simple measure, through the first six months of 2011 in the top-ten emerging stock markets, the weakest returns came in India, down 9 percent, and the best came in Indonesia, up 13 percent. This 22-percentage-point gap was unusually narrow, a clear indicator of herd behavior. In 2012, the gap climbed to 64 percentage points, with Brazil down 3 percent and Turkey, still a model for economic normalcy in the Muslim world, up 61 percent.

Broken BRICS

All of the BRICS economies are slowing sharply. China is on track to see its GDP growth fall well below the 8 percent target that Beijing had maintained for many years. The country's slowdown is in turn taking the wind out of economies that set sail in the last decade by selling commodities to China, particularly Russia and Brazil, where GDP growth rates have slipped to 3.5 percent and 1 percent, respectively, in 2012. The risk of relying so heavily on exports of raw materials is showing its ugly head.

The government in Brazil still prefers to fix the problem of *custo Brasil* (the high cost of doing business in Brazil) using the heavy hand of the state, and has cemented the country's status as one of the most closed emerging economies by tossing up new tariff barriers. In Russia, President Vladimir Putin continues to prove a key rule of the road—even the most effective economic leaders lose momentum after about a decade in power—as the Kremlin continues to talk about reform without following through.

India, as usual, is on a different path. Nations enter the breakout class by beating the rivals and the expectations in their income class, and India's prospects have improved only because its expectations for economic growth (as measured by consensus forecasts) have plummeted sharply, from more than 8 percent to around 6 percent. By the summer of 2012, the overconfidence in India had given way to fears of a balance-of-payments crisis, puncturing the widespread expectation that it is destined to be the "Next China." That's okay: 6 percent represents reasonable progress at India's income level, but so much for India as the next China. Meanwhile, South Africa—the least likely member of any large emerging-market grouping—is struggling to grow at even a 3 percent pace. Violent disruptions in the labor market, persistently high unemployment, and lack of policy cohesion are all working to undermine the country's growth prospects.

The Monks in the Marketplace

Sometimes the stars of a new decade make a splashy entrance, like China in the 1990s or India in the 2000s. At other times, the newcomers climb onto the fast track without attracting much notice, like South Korea and Taiwan in the 1960s. The current decade is one of those other times; the four largest and most hyped emerging markets are yielding the global stage to unsung leaders who are pushing productive reforms in largely unheralded nations.

These new stars are like monks in the marketplace—anonymous but enlightened figures who will eventually draw the eyes of the crowd. One top-performing emerging market so far in 2012 is the Philippines, where President Noynoy Aquino has shown the competence his nation needs to restore some of the luster its economy enjoyed half a century ago. Signs of a manufacturing comeback are beginning to appear as the Philippines benefits from shifts in its competitive position vis-à-vis China—a weakening currency, falling labor costs—shifts that are also benefiting economies across Southeast Asia. Thailand too is edging toward firm membership in the breakout class, as Prime Minister Yingluck Shinawatra works quietly to extinguish the political tension between the capital and the countryside that exploded under the regime of her brother Thaksin.

In Latin America, outside of the region's two largest economies—commodity-crazed Brazil and monopoly-ruled Mexico—a string of Pacific nations are attracting attention as the new Gold Coast. Since World War II, sustained rapid growth has tended to appear in clusters—in southern Europe, the Gulf oil states, East Asia, and perhaps now on the west coast of South America.

Take a map of South America, draw a line down the middle, and you see disappointment on the right, success on the left. After tracking each other closely for a decade, the Atlantic and Pacific coasts are starting to chart different growth paths. The prominent Atlantic economies—Venezuela, Argentina, and Brazil—have little chance of

keeping up with the expected emerging-market average of 4 to 5 percent GDP growth for the next five years. In stark contrast, the leading
Pacific economies—Chile, Peru, and Colombia—look likely to beat
the high end of that forecast.

Though the Chilean economy may be peaking under the administration of a billionaire president who does not have the street credibility to push reforms that can take the country to the next stage of
development, Chilean businessmen are systematically shifting investments to Peru and Colombia, countries whose Chilean-style business
environments prove equally welcoming. Peru was the fastest-growing
Latin nation in the 2000s, and both Peru and Colombia are currently
among the ten fastest-growing developing economies. Colombia may
have the best chance among the Gold Coast economies to become a
breakout nation: it has the largest population and consumer market;
with a deal in the works to end a long-running guerrilla rebellion,
it has more political stability than Peru; and it recently completed
landmark reforms—including a 2012 free trade deal with the United
States—that will give it momentum in the coming years.

New Role Models

The emerging class of developing countries is returning to a state of
churn, tossing up new ideas, new stars, and new role models. None
is more striking than Egypt, where a conservative Muslim Brotherhood government has replaced the pro-American autocracy toppled
by the Arab Spring of 2011. Americans are worrying, once again, that
promoting elections in the Muslim world is opening the door to anti-
American governments. Yet Egypt was one of the best-performing
stock markets in the world in 2012, even after its prices plunged in
November following some renewed political turmoil.

To be sure, the locals seem more excited than foreigners about
Egypt's prospects, but remember the rule: locals are always the first
to know. They see in the Muslim Brotherhood a regime that has signaled its basic moderation by trying to follow in the footsteps of the
Justice and Development (AK) Party in Turkey—the model for economic management in the Muslim world. The Cairo government has

also begun to institute reforms to help boost growth in the medium term, most notably in talks on a relief package with the IMF. Virtually all investors in the Cairo market now come from within Egypt or from the nearby Gulf oil states, which embrace Egypt as the largest country in the region that shares their predominantly Sunni culture and still has a low per capita income, and the potential to grow rapidly from this low base. This makes Egypt a natural outlet for the vast pool of oil wealth that is still sloshing around the Gulf. Though the Egyptian economy is contracting this year in the fallout from the Arab Spring, at least some locals still see reason to believe Egypt has the potential to become a breakout nation in the foreseeable future.

The new age of uneven growth should inspire a healthy skepticism of sweeping ideas about what makes economies grow. That includes a newly popularized notion that strong growth is all about strong institutions, particularly the open, inclusive institutions of democratic systems, which create the conditions for innovation. As chapter 2 shows, in the developing world, democracies are no more likely to produce rapid economic growth than autocracies are, and the fact is that innovation matters most when countries need to graduate to the developed world. Otherwise, even middle-income countries can grow by copying (Chile, for example, spends less than 1 percent of GDP on research and development), and the poorer economies can grow just by paving roads, erecting cell-phone towers, or giving young girls a bicycle to go to school.

A case-by-case look at emerging markets pokes holes in grand theories about what makes countries grow. If growth is driven by open institutions, how does this explain the rise of China, with its opaque bureaucracy and exclusive ruling party? And how does this theory make sense of South Africa, which has world-class financial institutions alongside a stagnant political system that has failed to reduce the increasingly restive ranks of the unskilled and unemployed? The result is a vicious cycle of low economic growth, aggravated by violent demonstrations in the crucial mining industry. The sweeping explanatory theories have two basic flaws: First, they tend to emphasize just one factor, such as institutions, geography, or even culture, to explain the rise and fall of nations, which distorts the complex growth process. Second, they often build on historical records that go back decades, if not centuries, and look forward for equally extended periods, coming up with forecasts as far off as 2050. As a result, they tend to miss what practical people care about, which is what is going to happen over the next few years.

America's Economic Renaissance

The breakout nations framework for picking likely winners—tracking individual economies against rivals in the same income class and against expectations for the next three to five years—applies just as well to developed nations as to emerging nations. The rich nations are not one faceless mass either, yet many analysts who confidently forecast the uniform rise of the world's other six billion also assume their rise will lead inevitably to the decline of the West, a phrase so loose it is often stretched to include Japan. The truth is that there are breakout nations in the West too.

As the global economy enters a long period of slow growth, the United States and some parts of Europe are in position to regain competitive ground. This shift is relative and unspectacular—a matter of certain wealthy nations slowing less sharply than their peers or emerging rivals—so it is easy to overlook. But the potential for a revival in America is growing, and it is spreading to parts of Europe for reasons that have to do with the upside of hard landings (discussed in chapter 14).

The big problem for most rich nations is high debt, and America's debt burden is among the heaviest. The total U.S. debt (combining government, corporate, and household debt) is now strikingly high, at 340 percent of GDP, but what often matters most for growth are the pace and direction of change. While the U.S. government has a lot of work left to do on its debt problem, American households and businesses are working down debt much faster than their peers in most other heavily indebted nations, including China. Across the Atlantic, severe belt-tightening has radically improved the competitive position of some Baltic and central European nations, and now a similar if slower process of streamlining is setting up parts of southern Europe for a rebound that echoes, in some respects, the comeback of the Asian tigers after the crisis of 1998.

Since the crisis of 2008, most Americans have grown accustomed to gloom. The high debt burden is indeed weighing on the long-term U.S. growth rate, which is widely believed to have fallen from 3.4 percent between 1950 and 2007 to 2 percent, which is slower than during the recovery phase of most postwar recessions. There is a widespread sense that America has lost its mojo. In a recent paper, however, Harvard economists Carmen Reinhart and Kenneth Rogoff point out that the relevant comparison is not previous U.S. recessions but the very different case of systemic financial crises. These are much more traumatic and rare, and by this standard the United States is recovering lost per capita output faster than it did following previous systemic crises, from the meltdown of 1873 through the Great Depression, and faster than most Western nations following the systemic crisis of 2008.

In 2012, the U.S. economy expanded at about the same pace as the global average for the first time since 2003, the year the boom in emerging markets began. That boom did a lot to popularize the notion that the poor nations are rapidly eclipsing the rich. Now, the poor are still catching up, but much more slowly and unevenly. As of 2007, the economies in the emerging markets were on average growing three times faster than the U.S. economy; today they are growing only twice as fast.

Evidence of an American revival, against both developed and emerging world competition, is mounting, driven by the traditional strengths of the U.S. economy—including its ability to innovate and adapt quickly, particularly in applying new technology. Many of America's worst worries—heavy debt, high gas prices, slow growth, the fall of the dollar, and the decline of manufacturing—will look much less troubling when compared to its direct rivals. One big reason is that advances in U.S. technology are having a significant positive impact on all these concerns.

The Debt Is the Threat

In a global economy that is increasingly defined by competing forms of capitalism, the American brand appears to be winning. Consider the key challenge of "deleveraging," or digging out from debt. A recent study from the McKinsey Global Institute shows that the United States is the only major developed economy that is even loosely following the path of countries that successfully negotiated similar debt crises, like Sweden and Finland in the 1990s. According to McKinsey, total debt as a share of GDP has fallen since 2008 by 16 percent in the United States, while it has been rising in Germany and increasing sharply in Japan, the United Kingdom, France, Italy, and Spain. As in Sweden during the 1990s, the fall in total U.S. debt is due entirely to sharp cuts in the private sector, particularly the finance industry and private households. It is a painful fact that much of this reduction has come from banks foreclosing on homeowners who can't make their mortgage payments, but it is also a tribute to America's willingness to take the necessary medicine.

The weak link in the U.S. response to the debt crisis is the government. The Scandinavian cases show that government needs to start cutting spending and debt roughly four years after the downturn—exactly the stage where the United States is currently. The next step depends on what President Barack Obama and the Congress do to tackle the debt threat. Research on previous crises shows very clearly that the recovery is likely to be much faster if the debt is disposed of through spending cuts rather than tax increases, because business investment responds positively to the former, negatively to the latter. The most recent addition to this research comes in an August 2012 paper from the National Bureau of Economic Research, and builds on data describing the efforts of seventeen developed nations to cut fiscal deficits in the period between 1980 and 2005. It finds that belt-tightening efforts based on spending cuts typically lead to mild and short-lived recessions, or to no recession at all, while similar efforts based on tax increases are often followed by prolonged and deep recessions. The authors, Alberto Alesina, Carlo Favero, and Francesco Giavazzi, conclude that the difference in impact "is remarkable in its size" and cannot be explained by differences in the way these countries were conducting monetary policy.

No matter how the United States chooses to tackle its deficit, the economy may have to take some pain in 2013, because any deal to tackle the debt problem will involve cutting government stimulus, which will act as a drag on growth in the short term, even as it strengthens the economy in the medium and long term. The bigger picture for 2013 is that if Washington can produce a credible road map to lowering public debt, it could put the United States on track to be a breakout nation this decade.

One simple reason is that America's troubles are less challenging than those of many countries in Europe and of Japan, which has a debt problem that virtually rules it out as a breakout nation in the rich world class. An aging and conservative society in which most old people save heavily, Japan is unusual in that most of its households are net creditors, not debtors. Because so many Japanese are creditors, they create a powerful support for a sluggish economic environment with low inflation, in which lenders do best. The vast creditor class also places little pressure on the government to bring down its startling debts, because creditors do well taking interest payments from the government. At 220 percent of GDP, the country's government debt has historical parallels in terms of its size—the government debts in the United States and the United Kingdom hit triple digits after World War II, but in both cases the governments worked hard to bring down the debt as quickly as possible after the war. Japan is conducting an experiment with no known parallel, by running a steady peacetime fiscal deficit of 8.5 percent of GDP, with no apparent strategy to close the gap.

If there is a positive surprise on the horizon in Japan, it will come from the private sector: over the last twenty years corporations have eliminated $6 trillion in debt, and there are signs that the long slide in Japanese private investment is over. If growth returns to the private sector, it may allow the government to stop propping up the country with deficits. That's a bright but, alas, still low-probability scenario.

So the United States is recovering from the crisis of 2008 faster than its competition in the rich world, and perhaps with more strength than rivals in the emerging world as well. It is important to keep America's debt problem in perspective. China is arguably worse off, with total debt equal to 180 percent of GDP. The wealthier you are, the more debt you can carry, so America's total debt (340 percent) is actually less of a challenge because its per capita income is still seven times that of China.

The Dollar Advantage

The decline of the dollar is also a major plus for the U.S. competitive position, but it has been widely misinterpreted as a minus. Americans became so accustomed to listening to Treasury secretaries defend the "strong dollar" that perhaps it was inevitable that its decline over the last decade would be interpreted as a national defeat. The big fear has been that the rise of the emerging markets will ultimately persuade countries that they would rather hold savings in Chinese yuan or other star emerging-market currencies than in dollars, ending the status the greenback has held for a century: the world's reserve currency.

This status is, indeed, a huge benefit to Americans, and its loss would be painful. The fact that foreigners are eager to store money in dollars (often in Treasury bills) lowers the cost of borrowing for the government and for consumers. Over many years, according to Berkeley political economist Barry Eichengreen, cheap borrowing costs have effectively raised U.S. income levels by as much as 3 percent. For all the worried talk about the dollar's demise, the facts show that its status has not slipped in decades, with the dollar share of the global reserve holding steady at more than 60 percent.

It is very difficult to gain reserve currency status, but that status is also difficult to lose. In theory, reserves should be held in various currencies in proportion to their weight in the global economy, and the U.S. share of the world economy is obviously nowhere near 60 percent, but old habits and relationships make governments slow to adjust. Officials seeking a safe, secure haven do not move their national treasure lightly. The United States surpassed Britain as the world's largest economy in the 1870s, but British sterling held on to its reserve status for another fifty years.

To become the world's reserve currency holder, a nation needs to have a large economy that dominates global transactions. It also has to offer a vast pool of ways to hold its currency that pose essentially zero risk of loss through confiscation or revolution, an example being U.S. government bonds. Right now, Europe has a large economy with no safe or vast pool of Eurobonds. China is becoming a large but not a dominant economy, and it severely limits foreign access to its primitive capital markets. There is no risk-free alternative to the dollar, and it does not look like there will be one in the foreseeable future.

The one serious threat to the dollar's reserve status would be if Washington fails to get U.S. public debt under control, in which case foreign holders might decide America is headed for default, leading to a crash of the dollar. If it came to pass, it would represent a serious threat, but the odds of that happening are slim.

Meanwhile, the dollar's depreciation over the past decade has made U.S. exports more competitive. The dollar has strengthened slightly in the last year, but it remains 25 percent below its 2002 peak, a situation that continues to feed a U.S. export recovery. The U.S. share of global exports is up a full point from its all-time low of 7.5 percent, hit in July 2008. Economist Tyler Cowen recently predicted that America's export success will not only revive the United States as a dominant global economic power but "largely cure its trade imbalance with China" and wipe away the view of America as "the borrowing supplicant in the US-China economic relationship."

The Manufacturing Revival

The most dramatic signs of a U.S. revival are in manufacturing. Even as it was losing out to emerging manufacturing powers in the last decade, the United States was reacting much more quickly than other rich nations. U.S. companies were restraining wage growth, boosting the productivity of remaining workers by using new technology, and

incorporating inexpensive new foreign manufacturers into their supply chains.

The U.S. export recovery is primarily due to the renaissance in
American manufacturing, which accounts for three-fourths of the
U.S. gain in global export market share and continues to gain momentum. For U.S. manufacturing exporters, the biggest gains have come
in airplanes, automobiles, and energy—led by the U.S. revolution
in shale gas production. The result is that China's rise as an export
manufacturer has continued largely at Europe's expense. Since 2004,
China has gained market share in the export of manufactured goods,
while Europe's share has fallen and the U.S. share has held steady.
After losing six million manufacturing jobs in the last decade, the
United States gained half a million in the eighteen months from 2011
through mid-2012, while Europe, Canada, and Japan lost jobs or saw
no change.

The manufacturing renaissance has unleashed a new factory construction boom. U.S. spending on manufacturing facilities had been
falling for years before it bottomed out in early 2011 and then started
to climb; over the last eighteen months it rose 60 percent, to just
under $50 billion. International Strategy & Investment, a Wall Street
advisory firm, has compiled a little book of anecdotal and statisti-
cal evidence for the renaissance that presents more than fifty recent
examples of domestic and foreign companies that have decided to
open manufacturing plants in the United States. Only five years ago,
these plants would almost certainly have located in China or some
other low-wage destination like Mexico.

The Energy Revolution

The manufacturing boom is closely tied to the U.S. energy revolution.
Energy, which until recently was seen as an obstacle to U.S. prosperity, has been transformed into an American competitive advantage.
After falling for twenty-five years, the share of the U.S. energy supply
that comes from domestic sources has been rising since 2005, from
69 percent to around 80 percent, aided by increasing production of

oil and particularly natural gas. This is pushing down U.S. natural gas prices to one of the lowest rates in the world, which helps explain why manufacturers are relocating to Iowa and Texas. The textile industry was one of the first to leave the developed world, but recently Santana Textiles turned history around by moving from Mexico to Texas to take advantage of lower energy costs.

The energy boom provides a major boost to American competitive strength, starting with the impact on the trade deficit. Five years ago, most analysts expected the United States to be a leading importer of natural gas, to the tune of $100 billion a year by 2012. Here we are in 2012, and the United States is now the leading producer of natural gas and a budding energy exporter as well. This is a positive step toward that ultimately unreachable ideal, so often talked up on the U.S. campaign trail, of "energy independence." Oil and gas production is now the fastest-growing industry in the United States, generating jobs that often pay in the $75,000 to $100,000 range—at least an isolated reversal of the worrisome decline in the manufacturing middle class.

America's shale gas advantage is likely to prove highly durable. Potential rivals like China and Saudi Arabia may have sizable stores of natural gas trapped in shale rock, but they lack the large supplies of water necessary for hydraulic "fracking," which uses blasts of water to fracture the shale and release the gas. Before these countries and European contenders, such as Poland, can tap shale gas, they will also have to work through legal disputes over whether landowners have the mineral rights to shale gas under their land. In the United States, landowners typically do control mineral rights.

The explosive pace of shale gas development in the United States has also given it a huge lead in building the basic infrastructure and cultivating experienced talent: there are now 425 gas rigs drilling on U.S. lands, compared to about 30 in Europe. Fracking technology took off in the United States because it took advantage of the country's long-standing strengths, including strong property rights and ready financing for promising entrepreneurial ventures. At its core, the American energy revolution is a technology revolution.

The Technology Edge

Today, an interesting debate is under way over whether the digital technology revolution is really a big deal in terms of improving U.S. productivity. Leading skeptics about America's productivity boom, such as Northwestern University economist Robert Gordon, say the computer and the Internet, even when rendered mobile in handheld devices, do less to raise productivity than inventions from previous technology revolutions—particularly the emergence in the late nineteenth century of electricity, the combustion engine, and indoor plumbing. The technology bulls say we haven't seen anything yet.

Everyone knows that today's PCs are faster than machines that three decades ago would fill a warehouse. Not everyone is fully aware that the next step—cloud computing—will allow home PCs to tap the computing power of an army of warehouse-size supercomputers. It's hard to imagine just what gains will emerge from this awesome capacity, but as a demonstration to provoke interest, Google recently used its cloud to decode the human genome . . . in eleven seconds. This shift—from merely crunching data to analyzing information— was illustrated in a viewer-friendly way by an IBM computer named "Watson" when, in early 2011, it dominated the most successful human champion of the popular American TV quiz show *Jeopardy!*

However large the impact of digital technology will be on economic productivity (and I believe it will be significant), it is likely to be disproportionately large in the leading economies, particularly the United States. As wages rise in emerging nations, they are starting to automate and digitize their manufacturing plants, but nations like Brazil, Russia, India, and China remain well below the global average on automation measures, such as number of robots per employee. The hot new thing is machines that can "print" a three-dimensional product, including anything from a machine tool part to a mobile phone case—straight from a digital image. And all of the top-fifteen companies that make 3D printers are based in the United States, Europe, and Japan.

Despite its inherent advantages as a technology-driven society, Japan seems almost to have given up on competing for the title of breakout nation in the top income category. Japan's companies suffer from low profitability, weighed down by a decades-old problem of over-capacity and inefficiency in its domestic industries. With a declining workforce, Japan turned to the use of robots early, but apparently not enough because Japan has the lowest productivity per capita among developed nations, outside only Portugal and Greece. When Japanese companies think about innovation, they think mainly about cool prod-ucts, not new ways to penetrate new markets, which helps explain Japan's stagnation as an export power. Nearly 70 percent of Japanese R&D is targeted at strengthening existing businesses, not exploring new ones. Without a more urgent push to compete more aggressively, Japan's share of global GDP seems likely to keep falling.

The American technology edge is especially critical in light of the slowdown in global growth. The question now is, what is the new driver, what will push the global economy to the next level of devel-opment? As the entrepreneur Peter Thiel has argued, the next driver usually comes in the form of material advances in new technology, and these are most likely to emerge in nations like the United States, where the system promotes innovation.

For example, as 3D manufacturing advances, it is expected to give manufacturers the capacity to custom build goods for individ-ual consumers more cheaply than the goods can be mass-produced in manned factories in Asia. And as developed nations like China grow richer, their consumers will demand the kind of advanced and custom-designed products that will be made mainly in America. As Tyler Cowen points out, the United States is a leading exporter of products that lie in the "sweet spot" for future demand from the emerging world, including civilian aircraft, semiconductors, cars, pharmaceuticals, machinery and equipment, automobile accessories, and entertainment.

Technology, Inequality, and the Debt Threat

There is an undeniable and scary connection between technology and persistent or rising income inequality, an issue that has remark-able resonance everywhere I travel, from Chile to South Korea. Kenneth Rogoff has called inequality "the single biggest threat to social stability around the world," and for good reason. A decade ago the technorati were predicting that a wireless, digital world would give working people a welcome windfall in leisure time, but the reality looks a lot less comfortable. As companies employ digital machines more efficiently, they need fewer people and will pay more for the relatively few people skilled in handling digital machines. But the more global the labor market becomes, the more wages tend to drift toward the level found in the lowest-wage countries, particularly for the unskilled but even for the skilled.

These forces are particularly powerful in the United States, precisely because companies here are the fastest to adapt to new technology and market realities. The stagnation of middle-class wages in the United States is in part a function of the fact that U.S. companies (and unions too) have been faster than their rivals to accept the need to reduce wages, or to institute two-tier pay scales that start new workers at lower wages. The resulting increase in productivity is driving up the profitably of large companies and the wealth of the richest Americans. Robert Gordon figures that between 1993 and 2008, real incomes in the United States rose by an annual average of 1.3 percent, but more than half of those gains went to the richest 1 percent of households. It's tough to make an economy more competitive and more fair at the same time.

Judged by my rules on how to read the billionaire lists, however, the United States does not rank too badly in terms of the economic impact of inequality. It's a bit misleading to compare the billionaire elites of emerging economies to those of developed economies, because it is normal for a wealthy establishment to appear over time in a developed country. Still, even when compared to emerging nations, the United States is not generating a disproportionately powerful billionaire class. In the United States, where the average fortune of the top-ten richest is $31 billion, far larger than in any emerging nation, the overall billionaire share of GDP (10.6 percent) would be about average by emerging-market standards.

America's billionaires have also survived the financial crisis relatively unscathed. The Japanese tycoons who once ruled the list of top-ten global billionaires were felled as a group by Japan's crisis in the early 1990s. But the U.S. billionaires who replaced them have held on to those positions despite the American-born crisis of 2008. The Americans, it seems, were much better at adapting to catastrophic global upheaval. Indeed what stands out on the U.S. list is that the greatest and most stable fortunes have been generated by independent and innovative leaders who founded exactly the kind of productive companies (particularly Microsoft, Berkshire Hathaway, and Wal-Mart) that would make any economy, developed or emerging, more globally competitive. They have little in common with the new class of oil tycoons rising in nations like Russia, who made their money by digging stuff out of the ground.

The technology edge is also mitigating the biggest threat to America's competitive position: debt. Rich nations have a much worse government debt problem than emerging nations, but the situation is reversed when you look at corporate debt. Despite slowing global growth, U.S. companies have been able to increase profits and pay down debt—as we saw earlier—largely because they have been sharply increasing productivity. This is, in good measure, a story of getting more out of digital technology. In many emerging markets such as China, where companies generate profit mainly by increasing revenue as opposed to increasing productivity, corporate profit margins remain low and debts remain stubbornly high.

Since it is likely that global economic growth will remain sluggish and volatile for the foreseeable future, the ability of U.S. companies to generate income in hard times is likely to be another enduring advantage. The dramatically different approaches of the developed nations to the basic challenges—deleveraging debt and maintaining a technological edge in a globalized world—is going to put them on very different growth paths. On balance, despite the high government debt and the risk of a sharp slowdown in 2013 due to a fiscal hit, the United States has more than an even chance of being a breakout nation in the coming decade.

The Rest of the West

Just as it makes no sense to analyze emerging markets in terms of generic rubrics like BRICS, developed markets also need to be analyzed as individual stories, and compared to rivals in the same income class. This is particularly true today in Europe, where nations of vastly different sizes and circumstances are often lumped together as interchangeable pieces of the troubled Eurozone.

One of the interesting differences between the Eurozone crisis and earlier regional debt crises is that money is fleeing within the region, not out of it, as investors seek safe haven in the two largest European economies, Germany and France. Germany's economic performance is the positive opposite of the troubles in some smaller Eurozone countries, because capital inflows are driving down borrowing costs in Germany, feeding a boomlet in the housing market, while the gradual decline of the euro is helping to push exports. Germany is also being rewarded for entering the crisis with its debts under control, and it now has its lowest unemployment level in twenty years. In contrast, unemployment levels in many of the periphery countries are at twenty-year highs, led by Spain at more than 20 percent. Meanwhile, France has used the windfall in cheaper borrowing costs mainly to put off the day of reckoning with its own debt. It went into the crisis increasingly uncompetitive, deep in debt, and with the state growing even larger as a share of the economy. Germany stands out as the breakout nation among the leading European states.

The next tier of Eurozone economies offers another striking contrast, between Italy and Spain, respectively the third and fourth largest economies in the region. Spain still has strong potential, but Italy increasingly resembles Japan after the crisis of 1990, when the Japanese never felt any deep pain or drama, but also never recovered any real economic momentum. The second-oldest population in the world after Japan, Italy too looks increasingly gray and unambitious. Much of the country's government debt is held at home by older Italians, who have created a political constituency that is content with the status quo. Italy and Japan share membership in the small and undesirable club of rich nations with a ratio of public debt to GDP in the triple digits, and the politics of both Rome and Tokyo have been shaped by a recent succession of leaders who make vague noises about change and then leave only a vague impression on the system. Spain, on the other hand, has suffered real drama and pain, with a deep housing crisis, but it is now moving more aggressively in the right direction, including serious labor market reform to deal with its high unemployment rate. Between these two southern rivals, Spain is more likely to bounce high off a hard landing, with a chance to become a breakout nation in the coming decade.

One way to gauge the impact of the crisis in Europe is through some simple comparisons to the Asian crisis of 1998. At bottom, Thailand's stock market was worth $30 billion, or less than the value of Chrysler, the troubled U.S. car company. Today the total value of the stock market in Greece is $41 billion, or less than the value of Costco, the U.S. discount retailer. The same calculation can be done across the crisis-hit region of "peripheral Europe," a term that covers Greece, Portugal, Ireland, and sometimes Spain and Italy, which now has a market capitalization lower than Apple's.

The point of this comparison is not to disparage these "peripheral" economies, quite the opposite. It now looks likely that at least some of the troubled nations of Europe are near bottom and that recovery is in sight, though it may lift the stock markets before it restores the economy to pre-crisis levels. At the low point in mid-1998, the combined stock market value of the key East Asian economies (Thailand, South Korea, Indonesia, Malaysia) was $250 billion, or less than the value of General Electric. Since then the East Asian stock markets have surged tenfold in dollar terms. In retrospect, 1998 offered investors a rare opportunity to buy into those markets.

In all of the regional financial crises going back to the Mexican Tequila Crisis of 1994, the country where the crisis started saw its stock market drop 85 percent on average (for example, Thailand in 1997–1998), while all of the markets in the region fell by an average of 65 percent. Europe is at a similar point today. The Eurozone crisis started in Greece, where the market is up slightly from a maximum decline of 90 percent, and the rest of peripheral Europe—Portugal, Italy, Ireland, and Spain—hit maximum declines that averaged 70 percent.

Europe's crisis echoes Asia's circumstances circa 1997 in other crucial ways. In both regions, the smaller economies went into crisis embracing what they thought was a tool of stability, the fixed exchange rate. Asian nations pegged their currencies to the dollar, and small European nations adopted the euro, hoping the link to a strong currency would make them look like safer places in which to lend and invest. The plan worked, attracting foreign investors and creditors, but it went awry when borrowing costs fell so low that both regions saw debt to foreigners rise sharply.

Both regions borrowed to pay for a binge of consumption and spending that began to undermine the current account balance, a broad measure of trade that covers goods, services, and investment income (including interest payments). The current account balance is of particular interest to analysts of global competition because it captures not only what countries are buying and selling but also their ability to pay for what they are buying. As this balance dipped deeply into the red, outsiders began wondering if these countries could continue to pay their creditors. When those doubts hit a fever pitch in one country—Thailand in Asia and Greece in Europe—the contagion quickly spread across the region, as investors (local and foreign) tried to pull out.

The Different Paths

The ensuing collapse was much more sudden in Asia than in peripheral Europe, but ultimately it was much less destructive. The Asian nations quickly abandoned the dollar peg, a move that sent their currencies plummeting by 40 percent on average and accelerated the flight of capital. However, the falling currency also began to restore balance to these inflated economies by making their exports cheaper and thus easier to sell, and by reducing consumer purchasing power, which greatly reduced imports. These forces quickly put current account balances back in surplus and made Asia much less reliant on foreign capital. The economies recovered rapidly and, on average, took just three and half years to surpass the real peak output of their pre-crisis years.

The smaller nations of the Eurozone have no such quick, almost automatic fix. They could not simply abandon the euro overnight. (The value of the euro has slipped, but by only 15 percent over four years.) Instead, they are undergoing a slow-motion crisis. To regain competitiveness, these countries have had to rein in spending and to lower wages, a difficult process anywhere but perhaps especially so in Europe, where governments and unions have spent decades writing rules that protect workers from the kind of pain that is called for now. As a result, the economies of peripheral Europe are still at or near bottoms that Asian economies had passed two to three years earlier in their recovery process.

In the unfolding drama of Europe, every tragic character has its alter ego in the Asian crisis. If you compare these economies to the level of output they established in the decade before the crisis, Greece's GDP has fallen 28 percent below its trend level and looks very similar to Thailand at its low point (down about 30 percent); Ireland looks as hard hit as Indonesia (–22 percent) was, while Spain (–16 percent) is even worse than Malaysia (–13 percent). Italy (–12 percent) and Portugal (–10 percent) have dropped as far as Korea (–10 percent) did.

The economies of peripheral Europe also face two key obstacles to recovery that Asia did not. First, it was easier for Asia to recover because in those years the global economy was growing at an average pace of more than 3 percent, almost twice as fast as it is today. Second, Asia's debt problem was confined to the corporate sector; its governments were in the black and in good shape to borrow and spend their way out of recession. Europe has a twin problem of corporate and government debt, and so much less room for maneuver. In Asia during its crisis years, the worst fiscal deficit was posted by Thailand, at 9 percent of GDP, while in peripheral Europe the peak deficits ranged from 10 percent in Italy to a high of 30 percent in Ireland (where the 2010 deficit spiked because of a major bank bailout). The likely result is that the long, slow contraction in Europe will be followed by a protracted, weak recovery.

The Asian experience shows that some recoveries will be much stronger than others, and it offers a clear lesson in how to spot recovery in a crisis-hit nation. It is not the depth of the decline in GDP or employment that matters, but how aggressively leaders accept the need to get control of debts and to create the competitive conditions in which lending, investment, and exports will bounce back. (Among the Asian countries, South Korea launched the most aggressive response from day one, and managed to sustain its long record of strong growth.) One of the strongest signs of recovery is the current account balance, which will signal a recovery at the moment it climbs out of deficit and back into positive territory, because it is only at this point that the country as a whole is generating the income to pay down foreign debts.

This climb came very fast in Asia (again, largely because of the collapse in currency values): Thailand saw its current account swing within a little over a year by 21 percentage points of GDP, or from a deficit equal to 8 percent of GDP to a surplus of 13 percent. By the first quarter of 1998—when the crisis was still seen as a rising threat to the rest of the globe—the end was in fact in sight because all of the current account balances of the crisis-hit economies were in the black.

Peripheral Europe is now approaching this critical turning point. Spain, Portugal, Greece, and even slow-moving Italy have seen some significant improvement in the current account, with deficits now on the verge of crossing into surpluses in 2013. The star, however, is Ireland, where a 15-percentage-point swing has created the only current account surplus in the region, at 8 percent of GDP.

The most political flammable aspect of crisis-recovery efforts is bringing down labor costs, and here too peripheral Europe is making progress. In the run-up to the crisis, citizens of the periphery enjoyed an increase in wages, which allowed them to spend heavily on imports, one reason why their economies are so heavily in debt now.

Since the crisis, the nations of peripheral Europe have begun to cut back. From their recent peaks, the costs of hiring workers (measured in terms of unit labor costs) have fallen by roughly 7 percent in Spain, Portugal, and Greece, where the government cut the minimum wage by 20 percent; in Italy, they have not fallen at all.

The biggest changes have come in Ireland, which has the most flexible labor market rules in the Eurozone and has seen unit labor costs fall about 18 percent. Ireland has done more than any Eurozone rival to regain its competitive position, starting with deep cuts that have brought its deficit down to 10 percent of GDP, from the 30 percent high of 2010. In Ireland, falling wages—including a 15 percent pay cut for all public employees—are helping to feed a boost in exports while reducing demand for imports (both factors are helping to push the current account into the black). Simply put, the Irish are accepting the necessary pain of a hard landing more stoically than any other nation of the periphery. While others voted out governments for imposing austerity, the Irish in early 2011 voted in a party that remains committed to tough measures to restore Ireland's competitive edge.

For the rest of peripheral Europe, the important point is that an economy can't bounce back unless it can see the bottom. Today, worldwide, the average ratio of stock market value to GDP in any given country is about 80 percent—a reflection of reasonably firm investor optimism in the future of the economy. The average for the entire Eurozone today is around 40 percent, and in peripheral Europe this ratio ranges from 23 percent in Greece to 38 percent in Portugal, very close to where their Asian alter egos were in 1998. At least some of them will probably rise out of this trough soon.

The Unlucky Countries

The new global landscape offers some surprises on the downside for developed nations too. In recent decades, the luckiest countries were those that rode the rising prices of commodities. Worldwide, capital spending in energy and raw material businesses rose sixfold in the last decade, and those investments will produce a surge in supply as new plants, mills, and mines come on line. Meanwhile the global slowdown is putting strong downward pressure on demand for virtually all raw materials; growth in demand for iron ore is down from 10 percent a year during the 2003–2007 boom to just 3 percent since then, and growth in demand for oil is down from 2 percent over the same period to 0.5 percent. The demand for raw materials in China, which accounted for more than half of the rise in demand for most commodities over the last decade, is slowing sharply, and China now has more supply than it can use, with stockpiles of coal and copper growing into small mountains. The bottom line is that with massive supplies entering the market, demand beginning to recede, and inventories rising, the price of commodities has begun to fall.

The commodity boom swept up not only countries in the emerging world, such as Brazil and Russia, but also two in the developed world, Australia and Canada. While in recent decades the business cycle had flattened out, with shorter recessions and longer recoveries across the world, nowhere in the world did it become as flat as in Australia, which has been living up to its self-image as the "Lucky Country." It has averaged 3 percent growth for twenty years and has not seen a single recession in that time.

Perhaps more than any other economy, Australia soared on the back of rising prices for its major export commodities, coal and iron ore, which paid for a neck-snapping rise in living standards. The phrase "terms of trade" is economic jargon for the difference between the prices a country pays for its imports and the prices it gets for its exports. It is hard to think of a more favorable turn in these terms than the one experienced by Australia in recent years. It was Australia's central banker who pointed out that in 2006, the price of a shipload of iron ore could pay for 2,200 flat-screen TVs, and five years later it could pay for 22,000. Amazingly, despite clear evidence that the business cycle is returning to normal, the consensus forecast for Australia is a continued run of 3 percent growth. However, as commodity prices fall—the price of iron ore has already dropped 40 percent since early 2011, for example—the terms of trade, which effectively boosted Australian household incomes, have started to ease and are likely to decline further. The investment in new mines that helped sustain Australia's growth is bound to weaken sharply. Corporate profits, which more than doubled to 14 percent during the 2000s, are likely to fall. Growth in wages, which on average rose at an annual pace of 5 percent during the boom years, will slow if not decline. To counteract the effects of falling prices for its raw material exports, Australia needs to focus on development outside the mining industry; for starters it should attempt to make the terribly overvalued Australian dollar more competitive by reducing interest rates.

Canada is the rich nation most dependent on selling raw materials, which account for more than half of the country's exports and about a fifth of its GDP. Interestingly, the Canadian economy proved more resilient than most of its rich peers after the crisis of 2008, attributable in part to the spending restraint that Ottawa learned the hard way, during fiscal fiascos of the 1990s, and in part to a housing market that never suffered the mortgage bankruptcies that burden the United States. However, Canada didn't benefit as much as Australia did from the recent boom in emerging markets, in part because it trades more with the developed world. Canada also saw no increase in productivity growth, a sluggish trait typical of many commodity-rich countries, and a major reason why it is not likely to enjoy an American-style manufacturing revival.

These rich commodity economies have run out of luck as the commodity supercycle has ebbed. The latest figures on industrial production also show very clearly that the growth paths of economies across the globe are starting to part ways, with clearer winners and losers. In Europe, as in the emerging markets, investors are beginning to think more carefully about individual storylines: through the first six months of 2011, the gap between the best- and the worst-performing European stock markets was 26 percentage points, but over the first nine months of 2012 that gap has climbed back up to 51 percentage points, with the Belgian markets up 28 percent and the Greek markets down 23 percent.

. . .

The first edition of this book offered a list of breakout nations that focused only on the developing world, including the Philippines, Indonesia, Thailand, Turkey, Poland, the Czech Republic, South Korea, Nigeria, and Sri Lanka. In the developed world, the breakout stories are likely to be America and Germany among the largest nations, and Spain and Ireland among the second-tier nations. After the debt binge of the last decade, which lifted all nations, the new era is one of moderate, uneven growth, with much wider gaps in performance between rival economies and markets. It's a tough age, but also very fair in the sense that there is no global tailwind for any nation, no matter whether it is developed or emerging. Now, everyone has to row.

ACKNOWLEDGMENTS

The idea of a book had long appealed to me, but it finally took shape in a matter of days when Tony Emerson, who for years had made my columns readable at *Newsweek International*, mentioned to me that he was looking to do something different. I could not have thought of a better person to help me write this book, and now it is hard to imagine how I could have done it without him, given his knowledge of my thought process and his easy grasp of the subject matter. Megha Khanduja, who worked tirelessly on numerous research assignments, assisted us.

In many ways, the book is an outgrowth of two decades of public writing. I had made it a habit to write for newspapers and journals following my visit to a country, because it helps in crystallizing my thoughts and in ensuring that I have all the facts right. The editors at *Newsweek* and *The Economic Times* were particularly indulgent of my copy, and I want to thank them for giving me the opportunity. That was an essential part of the journey en route to writing a book.

The one constant presence through all my writings has been my sister, Shumita Deveshwar. From maintaining clippings of my articles at the start, then growing up to become my main critic, diligently poring over my columns to tell me what worked and what did not, I am eternally grateful to her. Shumita read the manuscript of this book in detail, and her comments were incorporated in full. I am also deeply indebted to my friend and mentor, Simran Bhargava. I do not know of a writer with greater flair, and she has taught me many tricks of the trade over the years. She has a way with smart lines and crafted some for this book as well.

My writings are a product of my day job, and I owe various members of my emerging-markets investing team a lot for both their direct and their indirect contributions to the book. Jitania Khandari's suggestions were extremely insightful, while Dan Raghoonundon and Steven Quattry responded to data requests at a speed that would stun my editors. Meanwhile, the portfolio managers on the team shaped the thinking behind the various chapters. I would like to thank the following for their contributions on specific chapters or topics: Paul Psaila, Eric Carlson, and Frank Zheng for the chapters on Russia, Turkey, South Africa, and Eastern Europe; Tim Drinkall for the frontier-markets section; Munib Madni for the chapter on Southeast Asia; Samuel Rhee for the chapter on Korea and Taiwan; Swanand Kelkar and Amay Hattangadi for the chapter on India; and Cristina Piedrahita and Gaite Ali for the chapters on Mexico and Brazil.

Ashutosh Sinha and James Upton contributed with some very helpful advice. Meanwhile, Cyril Moulle-Berteaux read different parts of the manuscript and gave me extremely useful suggestions to smoothen the prose. It would have been terribly hard to manage this entire process without Paul Weiner, who knew how to direct the flow and keep the momentum going.

As a global investor, I am fortunate to have access to research reports prepared by brokerage firms all over the world and am able to speak with their analysts frequently. The reports and conversations influenced my thought process in many ways, and I would like to thank, in particular, Gyrogy Kovacs, Gyula Schuch, Banu Basar, Dan Fineman, Karim Salamatian, Deanne Gordon, Marianne Page, and Yolan Seimon for their specific contributions to this project. I also got some very valuable input from friends in journalism and academia, especially Simon Cameron Moore, Dorab Soparwala, and Ananthakrishnan Prasad for the Turkey, India, and GCC chapters, respectively. My sincere thanks to all of them.

After writing one-thousand- to two-thousand-word articles for so long, the thought of penning something many times that length was a bit intimidating, and I am grateful to friends who pushed me to take the plunge.

Nandan Nilekani, long familiar with my passion for emerging markets, had made it a point to ask me during every meeting in 2009 and 2010: Where is the book proposal? For some reason, he seemed convinced I had to move on from writing columns. Fareed Zakaria constantly guided me through the book process, and it was certainly inspiring to see how well both his books had done.

Still, without the specialists of the literary profession in the mix, the project would have never taken off. Scott Moyers at the Wylie Agency instantly took to the proposal and was able to sell the rights in what appeared to be record time. His colleagues James Pullen in London and the legendary Andrew Wylie shared his enthusiasm. It was Scott who put me in the magical hands of editors such as Brendan Curry at Norton and Stuart Proffitt at Penguin. Working with them has been a great learning experience in the art of communication.

It's always nice to have support for a new venture, but it matters even more when we step outside our comfort zone. In this regard, I truly appreciate the faith shown in this project by so many of my colleagues, friends, and associates. I sure hope the product justifies their confidence.

APPENDIX A:
THE EMERGING-MARKETS UNIVERSE

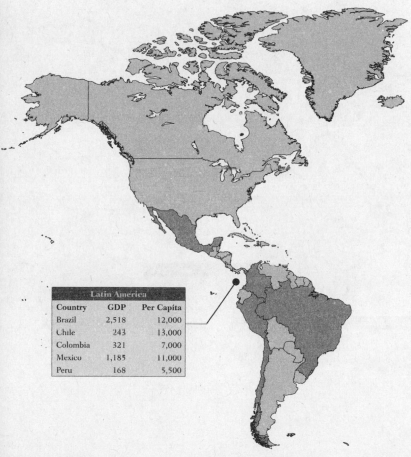

Latin America		
Country	GDP	Per Capita
Brazil	2,518	12,000
Chile	243	13,000
Colombia	321	7,000
Mexico	1,185	11,000
Peru	168	5,500

Eastern Europe		
Country	GDP	Per Capita
Czech Republic	220	21,000
Hungary	148	15,000
Poland	532	14,000
Russia	1,885	13,000
Turkey	763	10,500

Middle East & Africa		
Country	GDP	Per Capita
Egypt	232	3,000
Morocco	120	3,000
South Africa	422	8,000

Asia		
Country	GDP	Per Capita
China	6,988	5,000
India	1,843	1,400
Indonesia	834	3,500
Korea	1,164	23,500
Malaysia	248	8,000
Philippines	216	2,500
Taiwan	505	21,500
Thailand	339	5,000

APPENDIX B:
THE FRONTIER-MARKETS UNIVERSE

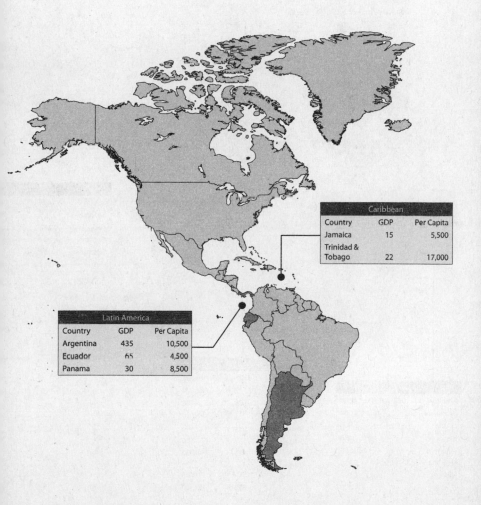

Caribbean		
Country	GDP	Per Capita
Jamaica	15	5,500
Trinidad & Tobago	22	17,000

Latin America		
Country	GDP	Per Capita
Argentina	435	10,500
Ecuador	65	4,500
Panama	30	8,500

Eastern Europe

Country	GDP	Per Capita
Bulgaria	54	7,000
Croatia	64	14,500
Estonia	23	17,000
Latvia	27	12,000
Lithuania	43	13,000
Romania	185	8,000
Serbia	46	6,000
Slovenia	52	26,000
Ukraine	163	3,500

Asia

Country	GDP	Per Ca
Bangladesh	115	
Kazakhstan	180	11
Pakistan	204	1
Sri Lanka	59	3
Vietnam	122	1

Africa

Country	GDP	Per Capita
Botswana	16	9,000
Ghana	39	1,500
Kenya	36	1,000
Mauritius	11	8,500
Namibia	13	6,000
Nigeria	247	1,500
Tunisia	49	4,500

Middle East

Country	GDP	Per Capita
Bahrain	26	23,000
Jordan	28	4,500
Kuwait	171	46,500
Lebanon	41	10,500
Oman	67	21,500
Qatar	173	98,000
Saudi Arabia	560	20,000
UAE	358	66,500

BIBLIOGRAPHY

2: China's After-Party

Capital Economics. "What Should We Make of the Lower Growth Target?" March 2, 2011. http://www.capitaleconomics.com/china-economics/china-watch/what-should-we-make-of-the-lower-growth-target.html

Gertken, Matthew, and Jennifer Richmond. "China and the End of the Deng Dynasty." STRATFOR Global Intelligence, April 19, 2011. http://www.stratfor.com/weekly/20110418-china-and-end-deng-dynasty

Gupta, Anil K., and Haiyan Wang. "China as an Innovation Center? Not So Fast." Wall Street Journal, July 28, 2011. http://online.wsj.com/article/SB10001424053 11190359110457646969670146238648.html

Hao, Yan. "Age Structural Transitions and Major Policy Implications in China." Paper prepared for CICRED Seminar on Age-Structural Transitions: Demographic Bonuses, but Emerging Challenges for Population and Sustainable Development, Paris, March 23, 2004. http://www.cicred.org/Eng/Seminars/Details/Seminars/Popwaves/PopwavesHao.pdf

Shirouzu, Norihiko. "Chinese Rail Projects Grind to a Halt as Funds Dry Up." Wall Street Journal, October 20, 2011. http://online.wsj.com/article/SB10001424052 97020461870457664066358445934.html

Tianyu, Yu. "Males Turn to Cosmetic Appearance." China Daily (U.S. edition), January 6, 2011. http://usa.chinadaily.com.cn/2011-01/06/content_11802981.htm

3: The Great Indian Hope Trick

Aon Hewitt. News from Aon: 15th Annual Salary Increase Survey. March 8, 2011.

Becerra, Jorge, Peter Damisch, Bruce Holley, Monish Kumar, Matthias Naumann,

Tjung Tang, and Anna Zakrzewski. *Global Wealth 2011: Shaping the New Tomorrow: How to Capitalize on the Momentum of Change*. Boston Consulting Group, May 31, 2011.

Capgemini and Merrill Lynch Global Wealth Management. *World Wealth Report 2011*. June 22, 2011.

French, Patrick. *India: A Portrait*. New York: Alfred A. Knopf, 2011.

Lahiri, Tripti. "India Passes 1.2 Billion Mark." *Wall Street Journal*, April 1, 2011. http://online.wsj.com/article/SB10001424052748703806304576233981941525872.html

Lamont, James, and James Fontanella-Khan. "'India: Writing Is on the Wall' by James and James Fontanella-Khan." *Financial Times*, March 21, 2011. http://www.ft.com/intl/cms/s/2/3c5009ba-53f2-11e0-8bd7-00144feab49a.html#axzz1eLU7PvxS

Mishra, Neelkanth, and Piyush Nahar. *Fresh Horses for the Economy.* Credit Suisse, Equity Research, India Market Strategy, February 17, 2011.

Takahashi, Kuni. "Turnaround of India State Could Serve as a Model." *New York Times*, April 10, 2011. http://www.nytimes.com/2010/04/11/world/asia/11bihar.html

4: Is God Brazilian?

Abreu, Marcelo de Paiva. *The Brazilian Economy, 1928–1980*. Pontifical Catholic University of Rio de Janeiro, November 2000.

———. *The Brazilian Economy, 1980–1994*. Pontifical Catholic University of Rio de Janeiro, November 2004.

Barro, Robert J. *Economic Growth in a Cross Section of Countries*. NBER Working Paper 3120. Cambridge, MA: National Bureau of Economic Research, May 2, 1991.

Evans, Leslie. "How Brazil Beat Hyperinflation." Latin American Center, UCLA International, February 22, 2002. http://www.econ.puc-rio.br/gfranco/How%20Brazil%20Beat%20Hyperinflation.htm

5: Mexico's Tycoon Economy

Mayer-Serra, Carlos Elizondo. "Perverse Equilibria: Unsuitable but Durable Institutions," in Santiago Levy and Michael Walton (eds.), *No Growth without Equity? Inequality, Interest and Competition in Mexico*. Washington, DC: World Bank; New York: Palgrave Macmillan UK, February 26, 2009. http://siteresources.worldbank.org/INTMEXICOINSPANISH/Resources/nogrowthwithoutequity.pdf

6: In Russia, There's Room Only at the Top

Becerra, Jorge, Peter Damisch, Bruce Holley, Monish Kumar, Matthias Naumann, Tjung Tang, and Anna Zakrzewski. *Global Wealth 2011: Shaping the New Tomorrow: How to Capitalize on the Momentum of Change*. Boston Consulting Group, May 31, 2011.

Citi. *The Russian Hunter: How to Invest in the Russian Rentier Market*. July 7, 2011.

"The World's Billionaires." *Forbes*, March 2011. http://www.forbes.com/wealth/billionaires/list

7: The Sweet Spot of Europe

Papic, Marko. "Portfolio: Poland Stalls on Eurozone Entry." STRATFOR Global Intelligence, May 19, 2011. http://www.stratfor.com/memberships/194854/analysis/20110518-portfolio-poland-stalls-eurozone-entry

8: The Monophonic Voice of Turkey

Gönenç, Rauf, Lukasz Rawdanowicz, Saygin Şahinöz, and Ozge Tuncel. *OECD Economic Surveys: Turkey, September 2010*. July 6, 2010. http://www.oecd.org/dataoecd/23/10/45951718.pdf

Meral, Ziya. *Prospects for Turkey*. London. Legatum Institute, September 2010. http://www.li.com/attachments/prospects%20for%20turkey.pdf

Stone, Norman. *Turkey: A Short History*. London: Thames and Hudson, March 2011.

STRATFOR Global Intelligence. "Islam, Secularism and the Battle for Turkey's Future." August 23, 2010. http://www.stratfor.com/memberships/163275/analysis/20100525_islam_secularism_battle_turkeys_future

Turgut, Pelin. "Erdogan Showdown with Generals Shows Advance of Turkey's Democracy." *Time*, August 3, 2011. http://www.time.com/time/world/article/0,8599,2086490,00.html

———. "Turning to the East." *Time*, July 5, 2010. http://www.time.com/time/magazine/article/0,9171,1999436,00.html

"The Turkish Model: A Hard Act to Follow." *Economist*, August 6, 2011.

10: The Gold Medalist

Bast, Andrew. "In Hard Times, Family Firms Do Better." *Newsweek*, December 29, 2011. http://www.thedailybeast.com/newsweek/2010/12/29/family-owned-businesses-get-through-hard-times.html (cites McKinsey studies)

Caspar, Christian, Ana Karina Dias, and Heinz-Peter Elstrodt. "The Five Attributes of Enduring Family Businesses." *McKinsey Quarterly*, January 2010.

11: The Endless Honeymoon

Abedian, Iraj, David Hale, and Lyric Hughes Hale. *South Africa after 2010—What's Next? Unconventional Wisdom on the Future of the World Economy.* New Haven, CT: Yale University Press, May 24, 2011.

Hirsch, Alan. *Season of Hope: Economic Reform under Mandela and Mbeki.* Scottsville, South Africa: University of KwaZulu-Natal Press, 2005.

Klein, Nir. *Measuring the Potential Output of South Africa.* Washington, DC: International Monetary Fund, November 2011.

Pike, Richard, Loane Sharp, and Ted Black. *The New Divide: Will High Wages and a Lack of Leadership Create an Unemployed Majority?* Johannesburg: TerraNova and Adcorp, 2010.

12: The Fourth World

Cabraal, Ajith Nivard. *Towards a Sri Lankan Renaissance: Simple Ideas That Will Change the Future.* Colombo, Sri Lanka: Ajith Cabraal 2000, 2002.

Collier, Paul. *The Bottom Billion: Why the Poorest Countries Are Failing and What Can Be Done about It.* New York: Oxford University Press, May 25, 2007.

Collier, Paul, Anke Hoeffler, and Mans Söderbom. "Post Conflict Risks." *Journal of Peace Research,* July 2008.

Goldstone, Jack. "Understanding the Revolutions of 2011." *Foreign Affairs,* May/June 2011.

A Guide to Economic Growth in Post-Conflict Countries. Bureau for Economic Growth, Agriculture and Trade, U.S Agency for International Development (USAID), January 2009. http://pdf.usaid.gov/pdf_docs/PNADO408.pdf

Quisenberry, Cliff. "Exploring the Frontier Emerging Markets." *Caravan Capital Management,* September 24, 2010.

Regional Economic Outlook: Sub-Saharan Africa: Resilience and Risks. World Economic and Financial Surveys. Washington, DC: International Monetary Fund, October 2010. (cites freight cost data)

Sheldrake, Rupert. *A New Science of Life: The Hypothesis of Formative Causation.* Los Angeles, CA: J. P. Tarcher, 1981.

"Sri Lanka's Constitutional Amendment: Eighteenth Time Unlucky." *Economist,* September 9, 2010. http://www.economist.com/node/1699214

"Sri Lanka's War: Two Years On." *Economist,* May 19, 2011. http://www.economist.com/blogs/banyan/2011/05/sri_lankas_war

13: After the Ecstasy, the Laundry

Andreessen, Marc. "Why Software Is Eating the World." *Wall Street Journal,* August 13, 2011. http://online.wsj.com/article/SB10001424053111903480904576512250915629460.html

CLSA Asia-Pacific Markets. *2020 Innovation: Pulling the Future towards US*. November 2011.

Commission on Growth and Development. *The Growth Report: Strategies for Sustained Growth and Inclusive Development*. Washington, DC: World Bank, 2008. http://cgd.s3.amazonaws.com/GrowthReportComplete.pdf

de la Torre, Ignacio. "Happiness Economics." business.in.com, January 15, 2010. http://business.in.com/article/ie/happiness-economics/9162/1#ixzz1eLBdRsxV

Goodman, George J. *The Money Game*. New York: Random House, 1968.

Gupta, Anil K., and Haiyan Wang. "China as an Innovation Center? Not So Fast." *Wall Street Journal*, July 28, 2011. http://online.wsj.com/article/SB10001424053 111903591104576469670146238648.html

Mullins, Brody, and Susan Pulliam. "Capital Gains: Hedge Funds Pay Top Dollar for Washington Intelligence." *Wall Street Journal*, October 4, 2011. http://online .wsj.com/article/SB10001424053111904070604576514791591319306.html

"The US Treasury Considers Housing Support." *GaveKal Dragonomics*, August 16, 2011.

14: The Third Coming

Reinhart, Carmen M., and Kenneth S. Rogoff. *This Time Is Different*. Princeton, NJ: Princeton University Press, 2009.

Rodrik, Dani. "The Future of Economic Convergence." Paper prepared for the 2011 Jackson Hole Symposium of the Federal Reserve Bank of Kansas City, August 25–27, 2011. http://www.hks.harvard.edu/fs/drodrik/Research%20papers/The% 20Future%20of%20Economic%20Convergence%20rev2.pdf

Saad, Lydia. "China Surges in Americans' View of Top World Economy." *Gallup Daily*, February 14, 2011. www.gallup.com

Sirkin, Harold L., Michael Zinser, and Douglas Hohner. *Made in America, Again: Why Manufacturing Will Return to the U.S*. Boston Consulting Group, August 2011.

Solnick, Sara J., and David Hemenway. "Is More Always Better? A Survey on Positional Concerns." *Journal of Economic Behavior and Organization*, vol. 37, no. 3, 1998, pp. 373–383. (Harvard School of Public Health survey)

Xie, Andy. "Don't Kill This Economy Softly." *Caixin Online*, June 21, 2011.

Epilogue

Alesina, Alberto, Carlo Favero, and Francesco Giavazzi. *The Output Effect of Fiscal Consolidations*. NBER Working Paper 18336. Cambridge, MA: National Bureau of Economic Research, August 2012. http://www.nber.org/papers/ w18336.

Cowen, Tyler. "What Export-Oriented America Means." *American Interest*, May/June 2012. http://www.the-american-interest.com/article.cfm?piece=1227.

Eichengreen, Barry, and Russ Roberts. "Eichengreen on the Dollar and International Finance." EconTalk presented by Library of Economics and Liberty, June 6, 2011. http://www.econtalk.org/archives/2011/06/eichengreen_on.html.

Gordon, Robert J. *Is U.S. Economic Growth Over? Faltering Innovation Confronts the Six Headwinds*. NBER Working Paper 18315. Cambridge, MA: National Bureau of Economic Research, August 2012. http://www.nber.org/papers/w18315.

Lazar, Nancy. *Manufacturing Renaissance—Update*. International Strategy & Investment, September 2012.

McKinsey Global Institute. *Debt and Deleveraging: Uneven Progress on the Path to Growth*. McKinsey & Company, January 2012.

Reinhart, Carmen, and Kenneth Rogoff. "The Aftermath of Financial Crises." *American Economic Review*, vol. 99, no. 2, 2009, pp. 466–472.

Rogoff, Kenneth. "Technology and Inequality." *Project Syndicate*, July 6, 2011. http://www.project-syndicate.org/commentary/technology-and-inequality.

Thiel, Peter. "The Technological Challenge." Speech given at Credit Suisse 2012 Global Macro Investors Conference, May 17, 2012.

INDEX

Page numbers in *italics* refer to illustrations, maps, and tables.